IMPORTANT RECORDS, IF YOU FOUND THIS NOTEBOOK, PLEASE CONTACT ME

NAME: ....

ADDRESS: ....

PHONE: .... EMAIL: ....

Flights Index

#	Description	#	Description
01		26	
02		27	
03		28	
04		29	
05		30	
06		31	
07		32	
08		33	
09		34	
10		35	
11		36	
12		37	
13		38	
14		39	
15		40	
16		41	
17		42	
18		43	
19		44	
20		45	
21		46	
22		47	
23		48	
24		49	
25		50	

FLIGHTS INDEX

#	DESCRIPTION	#	DESCRIPTION
1		76	
2		77	
3		78	
4		79	
5		80	
6		81	
7		82	
8		83	
9		84	
50		85	
51		86	
52		87	
53		88	
54		89	
55		90	
56		91	
57		92	
58		93	
59		94	
70		95	
71		96	
72		97	
73		98	
74		99	
75		100	

FLIGHT PLAN

PILOT NAME: .... FAA ID: ....

ADDRESS: .... PHONE: ....

VISUAL OBSERVER(S): ....

LOCATION: ....

DATE: .... AIRCRAFT TYPE/NAME: ....

PLANNED TIME: .... AIRCRAFT CERTIFICATE N°: ....

ESTIMATED FLIGHT DURATION: .... FLIGHT TYPE: ....

AIRPORTS WITHIN 5 MILES: ....

WAIVERS APPLIED FOR: ....

FLIGHT DESCRIPTION/ROUTE: ....

....

....

FLIGHT RECORD

FLIGHT 1

TAKEOFF LOC.: .... LAUNCH TIME: .... FLIGHT NOTES: ....

LANDING LOC.: .... LANDING TIME: ....

BATTERY VOLTAGE: .... ELAPSED TIME: ....

FLIGHT 2

TAKEOFF LOC.: .... LAUNCH TIME: .... FLIGHT NOTES: ....

LANDING LOC.: .... LANDING TIME: ....

BATTERY VOLTAGE: .... ELAPSED TIME: ....

FLIGHT 3

TAKEOFF LOC.: .... LAUNCH TIME: .... FLIGHT NOTES: ....

LANDING LOC.: .... LANDING TIME: ....

BATTERY VOLTAGE: .... ELAPSED TIME: ....

FLIGHT 4

TAKEOFF LOC.: .... LAUNCH TIME: .... FLIGHT NOTES: ....

LANDING LOC.: .... LANDING TIME: ....

BATTERY VOLTAGE: .... ELAPSED TIME: ....

GENERAL NOTES: ....

....

....

Flight Checklist

☐ Airport(s) Notified	☐ UAV Batteries Charged	☐ Gimbal Protector Installed
☐ Location is OK To Fly	Battery 1 volts:	☐ Propellers Packed
☐ Weather Forecast OK	Battery 2 volts:	☐ Cables Packed
Temperature:	Battery 3 volts:	☐ Camera Filters Packed
Wind:	Battery 4 volts:	☐ Sun Shade Packed
Precipitation:	☐ Controller Charged	☐ Tools Packed
☐ Firmware up-to-date	☐ Tablet Charged	☐ Flight Plan designed/entered in Software
☐ Memory Card Formatted	☐ Mobile Phone Charged	☐ Logbook Packed

Launch Site Checklist

☐ Verify Weather is OK To Fly	☐ Check For Obstacles, Interferences
Temperature:	☐ Check For Nearby Human Activity/ Dangerous
Wind:	☐ Verify Launch Pad Is Down-wind From Observers
Precipitation:	☐ Launch Pad/Barriers Placed
☐ **Safety Briefing**	

Equipment Checklist

☐ Airframe/Landing Gear Inspected	☐ Battery Installed
☐ Propellers Inspected/ Attached	☐ Gimbal/Lens Protector Removed
☐ Controller/Tablet Assembled	
☐ Memory Card Installed	☐ Camera Filters Installed

Pre-Flight Checklist

☐ Aircraft Placed on Lauch Pad	☐ Check The Aircraft Status LEDs	☐ Check Flight Mode Switch (P-Mode)
☐ Turn On Remote Controller/ Tablet/DJI Pilot App	☐ Verify the Gimbal is Level, Can Move Unobstructed	☐ Check Satellite And Compass Status
☐ Antennas Properly Positioned	☐ Check RC Battery Level	☐ Set RTH Location And Height
☐ Turn on Aircraft	☐ Check Aircraft Battery Level	☐ Check Camera Settings

Takeoff Checklist

☐ Check Launch site is Clear for Takeoff	☐ Takeoff and Hover	☐ Check Flight Controls, Make Sure They Respond As Expected
☐ Start the motors	☐ Make Sure The Aircraft Is Stable While Hovering	☐ Start Recording Video

Post Flight Checklist

☐ Remove Battery From Aircraft	☐ Repack All Equipment
☐ Install Gimbal Guard	☐ **Complete The Flight Log**

FLIGHT PLAN

PILOT NAME: ....   FAA ID: ....

ADDRESS: ....   PHONE: ....

VISUAL OBSERVER(S): ....

LOCATION: ....

DATE: ....   AIRCRAFT TYPE/NAME: ....

PLANNED TIME: ....   AIRCRAFT CERTIFICATE N°: ....

ESTIMATED FLIGHT DURATION: ....   FLIGHT TYPE: ....

AIRPORTS WITHIN 5 MILES: ....

WAIVERS APPLIED FOR: ....

FLIGHT DESCRIPTION/ROUTE: ....
....
....

FLIGHT RECORD

FLIGHT 1

TAKEOFF LOC.: ....   LAUNCH TIME: ....   FLIGHT NOTES: ....

LANDING LOC.: ....   LANDING TIME: ....

BATTERY VOLTAGE: ....   ELAPSED TIME: ....

FLIGHT 2

TAKEOFF LOC.: ....   LAUNCH TIME: ....   FLIGHT NOTES: ....

LANDING LOC.: ....   LANDING TIME: ....

BATTERY VOLTAGE: ....   ELAPSED TIME: ....

FLIGHT 3

TAKEOFF LOC.: ....   LAUNCH TIME: ....   FLIGHT NOTES: ....

LANDING LOC.: ....   LANDING TIME: ....

BATTERY VOLTAGE: ....   ELAPSED TIME: ....

FLIGHT 4

TAKEOFF LOC.: ....   LAUNCH TIME: ....   FLIGHT NOTES: ....

LANDING LOC.: ....   LANDING TIME: ....

BATTERY VOLTAGE: ....   ELAPSED TIME: ....

GENERAL NOTES: ....
....
....

Flight Checklist

☐ Airport(s) Notified	☐ UAV Batteries Charged	☐ Gimbal Protector Installed
☐ Location is OK To Fly	Battery 1 volts:	☐ Propellers Packed
☐ Weather Forecast OK	Battery 2 volts:	☐ Cables Packed
Temperature:	Battery 3 volts:	☐ Camera Filters Packed
Wind:	Battery 4 volts:	☐ Sun Shade Packed
Precipitation:	☐ Controller Charged	☐ Tools Packed
☐ Firmware up-to-date	☐ Tablet Charged	☐ Flight Plan designed/entered in Software
☐ Memory Card Formatted	☐ Mobile Phone Charged	☐ Logbook Packed

Launch Site Checklist

☐ Verify Weather is OK To Fly	☐ Check For Obstacles, Interferences
Temperature:	☐ Check For Nearby Human Activity/ Dangerous
Wind:	☐ Verify Launch Pad Is Down-wind From Observers
Precipitation:	
☐ **Safety Briefing**	☐ Launch Pad/Barriers Placed

Equipment Checklist

☐ Airframe/Landing Gear Inspected	☐ Battery Installed
☐ Propellers Inspected/ Attached	☐ Gimbal/Lens Protector Removed
☐ Controller/Tablet Assembled	
☐ Memory Card Installed	☐ Camera Filters Installed

Pre-Flight Checklist

☐ Aircraft Placed on Lauch Pad	☐ Check The Aircraft Status LEDs	☐ Check Flight Mode Switch (P-Mode)
☐ Turn On Remote Controller/ Tablet/DJI Pilot App	☐ Verify the Gimbal is Level, Can Move Unobstructed	☐ Check Satellite and Compass Status
☐ Antennas Properly Positioned	☐ Check RC Battery Level	☐ Set RTH Location And Height
☐ Turn on Aircraft	☐ Check Aircraft Battery Level	☐ Check Camera Settings

Takeoff Checklist

☐ Check Launch site is Clear for Takeoff	☐ Takeoff and Hover	☐ Check Flight Controls, Make Sure They Respond As Expected
☐ Start the motors	☐ Make Sure The Aircraft Is Stable While Hovering	☐ Start Recording Video

Post Flight Checklist

☐ Remove Battery From Aircraft	☐ Repack All Equipment
☐ Install Gimbal Guard	☐ **Complete The Flight Log**

Flight Plan

Pilot Name: ....   FAA ID: ....

Address: ....   Phone: ....

Visual Observer(s): ....

Location: ....

Date: ....   Aircraft Type/Name: ....

Planned Time: ....   Aircraft Certificate n°: ....

Estimated Flight Duration: ....   Flight Type: ....

Airports Within 5 Miles: ....

Waivers Applied For: ....

Flight Description/Route: ....

....

....

Flight Record

FLIGHT 1
Takeoff Loc.: ....   Launch Time: ....   Flight Notes: ....
Landing Loc.: ....   Landing Time: ....
Battery Voltage: ....   Elapsed Time: ....

FLIGHT 2
Takeoff Loc.: ....   Launch Time: ....   Flight Notes: ....
Landing Loc.: ....   Landing Time: ....
Battery Voltage: ....   Elapsed Time: ....

FLIGHT 3
Takeoff Loc.: ....   Launch Time: ....   Flight Notes: ....
Landing Loc.: ....   Landing Time: ....
Battery Voltage: ....   Elapsed Time: ....

FLIGHT 4
Takeoff Loc.: ....   Launch Time: ....   Flight Notes: ....
Landing Loc.: ....   Landing Time: ....
Battery Voltage: ....   Elapsed Time: ....

General Notes: ....

....

....

Flight Checklist

☐ Airport(s) Notified	☐ UAV Batteries Charged	☐ Gimbal Protector Installed
☐ Location is OK To Fly	Battery 1 volts:	☐ Propellers Packed
☐ Weather Forecast OK	Battery 2 volts:	☐ Cables Packed
Temperature:	Battery 3 volts:	☐ Camera Filters Packed
Wind:	Battery 4 volts:	☐ Sun Shade Packed
Precipitation:	☐ Controller Charged	☐ Tools Packed
☐ Firmware up-to-date	☐ Tablet Charged	☐ Flight Plan designed/entered in Software
☐ Memory Card Formatted	☐ Mobile Phone Charged	☐ Logbook Packed

Launch Site Checklist

☐ Verify Weather is OK To Fly	☐ Check For Obstacles, Interferences
Temperature:	☐ Check For Nearby Human Activity/ Dangerous
Wind:	☐ Verify Launch Pad is Down-wind From Observers
Precipitation:	☐ Launch Pad/Barriers Placed
☐ **Safety Briefing**	

Equipment Checklist

☐ Airframe/Landing Gear Inspected	☐ Battery Installed
☐ Propellers Inspected/ Attached	☐ Gimbal/Lens Protector Removed
☐ Controller/Tablet Assembled	
☐ Memory Card Installed	☐ Camera Filters Installed

Pre-Flight Checklist

☐ Aircraft Placed on Lauch Pad	☐ Check The Aircraft Status LEDs	☐ Check Flight Mode Switch (P-Mode)
☐ Turn On Remote Controller/ Tablet/DJI Pilot App	☐ Verify the Gimbal is Level, Can Move Unobstructed	☐ Check Satellite and Compass Status
☐ Antennas Properly Positioned	☐ Check RC Battery Level	☐ Set RTH Location And Height
☐ Turn on Aircraft	☐ Check Aircraft Battery Level	☐ Check Camera Settings

Takeoff Checklist

☐ Check Launch site is Clear for Takeoff	☐ Takeoff and Hover	☐ Check Flight Controls, Make Sure They Respond As Expected
☐ Start the motors	☐ Make Sure The Aircraft is Stable While Hovering	☐ Start Recording Video

Post Flight Checklist

☐ Remove Battery From Aircraft	☐ Repack All Equipment
☐ Install Gimbal Guard	☐ **Complete The Flight Log**

FLIGHT 04

FLIGHT PLAN

PILOT NAME: .... FAA ID: ....

ADDRESS: .... PHONE: ....

VISUAL OBSERVER(S): ....

LOCATION: ....

DATE: .... AIRCRAFT TYPE/NAME: ....

PLANNED TIME: .... AIRCRAFT CERTIFICATE N°: ....

ESTIMATED FLIGHT DURATION: .... FLIGHT TYPE: ....

AIRPORTS WITHIN 5 MILES: ....

WAIVERS APPLIED FOR: ....

FLIGHT DESCRIPTION/ROUTE: ....

....

....

FLIGHT RECORD

FLIGHT 1
TAKEOFF LOC.: .... LAUNCH TIME: .... FLIGHT NOTES: ....

LANDING LOC.: .... LANDING TIME: ....

BATTERY VOLTAGE: .... ELAPSED TIME: ....

FLIGHT 2
TAKEOFF LOC.: .... LAUNCH TIME: .... FLIGHT NOTES: ....

LANDING LOC.: .... LANDING TIME: ....

BATTERY VOLTAGE: .... ELAPSED TIME: ....

FLIGHT 3
TAKEOFF LOC.: .... LAUNCH TIME: .... FLIGHT NOTES: ....

LANDING LOC.: .... LANDING TIME: ....

BATTERY VOLTAGE: .... ELAPSED TIME: ....

FLIGHT 4
TAKEOFF LOC.: .... LAUNCH TIME: .... FLIGHT NOTES: ....

LANDING LOC.: .... LANDING TIME: ....

BATTERY VOLTAGE: .... ELAPSED TIME: ....

GENERAL NOTES: ....

....

....

FLIGHT CHECKLIST

☐ Airport(s) Notified	☐ UAV Batteries Charged	☐ Gimbal Protector Installed
☐ Location is OK To Fly	Battery 1 volts:	☐ Propellers Packed
☐ Weather Forecast OK	Battery 2 volts:	☐ Cables Packed
Temperature:	Battery 3 volts:	☐ Camera Filters Packed
Wind:	Battery 4 volts:	☐ Sun Shade Packed
Precipitation:	☐ Controller Charged	☐ Tools Packed
☐ Firmware up-to-date	☐ Tablet Charged	☐ Flight Plan designed/entered in Software
☐ Memory Card Formatted	☐ Mobile Phone Charged	☐ Logbook Packed

LAUNCH SITE CHECKLIST

☐ Verify Weather is OK To Fly	☐ Check For Obstacles, Interferences
Temperature:	☐ Check For Nearby Human Activity/ Dangerous
Wind:	☐ Verify Launch Pad Is Down-wind From Observers
Precipitation:	☐ Launch Pad/Barriers Placed
☐ **Safety Briefing**	

EQUIPMENT CHECKLIST

☐ Airframe/Landing Gear Inspected	☐ Battery Installed
☐ Propellers Inspected/ Attached	☐ Gimbal/Lens Protector Removed
☐ Controller/Tablet Assembled	
☐ Memory Card Installed	☐ Camera Filters Installed

PRE-FLIGHT CHECKLIST

☐ Aircraft Placed on Lauch Pad	☐ Check The Aircraft Status LEDs	☐ Check Flight Mode Switch (P-Mode)
☐ Turn On Remote Controller/ Tablet/DJI Pilot App	☐ Verify the Gimbal is Level, Can Move Unobstructed	☐ Check Satellite And Compass Status
☐ Antennas Properly Positioned	☐ Check RC Battery Level	☐ Set RTH Location And Height
☐ Turn on Aircraft	☐ Check Aircraft Battery Level	☐ Check Camera Settings

TAKEOFF CHECKLIST

☐ Check Launch site is Clear for Takeoff	☐ Takeoff and Hover	☐ Check Flight Controls, Make Sure They Respond As Expected
☐ Start the motors	☐ Make Sure The Aircraft Is Stable While Hovering	☐ Start Recording Video

POST FLIGHT CHECKLIST

☐ Remove Battery From Aircraft	☐ Repack All Equipment
☐ Install Gimbal Guard	☐ **Complete The Flight Log**

FLIGHT 05

Flight Plan

Pilot Name: ....   FAA ID: ....

Address: ....   Phone: ....

Visual Observer(s): ....

Location: ....

Date: ....   Aircraft Type/Name: ....

Planned Time: ....   Aircraft Certificate n°: ....

Estimated Flight Duration: ....   Flight Type: ....

Airports Within 5 Miles: ....

Waivers Applied For: ....

Flight Description/Route: ....

....

....

Flight Record

FLIGHT 1

Takeoff Loc.: ....   Launch Time: ....   Flight Notes: ....

Landing Loc.: ....   Landing Time: ....

Battery Voltage: ....   Elapsed Time: ....

FLIGHT 2

Takeoff Loc.: ....   Launch Time: ....   Flight Notes: ....

Landing Loc.: ....   Landing Time: ....

Battery Voltage: ....   Elapsed Time: ....

FLIGHT 3

Takeoff Loc.: ....   Launch Time: ....   Flight Notes: ....

Landing Loc.: ....   Landing Time: ....

Battery Voltage: ....   Elapsed Time: ....

FLIGHT 4

Takeoff Loc.: ....   Launch Time: ....   Flight Notes: ....

Landing Loc.: ....   Landing Time: ....

Battery Voltage: ....   Elapsed Time: ....

General Notes: ....

....

....

FLIGHT CHECKLIST

☐ Airport(s) Notified	☐ UAV Batteries Charged	☐ Gimbal Protector Installed
☐ Location is OK To Fly	Battery 1 volts:	☐ Propellers Packed
☐ Weather Forecast OK	Battery 2 volts:	☐ Cables Packed
Temperature:	Battery 3 volts:	☐ Camera Filters Packed
Wind:	Battery 4 volts:	☐ Sun Shade Packed
Precipitation:	☐ Controller Charged	☐ Tools Packed
☐ Firmware up-to-date	☐ Tablet Charged	☐ Flight Plan designed/entered in Software
☐ Memory Card Formatted	☐ Mobile Phone Charged	☐ Logbook Packed

LAUNCH SITE CHECKLIST

☐ Verify Weather is OK To Fly	☐ Check For Obstacles, Interferences
Temperature:	☐ Check For Nearby Human Activity/ Dangerous
Wind:	☐ Verify Launch Pad Is Down-wind From Observers
Precipitation:	☐ Launch Pad/Barriers Placed
☐ **Safety Briefing**	

EQUIPMENT CHECKLIST

☐ Airframe/Landing Gear Inspected	☐ Battery Installed
☐ Propellers Inspected/ Attached	☐ Gimbal/Lens Protector Removed
☐ Controller/Tablet Assembled	
☐ Memory Card Installed	☐ Camera Filters Installed

PRE-FLIGHT CHECKLIST

☐ Aircraft Placed on Lauch Pad	☐ Check The Aircraft Status LEDs	☐ Check Flight Mode Switch (P-Mode)
☐ Turn On Remote Controller/ Tablet/DJI Pilot App	☐ Verify the Gimbal is Level, Can Move Unobstructed	☐ Check Satellite and Compass Status
☐ Antennas Properly Positioned	☐ Check RC Battery Level	☐ Set RTH Location And Height
☐ Turn on Aircraft	☐ Check Aircraft Battery Level	☐ Check Camera Settings

TAKEOFF CHECKLIST

☐ Check Launch site is Clear for Takeoff	☐ Takeoff and Hover	☐ Check Flight Controls, Make Sure They Respond As Expected
☐ Start the motors	☐ Make Sure The Aircraft Is Stable While Hovering	☐ Start Recording Video

POST FLIGHT CHECKLIST

☐ Remove Battery From Aircraft	☐ Repack All Equipment
☐ Install Gimbal Guard	☐ **Complete The Flight Log**

FLIGHT 06

Flight Plan

Pilot Name: .... FAA ID: ....

Address: .... Phone: ....

Visual Observer(s): ....

Location: ....

Date: .... Aircraft Type/Name: ....

Planned Time: .... Aircraft Certificate n°: ....

Estimated Flight Duration: .... Flight Type: ....

Airports Within 5 Miles: ....

Waivers Applied For: ....

Flight Description/Route: ....

....

....

Flight Record

FLIGHT 1
Takeoff Loc.: .... Launch Time: .... Flight Notes: ....

Landing Loc.: .... Landing Time: ....

Battery Voltage: .... Elapsed Time: ....

FLIGHT 2
Takeoff Loc.: .... Launch Time: .... Flight Notes: ....

Landing Loc.: .... Landing Time: ....

Battery Voltage: .... Elapsed Time: ....

FLIGHT 3
Takeoff Loc.: .... Launch Time: .... Flight Notes: ....

Landing Loc.: .... Landing Time: ....

Battery Voltage: .... Elapsed Time: ....

FLIGHT 4
Takeoff Loc.: .... Launch Time: .... Flight Notes: ....

Landing Loc.: .... Landing Time: ....

Battery Voltage: .... Elapsed Time: ....

General Notes: ....

....

....

Flight Checklist

☐ Airport(s) Notified	☐ UAV Batteries Charged	☐ Gimbal Protector Installed
☐ Location is OK To Fly	Battery 1 volts:	☐ Propellers Packed
☐ Weather Forecast OK	Battery 2 volts:	☐ Cables Packed
Temperature:	Battery 3 volts:	☐ Camera Filters Packed
Wind:	Battery 4 volts:	☐ Sun Shade Packed
Precipitation:	☐ Controller Charged	☐ Tools Packed
☐ Firmware up-to-date	☐ Tablet Charged	☐ Flight Plan designed/entered in Software
☐ Memory Card Formatted	☐ Mobile Phone Charged	☐ Logbook Packed

Launch Site Checklist

☐ Verify Weather is OK To Fly	☐ Check For Obstacles, Interferences
Temperature:	☐ Check For Nearby Human Activity/ Dangerous
Wind:	☐ Verify Launch Pad Is Down-wind From Observers
Precipitation:	
☐ **Safety Briefing**	☐ Launch Pad/Barriers Placed

Equipment Checklist

☐ Airframe/Landing Gear Inspected	☐ Battery Installed
☐ Propellers Inspected/ Attached	☐ Gimbal/Lens Protector Removed
☐ Controller/Tablet Assembled	
☐ Memory Card Installed	☐ Camera Filters Installed

Pre-Flight Checklist

☐ Aircraft Placed on Lauch Pad	☐ Check The Aircraft Status LEDs	☐ Check Flight Mode Switch (P-Mode)
☐ Turn On Remote Controller/ Tablet/DJI Pilot App	☐ Verify the Gimbal is Level, Can Move Unobstructed	☐ Check Satellite and Compass Status
☐ Antennas Properly Positioned	☐ Check RC Battery Level	☐ Set RTH Location And Height
☐ Turn on Aircraft	☐ Check Aircraft Battery Level	☐ Check Camera Settings

Takeoff Checklist

☐ Check Launch site is Clear for Takeoff	☐ Takeoff and Hover	☐ Check Flight Controls, Make Sure They Respond As Expected
☐ Start the motors	☐ Make Sure The Aircraft Is Stable While Hovering	☐ Start Recording Video

Post Flight Checklist

☐ Remove Battery From Aircraft	☐ Repack All Equipment
☐ Install Gimbal Guard	☐ **Complete The Flight Log**

FLIGHT 07

FLIGHT PLAN

PILOT NAME: .... FAA ID: ....

ADDRESS: .... PHONE: ....

VISUAL OBSERVER(S): ....

LOCATION: ....

DATE: .... AIRCRAFT TYPE/NAME: ....

PLANNED TIME: .... AIRCRAFT CERTIFICATE N°: ....

ESTIMATED FLIGHT DURATION: .... FLIGHT TYPE: ....

AIRPORTS WITHIN 5 MILES: ....

WAIVERS APPLIED FOR: ....

FLIGHT DESCRIPTION/ROUTE: ....

....

....

FLIGHT RECORD

FLIGHT 1

TAKEOFF LOC.: .... LAUNCH TIME: .... FLIGHT NOTES: ....

LANDING LOC.: .... LANDING TIME: ....

BATTERY VOLTAGE: .... ELAPSED TIME: ....

FLIGHT 2

TAKEOFF LOC.: .... LAUNCH TIME: .... FLIGHT NOTES: ....

LANDING LOC.: .... LANDING TIME: ....

BATTERY VOLTAGE: .... ELAPSED TIME: ....

FLIGHT 3

TAKEOFF LOC.: .... LAUNCH TIME: .... FLIGHT NOTES: ....

LANDING LOC.: .... LANDING TIME: ....

BATTERY VOLTAGE: .... ELAPSED TIME: ....

FLIGHT 4

TAKEOFF LOC.: .... LAUNCH TIME: .... FLIGHT NOTES: ....

LANDING LOC.: .... LANDING TIME: ....

BATTERY VOLTAGE: .... ELAPSED TIME: ....

GENERAL NOTES: ....

....

....

Flight Checklist

☐ Airport(s) Notified	☐ UAV Batteries Charged	☐ Gimbal Protector Installed
☐ Location is OK To Fly	Battery 1 volts:	☐ Propellers Packed
☐ Weather Forecast OK	Battery 2 volts:	☐ Cables Packed
Temperature:	Battery 3 volts:	☐ Camera Filters Packed
Wind:	Battery 4 volts:	☐ Sun Shade Packed
Precipitation:	☐ Controller Charged	☐ Tools Packed
☐ Firmware up-to-date	☐ Tablet Charged	☐ Flight Plan designed/entered in Software
☐ Memory Card Formatted	☐ Mobile Phone Charged	☐ Logbook Packed

Launch Site Checklist

☐ Verify Weather is OK To Fly	☐ Check For Obstacles, Interferences
Temperature:	☐ Check For Nearby Human Activity/ Dangerous
Wind:	☐ Verify Launch Pad is Down-wind From Observers
Precipitation:	☐ Launch Pad/Barriers Placed
☐ **Safety Briefing**	

Equipment Checklist

☐ Airframe/Landing Gear Inspected	☐ Battery Installed
☐ Propellers Inspected/ Attached	☐ Gimbal/Lens Protector Removed
☐ Controller/Tablet Assembled	
☐ Memory Card Installed	☐ Camera Filters Installed

Pre-Flight Checklist

☐ Aircraft Placed on Lauch Pad	☐ Check The Aircraft Status LEDs	☐ Check Flight Mode Switch (P-Mode)
☐ Turn On Remote Controller/ Tablet/DJI Pilot App	☐ Verify the Gimbal is Level, Can Move Unobstructed	☐ Check Satellite And Compass Status
☐ Antennas Properly Positioned	☐ Check RC Battery Level	☐ Set RTH Location And Height
☐ Turn on Aircraft	☐ Check Aircraft Battery Level	☐ Check Camera Settings

Takeoff Checklist

☐ Check Launch site is Clear for Takeoff	☐ Takeoff and Hover	☐ Check Flight Controls, Make Sure They Respond As Expected
☐ Start the motors	☐ Make Sure The Aircraft Is Stable While Hovering	☐ Start Recording Video

Post Flight Checklist

☐ Remove Battery From Aircraft	☐ Repack All Equipment
☐ Install Gimbal Guard	☐ **Complete The Flight Log**

FLIGHT PLAN

PILOT NAME: .... FAA ID: ....

ADDRESS: .... PHONE: ....

VISUAL OBSERVER(S): ....

LOCATION: ....

DATE: .... AIRCRAFT TYPE/NAME: ....

PLANNED TIME: .... AIRCRAFT CERTIFICATE N°: ....

ESTIMATED FLIGHT DURATION: .... FLIGHT TYPE: ....

AIRPORTS WITHIN 5 MILES: ....

WAIVERS APPLIED FOR: ....

FLIGHT DESCRIPTION/ROUTE: ....

....

....

FLIGHT RECORD

FLIGHT 1

TAKEOFF LOC.: .... LAUNCH TIME: .... FLIGHT NOTES: ....

LANDING LOC.: .... LANDING TIME: ....

BATTERY VOLTAGE: .... ELAPSED TIME: ....

FLIGHT 2

TAKEOFF LOC.: .... LAUNCH TIME: .... FLIGHT NOTES: ....

LANDING LOC.: .... LANDING TIME: ....

BATTERY VOLTAGE: .... ELAPSED TIME: ....

FLIGHT 3

TAKEOFF LOC.: .... LAUNCH TIME: .... FLIGHT NOTES: ....

LANDING LOC.: .... LANDING TIME: ....

BATTERY VOLTAGE: .... ELAPSED TIME: ....

FLIGHT 4

TAKEOFF LOC.: .... LAUNCH TIME: .... FLIGHT NOTES: ....

LANDING LOC.: .... LANDING TIME: ....

BATTERY VOLTAGE: .... ELAPSED TIME: ....

GENERAL NOTES: ....

....

....

Flight Checklist

☐ Airport(s) Notified	☐ UAV Batteries Charged	☐ Gimbal Protector Installed
☐ Location is OK To Fly	Battery 1 volts:	☐ Propellers Packed
☐ Weather Forecast OK	Battery 2 volts:	☐ Cables Packed
Temperature:	Battery 3 volts:	☐ Camera Filters Packed
Wind:	Battery 4 volts:	☐ Sun Shade Packed
Precipitation:	☐ Controller Charged	☐ Tools Packed
☐ Firmware up-to-date	☐ Tablet Charged	☐ Flight Plan designed/entered in Software
☐ Memory Card Formatted	☐ Mobile Phone Charged	☐ Logbook Packed

Launch Site Checklist

☐ Verify Weather is OK To Fly	☐ Check For Obstacles, Interferences
Temperature:	☐ Check For Nearby Human Activity/ Dangerous
Wind:	☐ Verify Launch Pad Is Down-wind From Observers
Precipitation:	
☐ **Safety Briefing**	☐ Launch Pad/Barriers Placed

Equipment Checklist

☐ Airframe/Landing Gear Inspected	☐ Battery Installed
☐ Propellers Inspected/ Attached	☐ Gimbal/Lens Protector Removed
☐ Controller/Tablet Assembled	
☐ Memory Card Installed	☐ Camera Filters Installed

Pre-Flight Checklist

☐ Aircraft Placed on Lauch Pad	☐ Check The Aircraft Status LEDs	☐ Check Flight Mode Switch (P-Mode)
☐ Turn On Remote Controller/ Tablet/DJI Pilot App	☐ Verify the Gimbal is Level, Can Move Unobstructed	☐ Check Satellite and Compass Status
☐ Antennas Properly Positioned	☐ Check RC Battery Level	☐ Set RTH Location And Height
☐ Turn on Aircraft	☐ Check Aircraft Battery Level	☐ Check Camera Settings

Takeoff Checklist

☐ Check Launch site is Clear for Takeoff	☐ Takeoff and Hover	☐ Check Flight Controls, Make Sure They Respond As Expected
☐ Start the motors	☐ Make Sure The Aircraft Is Stable While Hovering	☐ Start Recording Video

Post Flight Checklist

☐ Remove Battery From Aircraft	☐ Repack All Equipment
☐ Install Gimbal Guard	☐ **Complete The Flight Log**

FLIGHT 09

FLIGHT PLAN

PILOT NAME: .... FAA ID: ....

ADDRESS: .... PHONE: ....

VISUAL OBSERVER(S): ....

LOCATION: ....

DATE: .... AIRCRAFT TYPE/NAME: ....

PLANNED TIME: .... AIRCRAFT CERTIFICATE N°: ....

ESTIMATED FLIGHT DURATION: .... FLIGHT TYPE: ....

AIRPORTS WITHIN 5 MILES: ....

WAIVERS APPLIED FOR: ....

FLIGHT DESCRIPTION/ROUTE: ....

....

....

FLIGHT RECORD

FLIGHT 1

TAKEOFF LOC.: .... LAUNCH TIME: .... FLIGHT NOTES: ....

LANDING LOC.: .... LANDING TIME: ....

BATTERY VOLTAGE: .... ELAPSED TIME: ....

FLIGHT 2

TAKEOFF LOC.: .... LAUNCH TIME: .... FLIGHT NOTES: ....

LANDING LOC.: .... LANDING TIME: ....

BATTERY VOLTAGE: .... ELAPSED TIME: ....

FLIGHT 3

TAKEOFF LOC.: .... LAUNCH TIME: .... FLIGHT NOTES: ....

LANDING LOC.: .... LANDING TIME: ....

BATTERY VOLTAGE: .... ELAPSED TIME: ....

FLIGHT 4

TAKEOFF LOC.: .... LAUNCH TIME: .... FLIGHT NOTES: ....

LANDING LOC.: .... LANDING TIME: ....

BATTERY VOLTAGE: .... ELAPSED TIME: ....

GENERAL NOTES: ....

....

....

Flight Checklist

☐ Airport(s) Notified	☐ UAV Batteries Charged	☐ Gimbal Protector Installed
☐ Location is OK To Fly	Battery 1 volts:	☐ Propellers Packed
☐ Weather Forecast OK	Battery 2 volts:	☐ Cables Packed
Temperature:	Battery 3 volts:	☐ Camera Filters Packed
Wind:	Battery 4 volts:	☐ Sun Shade Packed
Precipitation:	☐ Controller Charged	☐ Tools Packed
☐ Firmware up-to-date	☐ Tablet Charged	☐ Flight Plan designed/entered in Software
☐ Memory Card Formatted	☐ Mobile Phone Charged	☐ Logbook Packed

Launch Site Checklist

☐ Verify Weather is OK To Fly	☐ Check For Obstacles, Interferences
Temperature:	☐ Check For Nearby Human Activity/ Dangerous
Wind:	☐ Verify Launch Pad Is Down-wind From Observers
Precipitation:	
☐ **Safety Briefing**	☐ Launch Pad/Barriers Placed

Equipment Checklist

☐ Airframe/Landing Gear Inspected	☐ Battery Installed
☐ Propellers Inspected/ Attached	☐ Gimbal/Lens Protector Removed
☐ Controller/Tablet Assembled	
☐ Memory Card Installed	☐ Camera Filters Installed

Pre-Flight Checklist

☐ Aircraft Placed on Lauch Pad	☐ Check The Aircraft Status LEDs	☐ Check Flight Mode Switch (P-Mode)
☐ Turn On Remote Controller/ Tablet/DJI Pilot App	☐ Verify the Gimbal is Level, Can Move Unobstructed	☐ Check Satellite and Compass Status
☐ Antennas Properly Positioned	☐ Check RC Battery Level	☐ Set RTH Location And Height
☐ Turn on Aircraft	☐ Check Aircraft Battery Level	☐ Check Camera Settings

Takeoff Checklist

☐ Check Launch site is Clear for Takeoff	☐ Takeoff and Hover	☐ Check Flight Controls, Make Sure They Respond As Expected
☐ Start the motors	☐ Make Sure The Aircraft Is Stable While Hovering	☐ Start Recording Video

Post Flight Checklist

☐ Remove Battery From Aircraft	☐ Repack All Equipment
☐ Install Gimbal Guard	☐ **Complete The Flight Log**

FLIGHT 10

FLIGHT PLAN

PILOT NAME: .... FAA ID: ....

ADDRESS: .... PHONE: ....

VISUAL OBSERVER(S): ....

LOCATION: ....

DATE: .... AIRCRAFT TYPE/NAME: ....

PLANNED TIME: .... AIRCRAFT CERTIFICATE n°: ....

ESTIMATED FLIGHT DURATION: .... FLIGHT TYPE: ....

AIRPORTS WITHIN 5 MILES: ....

WAIVERS APPLIED FOR: ....

FLIGHT DESCRIPTION/ROUTE: ....

....

....

FLIGHT RECORD

FLIGHT 1
TAKEOFF LOC.: .... LAUNCH TIME: .... FLIGHT NOTES: ....

LANDING LOC.: .... LANDING TIME: ....

BATTERY VOLTAGE: .... ELAPSED TIME: ....

FLIGHT 2
TAKEOFF LOC.: .... LAUNCH TIME: .... FLIGHT NOTES: ....

LANDING LOC.: .... LANDING TIME: ....

BATTERY VOLTAGE: .... ELAPSED TIME: ....

FLIGHT 3
TAKEOFF LOC.: .... LAUNCH TIME: .... FLIGHT NOTES: ....

LANDING LOC.: .... LANDING TIME: ....

BATTERY VOLTAGE: .... ELAPSED TIME: ....

FLIGHT 4
TAKEOFF LOC.: .... LAUNCH TIME: .... FLIGHT NOTES: ....

LANDING LOC.: .... LANDING TIME: ....

BATTERY VOLTAGE: .... ELAPSED TIME: ....

GENERAL NOTES: ....

....

....

Flight Checklist

☐ Airport(s) Notified	☐ UAV Batteries Charged	☐ Gimbal Protector Installed
☐ Location is OK To Fly	Battery 1 volts:	☐ Propellers Packed
☐ Weather Forecast OK	Battery 2 volts:	☐ Cables Packed
Temperature:	Battery 3 volts:	☐ Camera Filters Packed
Wind:	Battery 4 volts:	☐ Sun Shade Packed
Precipitation:	☐ Controller Charged	☐ Tools Packed
☐ Firmware up-to-date	☐ Tablet Charged	☐ Flight Plan designed/entered in Software
☐ Memory Card Formatted	☐ Mobile Phone Charged	☐ Logbook Packed

Launch Site Checklist

☐ Verify Weather is OK To Fly	☐ Check For Obstacles, Interferences
Temperature:	☐ Check For Nearby Human Activity/ Dangerous
Wind:	☐ Verify Launch Pad Is Down-wind From Observers
Precipitation:	
☐ **Safety Briefing**	☐ Launch Pad/Barriers Placed

Equipment Checklist

☐ Airframe/Landing Gear Inspected	☐ Battery Installed
☐ Propellers Inspected/ Attached	☐ Gimbal/Lens Protector Removed
☐ Controller/Tablet Assembled	
☐ Memory Card Installed	☐ Camera Filters Installed

Pre-Flight Checklist

☐ Aircraft Placed on Lauch Pad	☐ Check The Aircraft Status LEDs	☐ Check Flight Mode Switch (P-Mode)
☐ Turn On Remote Controller/ Tablet/DJI Pilot App	☐ Verify the Gimbal is Level, Can Move Unobstructed	☐ Check Satellite and Compass Status
☐ Antennas Properly Positioned	☐ Check RC Battery Level	☐ Set RTH Location And Height
☐ Turn on Aircraft	☐ Check Aircraft Battery Level	☐ Check Camera Settings

Takeoff Checklist

☐ Check Launch site is Clear for Takeoff	☐ Takeoff and Hover	☐ Check Flight Controls, Make Sure They Respond As Expected
☐ Start the motors	☐ Make Sure The Aircraft Is Stable While Hovering	☐ Start Recording Video

Post Flight Checklist

☐ Remove Battery From Aircraft	☐ Repack All Equipment
☐ Install Gimbal Guard	☐ **Complete The Flight Log**

FLIGHT 11

FLIGHT PLAN

PILOT NAME: .... FAA ID: ....

ADDRESS: .... PHONE: ....

VISUAL OBSERVER(S): ....

LOCATION: ....

DATE: .... AIRCRAFT TYPE/NAME: ....

PLANNED TIME: .... AIRCRAFT CERTIFICATE N°: ....

ESTIMATED FLIGHT DURATION: .... FLIGHT TYPE: ....

AIRPORTS WITHIN 5 MILES: ....

WAIVERS APPLIED FOR: ....

FLIGHT DESCRIPTION/ROUTE: ....

....

....

FLIGHT RECORD

FLIGHT 1
TAKEOFF LOC.: .... LAUNCH TIME: .... FLIGHT NOTES: ....

LANDING LOC.: .... LANDING TIME: ....

BATTERY VOLTAGE: .... ELAPSED TIME: ....

FLIGHT 2
TAKEOFF LOC.: .... LAUNCH TIME: .... FLIGHT NOTES: ....

LANDING LOC.: .... LANDING TIME: ....

BATTERY VOLTAGE: .... ELAPSED TIME: ....

FLIGHT 3
TAKEOFF LOC.: .... LAUNCH TIME: .... FLIGHT NOTES: ....

LANDING LOC.: .... LANDING TIME: ....

BATTERY VOLTAGE: .... ELAPSED TIME: ....

FLIGHT 4
TAKEOFF LOC.: .... LAUNCH TIME: .... FLIGHT NOTES: ....

LANDING LOC.: .... LANDING TIME: ....

BATTERY VOLTAGE: .... ELAPSED TIME: ....

GENERAL NOTES: ....

....

....

FLIGHT CHECKLIST

☐ Airport(s) Notified	☐ UAV Batteries Charged	☐ Gimbal Protector Installed
☐ Location is OK To Fly	Battery 1 volts:	☐ Propellers Packed
☐ Weather Forecast OK	Battery 2 volts:	☐ Cables Packed
Temperature:	Battery 3 volts:	☐ Camera Filters Packed
Wind:	Battery 4 volts:	☐ Sun Shade Packed
Precipitation:	☐ Controller Charged	☐ Tools Packed
☐ Firmware up-to-date	☐ Tablet Charged	☐ Flight Plan designed/entered in Software
☐ Memory Card Formatted	☐ Mobile Phone Charged	☐ Logbook Packed

LAUNCH SITE CHECKLIST

☐ Verify Weather is OK To Fly	☐ Check For Obstacles, Interferences
Temperature:	☐ Check For Nearby Human Activity/ Dangerous
Wind:	☐ Verify Launch Pad Is Down-wind From Observers
Precipitation:	
☐ **Safety Briefing**	☐ Launch Pad/Barriers Placed

EQUIPMENT CHECKLIST

☐ Airframe/Landing Gear Inspected	☐ Battery Installed
☐ Propellers Inspected/ Attached	☐ Gimbal/Lens Protector Removed
☐ Controller/Tablet Assembled	
☐ Memory Card Installed	☐ Camera Filters Installed

PRE-FLIGHT CHECKLIST

☐ Aircraft Placed on Lauch Pad	☐ Check The Aircraft Status LEDs	☐ Check Flight Mode Switch (P-Mode)
☐ Turn On Remote Controller/ Tablet/DJI Pilot App	☐ Verify the Gimbal is Level, Can Move Unobstructed	☐ Check Satellite and Compass Status
☐ Antennas Properly Positioned	☐ Check RC Battery Level	☐ Set RTH Location And Height
☐ Turn on Aircraft	☐ Check Aircraft Battery Level	☐ Check Camera Settings

TAKEOFF CHECKLIST

☐ Check Launch site is Clear for Takeoff	☐ Takeoff and Hover	☐ Check Flight Controls, Make Sure They Respond As Expected
☐ Start the motors	☐ Make Sure The Aircraft Is Stable While Hovering	☐ Start Recording Video

POST FLIGHT CHECKLIST

☐ Remove Battery From Aircraft	☐ Repack All Equipment
☐ Install Gimbal Guard	☐ **Complete The Flight Log**

FLIGHT 12

FLIGHT PLAN

PILOT NAME: ....

FAA ID: ....

ADDRESS: ....

PHONE: ....

VISUAL OBSERVER(S): ....

LOCATION: ....

DATE: ....

AIRCRAFT TYPE/NAME: ....

PLANNED TIME: ....

AIRCRAFT CERTIFICATE N°: ....

ESTIMATED FLIGHT DURATION: ....

FLIGHT TYPE: ....

AIRPORTS WITHIN 5 MILES: ....

....

WAIVERS APPLIED FOR: ....

FLIGHT DESCRIPTION/ROUTE: ....

....

....

FLIGHT RECORD

FLIGHT 1

TAKEOFF LOC.: ....

LAUNCH TIME: ....

FLIGHT NOTES: ....

LANDING LOC.: ....

LANDING TIME: ....

BATTERY VOLTAGE: ....

ELAPSED TIME: ....

FLIGHT 2

TAKEOFF LOC.: ....

LAUNCH TIME: ....

FLIGHT NOTES: ....

LANDING LOC.: ....

LANDING TIME: ....

BATTERY VOLTAGE: ....

ELAPSED TIME: ....

FLIGHT 3

TAKEOFF LOC.: ....

LAUNCH TIME: ....

FLIGHT NOTES: ....

LANDING LOC.: ....

LANDING TIME: ....

BATTERY VOLTAGE: ....

ELAPSED TIME: ....

FLIGHT 4

TAKEOFF LOC.: ....

LAUNCH TIME: ....

FLIGHT NOTES: ....

LANDING LOC.: ....

LANDING TIME: ....

BATTERY VOLTAGE: ....

ELAPSED TIME: ....

GENERAL NOTES: ....

....

....

Flight Checklist

☐ Airport(s) Notified	☐ UAV Batteries Charged	☐ Gimbal Protector Installed
☐ Location is OK To Fly	Battery 1 volts:	☐ Propellers Packed
☐ Weather Forecast OK	Battery 2 volts:	☐ Cables Packed
Temperature:	Battery 3 volts:	☐ Camera Filters Packed
Wind:	Battery 4 volts:	☐ Sun Shade Packed
Precipitation:	☐ Controller Charged	☐ Tools Packed
☐ Firmware up-to-date	☐ Tablet Charged	☐ Flight Plan designed/entered in Software
☐ Memory Card Formatted	☐ Mobile Phone Charged	☐ Logbook Packed

Launch Site Checklist

☐ Verify Weather is OK To Fly	☐ Check For Obstacles, Interferences
Temperature:	☐ Check For Nearby Human Activity/ Dangerous
Wind:	☐ Verify Launch Pad Is Down-wind From Observers
Precipitation:	☐ Launch Pad/Barriers Placed
☐ **Safety Briefing**	

Equipment Checklist

☐ Airframe/Landing Gear Inspected	☐ Battery Installed
☐ Propellers Inspected/ Attached	☐ Gimbal/Lens Protector Removed
☐ Controller/Tablet Assembled	
☐ Memory Card Installed	☐ Camera Filters Installed

Pre-Flight Checklist

☐ Aircraft Placed on Lauch Pad	☐ Check The Aircraft Status LEDs	☐ Check Flight Mode Switch (P-Mode)
☐ Turn On Remote Controller/ Tablet/DJI Pilot App	☐ Verify the Gimbal is Level, Can Move Unobstructed	☐ Check Satellite and Compass Status
☐ Antennas Properly Positioned	☐ Check RC Battery Level	☐ Set RTH Location And Height
☐ Turn on Aircraft	☐ Check Aircraft Battery Level	☐ Check Camera Settings

Takeoff Checklist

☐ Check Launch site is Clear for Takeoff	☐ Takeoff and Hover	☐ Check Flight Controls, Make Sure They Respond As Expected
☐ Start the motors	☐ Make Sure The Aircraft Is Stable While Hovering	☐ Start Recording Video

Post Flight Checklist

☐ Remove Battery From Aircraft	☐ Repack All Equipment
☐ Install Gimbal Guard	☐ **Complete The Flight Log**

FLIGHT 13

Flight Plan

Pilot Name: .... FAA ID: ....

Address: .... Phone: ....

Visual Observer(s): ....

Location: ....

Date: .... Aircraft Type/Name: ....

Planned Time: .... Aircraft Certificate n°: ....

Estimated Flight Duration: .... Flight Type: ....

Airports Within 5 Miles: ....

Waivers Applied For: ....

Flight Description/Route: ....

....

....

Flight Record

Flight 1
Takeoff Loc.: .... Launch Time: .... Flight Notes: ....
Landing Loc.: .... Landing Time: ....
Battery Voltage: .... Elapsed Time: ....

Flight 2
Takeoff Loc.: .... Launch Time: .... Flight Notes: ....
Landing Loc.: .... Landing Time: ....
Battery Voltage: .... Elapsed Time: ....

Flight 3
Takeoff Loc.: .... Launch Time: .... Flight Notes: ....
Landing Loc.: .... Landing Time: ....
Battery Voltage: .... Elapsed Time: ....

Flight 4
Takeoff Loc.: .... Launch Time: .... Flight Notes: ....
Landing Loc.: .... Landing Time: ....
Battery Voltage: .... Elapsed Time: ....

General Notes: ....

....

....

FLIGHT CHECKLIST

☐ Airport(s) Notified	☐ UAV Batteries Charged	☐ Gimbal Protector Installed
☐ Location is OK To Fly	Battery 1 volts:	☐ Propellers Packed
☐ Weather Forecast OK	Battery 2 volts:	☐ Cables Packed
Temperature:	Battery 3 volts:	☐ Camera Filters Packed
Wind:	Battery 4 volts:	☐ Sun Shade Packed
Precipitation:	☐ Controller Charged	☐ Tools Packed
☐ Firmware up-to-date	☐ Tablet Charged	☐ Flight Plan designed/entered in Software
☐ Memory Card Formatted	☐ Mobile Phone Charged	☐ Logbook Packed

LAUNCH SITE CHECKLIST

☐ Verify Weather is OK To Fly	☐ Check For Obstacles, Interferences
Temperature:	☐ Check For Nearby Human Activity/ Dangerous
Wind:	☐ Verify Launch Pad Is Down-wind From Observers
Precipitation:	☐ Launch Pad/Barriers Placed
☐ **Safety Briefing**	

EQUIPMENT CHECKLIST

☐ Airframe/Landing Gear Inspected	☐ Battery Installed
☐ Propellers Inspected/ Attached	☐ Gimbal/Lens Protector Removed
☐ Controller/Tablet Assembled	
☐ Memory Card Installed	☐ Camera Filters Installed

PRE-FLIGHT CHECKLIST

☐ Aircraft Placed on Lauch Pad	☐ Check The Aircraft Status LEDs	☐ Check Flight Mode Switch (P-Mode)
☐ Turn On Remote Controller/ Tablet/DJI Pilot App	☐ Verify the Gimbal is Level, Can Move Unobstructed	☐ Check Satellite and Compass Status
☐ Antennas Properly Positioned	☐ Check RC Battery Level	☐ Set RTH Location And Height
☐ Turn on Aircraft	☐ Check Aircraft Battery Level	☐ Check Camera Settings

TAKEOFF CHECKLIST

☐ Check Launch site is Clear for Takeoff	☐ Takeoff and Hover	☐ Check Flight Controls, Make Sure They Respond As Expected
☐ Start the motors	☐ Make Sure The Aircraft Is Stable While Hovering	☐ Start Recording Video

POST FLIGHT CHECKLIST

☐ Remove Battery From Aircraft	☐ Repack All Equipment
☐ Install Gimbal Guard	☐ **Complete The Flight Log**

FLIGHT 14

Flight Plan

PILOT NAME: ....   FAA ID: ....

ADDRESS: ....   PHONE: ....

VISUAL OBSERVER(S): ....

LOCATION: ....

DATE: ....   AIRCRAFT TYPE/NAME: ....

PLANNED TIME: ....   AIRCRAFT CERTIFICATE n°: ....

ESTIMATED FLIGHT DURATION: ....   FLIGHT TYPE: ....

AIRPORTS WITHIN 5 MILES: ....

WAIVERS APPLIED FOR: ....

FLIGHT DESCRIPTION/ROUTE: ....

....

....

Flight Record

FLIGHT 1

TAKEOFF LOC.: ....   LAUNCH TIME: ....   FLIGHT NOTES: ....

LANDING LOC.: ....   LANDING TIME: ....

BATTERY VOLTAGE: ....   ELAPSED TIME: ....

FLIGHT 2

TAKEOFF LOC.: ....   LAUNCH TIME: ....   FLIGHT NOTES: ....

LANDING LOC.: ....   LANDING TIME: ....

BATTERY VOLTAGE: ....   ELAPSED TIME: ....

FLIGHT 3

TAKEOFF LOC.: ....   LAUNCH TIME: ....   FLIGHT NOTES: ....

LANDING LOC.: ....   LANDING TIME: ....

BATTERY VOLTAGE: ....   ELAPSED TIME: ....

FLIGHT 4

TAKEOFF LOC.: ....   LAUNCH TIME: ....   FLIGHT NOTES: ....

LANDING LOC.: ....   LANDING TIME: ....

BATTERY VOLTAGE: ....   ELAPSED TIME: ....

GENERAL NOTES: ....

....

....

Flight Checklist

☐ Airport(s) Notified	☐ UAV Batteries Charged	☐ Gimbal Protector Installed
☐ Location is OK To Fly	Battery 1 volts:	☐ Propellers Packed
☐ Weather Forecast OK	Battery 2 volts:	☐ Cables Packed
Temperature:	Battery 3 volts:	☐ Camera Filters Packed
Wind:	Battery 4 volts:	☐ Sun Shade Packed
Precipitation:	☐ Controller Charged	☐ Tools Packed
☐ Firmware up-to-date	☐ Tablet Charged	☐ Flight Plan designed/entered in Software
☐ Memory Card Formatted	☐ Mobile Phone Charged	☐ Logbook Packed

Launch Site Checklist

☐ Verify Weather is OK To Fly	☐ Check For Obstacles, Interferences
Temperature:	☐ Check For Nearby Human Activity/ Dangerous
Wind:	☐ Verify Launch Pad Is Down-wind From Observers
Precipitation:	
☐ **Safety Briefing**	☐ Launch Pad/Barriers Placed

Equipment Checklist

☐ Airframe/Landing Gear Inspected	☐ Battery Installed
☐ Propellers Inspected/ Attached	☐ Gimbal/Lens Protector Removed
☐ Controller/Tablet Assembled	
☐ Memory Card Installed	☐ Camera Filters Installed

Pre-Flight Checklist

☐ Aircraft Placed on Launch Pad	☐ Check The Aircraft Status LEDs	☐ Check Flight Mode Switch (P-Mode)
☐ Turn On Remote Controller/ Tablet/DJI Pilot App	☐ Verify the Gimbal is Level, Can Move Unobstructed	☐ Check Satellite and Compass Status
☐ Antennas Properly Positioned	☐ Check RC Battery Level	☐ Set RTH Location And Height
☐ Turn on Aircraft	☐ Check Aircraft Battery Level	☐ Check Camera Settings

Takeoff Checklist

☐ Check Launch site is Clear for Takeoff	☐ Takeoff and Hover	☐ Check Flight Controls, Make Sure They Respond As Expected
☐ Start the motors	☐ Make Sure The Aircraft Is Stable While Hovering	☐ Start Recording Video

Post Flight Checklist

☐ Remove Battery From Aircraft	☐ Repack All Equipment
☐ Install Gimbal Guard	☐ **Complete The Flight Log**

FLIGHT 15

FLIGHT PLAN

PILOT NAME: .... FAA ID: ....

ADDRESS: .... PHONE: ....

VISUAL OBSERVER(S): ....

LOCATION: ....

DATE: .... AIRCRAFT TYPE/NAME: ....

PLANNED TIME: .... AIRCRAFT CERTIFICATE n°: ....

ESTIMATED FLIGHT DURATION: .... FLIGHT TYPE: ....

AIRPORTS WITHIN 5 MILES: ....

WAIVERS APPLIED FOR: ....

FLIGHT DESCRIPTION/ROUTE: ....
....
....

FLIGHT RECORD

FLIGHT 1

TAKEOFF LOC.: .... LAUNCH TIME: .... FLIGHT NOTES: ....

LANDING LOC.: .... LANDING TIME: ....

BATTERY VOLTAGE: .... ELAPSED TIME: ....

FLIGHT 2

TAKEOFF LOC.: .... LAUNCH TIME: .... FLIGHT NOTES: ....

LANDING LOC.: .... LANDING TIME: ....

BATTERY VOLTAGE: .... ELAPSED TIME: ....

FLIGHT 3

TAKEOFF LOC.: .... LAUNCH TIME: .... FLIGHT NOTES: ....

LANDING LOC.: .... LANDING TIME: ....

BATTERY VOLTAGE: .... ELAPSED TIME: ....

FLIGHT 4

TAKEOFF LOC.: .... LAUNCH TIME: .... FLIGHT NOTES: ....

LANDING LOC.: .... LANDING TIME: ....

BATTERY VOLTAGE: .... ELAPSED TIME: ....

GENERAL NOTES: ....
....
....

Flight Checklist

☐ Airport(s) Notified	☐ UAV Batteries Charged	☐ Gimbal Protector Installed
☐ Location is OK To Fly	Battery 1 volts:	☐ Propellers Packed
☐ Weather Forecast OK	Battery 2 volts:	☐ Cables Packed
Temperature:	Battery 3 volts:	☐ Camera Filters Packed
Wind:	Battery 4 volts:	☐ Sun Shade Packed
Precipitation:	☐ Controller Charged	☐ Tools Packed
☐ Firmware up-to-date	☐ Tablet Charged	☐ Flight Plan designed/entered in Software
☐ Memory Card Formatted	☐ Mobile Phone Charged	☐ Logbook Packed

Launch Site Checklist

☐ Verify Weather is OK To Fly	☐ Check For Obstacles, Interferences
Temperature:	☐ Check For Nearby Human Activity/ Dangerous
Wind:	☐ Verify Launch Pad Is Down-wind From Observers
Precipitation:	☐ Launch Pad/Barriers Placed
☐ **Safety Briefing**	

Equipment Checklist

☐ Airframe/Landing Gear Inspected	☐ Battery Installed
☐ Propellers Inspected/ Attached	☐ Gimbal/Lens Protector Removed
☐ Controller/Tablet Assembled	
☐ Memory Card Installed	☐ Camera Filters Installed

Pre-Flight Checklist

☐ Aircraft Placed on Lauch Pad	☐ Check The Aircraft Status LEDs	☐ Check Flight Mode Switch (P-Mode)
☐ Turn On Remote Controller/ Tablet/DJI Pilot App	☐ Verify the Gimbal is Level, Can Move Unobstructed	☐ Check Satellite and Compass Status
☐ Antennas Properly Positioned	☐ Check RC Battery Level	☐ Set RTH Location And Height
☐ Turn on Aircraft	☐ Check Aircraft Battery Level	☐ Check Camera Settings

Takeoff Checklist

☐ Check Launch site is Clear for Takeoff	☐ Takeoff and Hover	☐ Check Flight Controls, Make Sure They Respond As Expected
☐ Start the motors	☐ Make Sure The Aircraft Is Stable While Hovering	☐ Start Recording Video

Post Flight Checklist

☐ Remove Battery From Aircraft	☐ Repack All Equipment
☐ Install Gimbal Guard	☐ **Complete The Flight Log**

FLIGHT 16

FLIGHT PLAN

PILOT NAME: .... FAA ID: ....

ADDRESS: .... PHONE: ....

VISUAL OBSERVER(S): ....

LOCATION: ....

DATE: .... AIRCRAFT TYPE/NAME: ....

PLANNED TIME: .... AIRCRAFT CERTIFICATE n°: ....

ESTIMATED FLIGHT DURATION: .... FLIGHT TYPE: ....

AIRPORTS WITHIN 5 MILES: ....

WAIVERS APPLIED FOR: ....

FLIGHT DESCRIPTION/ROUTE: ....

....

....

FLIGHT RECORD

FLIGHT 1

TAKEOFF LOC.: .... LAUNCH TIME: .... FLIGHT NOTES: ....

LANDING LOC.: .... LANDING TIME: ....

BATTERY VOLTAGE: .... ELAPSED TIME: ....

FLIGHT 2

TAKEOFF LOC.: .... LAUNCH TIME: .... FLIGHT NOTES: ....

LANDING LOC.: .... LANDING TIME: ....

BATTERY VOLTAGE: .... ELAPSED TIME: ....

FLIGHT 3

TAKEOFF LOC.: .... LAUNCH TIME: .... FLIGHT NOTES: ....

LANDING LOC.: .... LANDING TIME: ....

BATTERY VOLTAGE: .... ELAPSED TIME: ....

FLIGHT 4

TAKEOFF LOC.: .... LAUNCH TIME: .... FLIGHT NOTES: ....

LANDING LOC.: .... LANDING TIME: ....

BATTERY VOLTAGE: .... ELAPSED TIME: ....

GENERAL NOTES: ....

....

....

Flight Checklist

☐ Airport(s) Notified	☐ UAV Batteries Charged	☐ Gimbal Protector Installed
☐ Location is OK To Fly	Battery 1 volts:	☐ Propellers Packed
☐ Weather Forecast OK	Battery 2 volts:	☐ Cables Packed
Temperature:	Battery 3 volts:	☐ Camera Filters Packed
Wind:	Battery 4 volts:	☐ Sun Shade Packed
Precipitation:	☐ Controller Charged	☐ Tools Packed
☐ Firmware up-to-date	☐ Tablet Charged	☐ Flight Plan designed/entered in Software
☐ Memory Card Formatted	☐ Mobile Phone Charged	☐ Logbook Packed

Launch Site Checklist

☐ Verify Weather is OK To Fly	☐ Check For Obstacles, Interferences
Temperature:	☐ Check For Nearby Human Activity/ Dangerous
Wind:	☐ Verify Launch Pad Is Down-wind From Observers
Precipitation:	
☐ **Safety Briefing**	☐ Launch Pad/Barriers Placed

Equipment Checklist

☐ Airframe/Landing Gear Inspected	☐ Battery Installed
☐ Propellers Inspected/ Attached	☐ Gimbal/Lens Protector Removed
☐ Controller/Tablet Assembled	
☐ Memory Card Installed	☐ Camera Filters Installed

Pre-Flight Checklist

☐ Aircraft Placed on Lauch Pad	☐ Check The Aircraft Status LEDs	☐ Check Flight Mode Switch (P-Mode)
☐ Turn On Remote Controller/ Tablet/DJI Pilot App	☐ Verify the Gimbal is Level, Can Move Unobstructed	☐ Check Satellite and Compass Status
☐ Antennas Properly Positioned	☐ Check RC Battery Level	☐ Set RTH Location And Height
☐ Turn on Aircraft	☐ Check Aircraft Battery Level	☐ Check Camera Settings

Takeoff Checklist

☐ Check Launch site is Clear for Takeoff	☐ Takeoff and Hover	☐ Check Flight Controls, Make Sure They Respond As Expected
☐ Start the motors	☐ Make Sure The Aircraft Is Stable While Hovering	☐ Start Recording Video

Post Flight Checklist

☐ Remove Battery From Aircraft	☐ Repack All Equipment
☐ Install Gimbal Guard	☐ **Complete The Flight Log**

FLIGHT 17

FLIGHT PLAN

PILOT NAME: .... FAA ID: ....

ADDRESS: .... PHONE: ....

VISUAL OBSERVER(S): ....

LOCATION: ....

DATE: .... AIRCRAFT TYPE/NAME: ....

PLANNED TIME: .... AIRCRAFT CERTIFICATE N°: ....

ESTIMATED FLIGHT DURATION: .... FLIGHT TYPE: ....

AIRPORTS WITHIN 5 MILES: ....

WAIVERS APPLIED FOR: ....

FLIGHT DESCRIPTION/ROUTE: ....

....

....

FLIGHT RECORD

FLIGHT 1

TAKEOFF LOC.: .... LAUNCH TIME: .... FLIGHT NOTES: ....

LANDING LOC.: .... LANDING TIME: ....

BATTERY VOLTAGE: .... ELAPSED TIME: ....

FLIGHT 2

TAKEOFF LOC.: .... LAUNCH TIME: .... FLIGHT NOTES: ....

LANDING LOC.: .... LANDING TIME: ....

BATTERY VOLTAGE: .... ELAPSED TIME: ....

FLIGHT 3

TAKEOFF LOC.: .... LAUNCH TIME: .... FLIGHT NOTES: ....

LANDING LOC.: .... LANDING TIME: ....

BATTERY VOLTAGE: .... ELAPSED TIME: ....

FLIGHT 4

TAKEOFF LOC.: .... LAUNCH TIME: .... FLIGHT NOTES: ....

LANDING LOC.: .... LANDING TIME: ....

BATTERY VOLTAGE: .... ELAPSED TIME: ....

GENERAL NOTES: ....

....

....

Flight Checklist

☐ Airport(s) Notified	☐ UAV Batteries Charged	☐ Gimbal Protector Installed
☐ Location is OK To Fly	Battery 1 volts:	☐ Propellers Packed
☐ Weather Forecast OK	Battery 2 volts:	☐ Cables Packed
Temperature:	Battery 3 volts:	☐ Camera Filters Packed
Wind:	Battery 4 volts:	☐ Sun Shade Packed
Precipitation:	☐ Controller Charged	☐ Tools Packed
☐ Firmware up-to-date	☐ Tablet Charged	☐ Flight Plan designed/entered in Software
☐ Memory Card Formatted	☐ Mobile Phone Charged	☐ Logbook Packed

Launch Site Checklist

☐ Verify Weather is OK To Fly	☐ Check For Obstacles, Interferences
Temperature:	☐ Check For Nearby Human Activity/ Dangerous
Wind:	☐ Verify Launch Pad Is Down-wind From Observers
Precipitation:	☐ Launch Pad/Barriers Placed
☐ **Safety Briefing**	

Equipment Checklist

☐ Airframe/Landing Gear Inspected	☐ Battery Installed
☐ Propellers Inspected/ Attached	☐ Gimbal/Lens Protector Removed
☐ Controller/Tablet Assembled	
☐ Memory Card Installed	☐ Camera Filters Installed

Pre-Flight Checklist

☐ Aircraft Placed on Lauch Pad	☐ Check The Aircraft Status LEDs	☐ Check Flight Mode Switch (P-Mode)
☐ Turn On Remote Controller/ Tablet/DJI Pilot App	☐ Verify the Gimbal is Level, Can Move Unobstructed	☐ Check Satellite and Compass Status
☐ Antennas Properly Positioned	☐ Check RC Battery Level	☐ Set RTH Location And Height
☐ Turn on Aircraft	☐ Check Aircraft Battery Level	☐ Check Camera Settings

Takeoff Checklist

☐ Check Launch site is Clear for Takeoff	☐ Takeoff and Hover	☐ Check Flight Controls, Make Sure They Respond As Expected
☐ Start the motors	☐ Make Sure The Aircraft Is Stable While Hovering	☐ Start Recording Video

Post Flight Checklist

☐ Remove Battery From Aircraft	☐ Repack All Equipment
☐ Install Gimbal Guard	☐ **Complete The Flight Log**

FLIGHT 18

FLIGHT PLAN

PILOT NAME: ....   FAA ID: ....

ADDRESS: ....   PHONE: ....

VISUAL OBSERVER(S): ....

LOCATION: ....

DATE: ....   AIRCRAFT TYPE/NAME: ....

PLANNED TIME: ....   AIRCRAFT CERTIFICATE N°: ....

ESTIMATED FLIGHT DURATION: ....   FLIGHT TYPE: ....

AIRPORTS WITHIN 5 MILES: ....

WAIVERS APPLIED FOR: ....

FLIGHT DESCRIPTION/ROUTE: ....
....
....

FLIGHT RECORD

FLIGHT 1
TAKEOFF LOC.: ....   LAUNCH TIME: ....   FLIGHT NOTES: ....
LANDING LOC.: ....   LANDING TIME: ....
BATTERY VOLTAGE: ....   ELAPSED TIME: ....

FLIGHT 2
TAKEOFF LOC.: ....   LAUNCH TIME: ....   FLIGHT NOTES: ....
LANDING LOC.: ....   LANDING TIME: ....
BATTERY VOLTAGE: ....   ELAPSED TIME: ....

FLIGHT 3
TAKEOFF LOC.: ....   LAUNCH TIME: ....   FLIGHT NOTES: ....
LANDING LOC.: ....   LANDING TIME: ....
BATTERY VOLTAGE: ....   ELAPSED TIME: ....

FLIGHT 4
TAKEOFF LOC.: ....   LAUNCH TIME: ....   FLIGHT NOTES: ....
LANDING LOC.: ....   LANDING TIME: ....
BATTERY VOLTAGE: ....   ELAPSED TIME: ....

GENERAL NOTES: ....
....
....

Flight Checklist

☐ Airport(s) Notified	☐ UAV Batteries Charged	☐ Gimbal Protector Installed
☐ Location is OK To Fly	Battery 1 volts:	☐ Propellers Packed
☐ Weather Forecast OK	Battery 2 volts:	☐ Cables Packed
Temperature:	Battery 3 volts:	☐ Camera Filters Packed
Wind:	Battery 4 volts:	☐ Sun Shade Packed
Precipitation:	☐ Controller Charged	☐ Tools Packed
☐ Firmware up-to-date	☐ Tablet Charged	☐ Flight Plan designed/entered in Software
☐ Memory Card Formatted	☐ Mobile Phone Charged	☐ Logbook Packed

Launch Site Checklist

☐ Verify Weather is OK To Fly	☐ Check For Obstacles, Interferences
Temperature:	☐ Check For Nearby Human Activity/ Dangerous
Wind:	☐ Verify Launch Pad Is Down-wind From Observers
Precipitation:	☐ Launch Pad/Barriers Placed
☐ **Safety Briefing**	

Equipment Checklist

☐ Airframe/Landing Gear Inspected	☐ Battery Installed
☐ Propellers Inspected/ Attached	☐ Gimbal/Lens Protector Removed
☐ Controller/Tablet Assembled	
☐ Memory Card Installed	☐ Camera Filters Installed

Pre-Flight Checklist

☐ Aircraft Placed on Lauch Pad	☐ Check The Aircraft Status LEDs	☐ Check Flight Mode Switch (P-Mode)
☐ Turn On Remote Controller/ Tablet/DJI Pilot App	☐ Verify the Gimbal is Level, Can Move Unobstructed	☐ Check Satellite and Compass Status
☐ Antennas Properly Positioned	☐ Check RC Battery Level	☐ Set RTH Location And Height
☐ Turn on Aircraft	☐ Check Aircraft Battery Level	☐ Check Camera Settings

Takeoff Checklist

☐ Check Launch site is Clear for Takeoff	☐ Takeoff and Hover	☐ Check Flight Controls, Make Sure They Respond As Expected
☐ Start the motors	☐ Make Sure The Aircraft Is Stable While Hovering	☐ Start Recording Video

Post Flight Checklist

☐ Remove Battery From Aircraft	☐ Repack All Equipment
☐ Install Gimbal Guard	☐ **Complete The Flight Log**

FLIGHT 19

Flight Plan

PILOT NAME: .... FAA ID: ....

ADDRESS: .... PHONE: ....

VISUAL OBSERVER(S): ....

LOCATION: ....

DATE: .... AIRCRAFT TYPE/NAME: ....

PLANNED TIME: .... AIRCRAFT CERTIFICATE N°: ....

ESTIMATED FLIGHT DURATION: .... FLIGHT TYPE: ....

AIRPORTS WITHIN 5 MILES: ....

WAIVERS APPLIED FOR: ....

FLIGHT DESCRIPTION/ROUTE: ....

....

....

Flight Record

FLIGHT 1
TAKEOFF LOC.: .... LAUNCH TIME: .... FLIGHT NOTES: ....

LANDING LOC.: .... LANDING TIME: ....

BATTERY VOLTAGE: .... ELAPSED TIME: ....

FLIGHT 2
TAKEOFF LOC.: .... LAUNCH TIME: .... FLIGHT NOTES: ....

LANDING LOC.: .... LANDING TIME: ....

BATTERY VOLTAGE: .... ELAPSED TIME: ....

FLIGHT 3
TAKEOFF LOC.: .... LAUNCH TIME: .... FLIGHT NOTES: ....

LANDING LOC.: .... LANDING TIME: ....

BATTERY VOLTAGE: .... ELAPSED TIME: ....

FLIGHT 4
TAKEOFF LOC.: .... LAUNCH TIME: .... FLIGHT NOTES: ....

LANDING LOC.: .... LANDING TIME: ....

BATTERY VOLTAGE: .... ELAPSED TIME: ....

GENERAL NOTES: ....

....

....

Flight Checklist

☐ Airport(s) Notified	☐ UAV Batteries Charged	☐ Gimbal Protector Installed
☐ Location is OK To Fly	Battery 1 volts:	☐ Propellers Packed
☐ Weather Forecast OK	Battery 2 volts:	☐ Cables Packed
Temperature:	Battery 3 volts:	☐ Camera Filters Packed
Wind:	Battery 4 volts:	☐ Sun Shade Packed
Precipitation:	☐ Controller Charged	☐ Tools Packed
☐ Firmware up-to-date	☐ Tablet Charged	☐ Flight Plan designed/entered in Software
☐ Memory Card Formatted	☐ Mobile Phone Charged	☐ Logbook Packed

Launch Site Checklist

☐ Verify Weather is OK To Fly	☐ Check For Obstacles, Interferences
Temperature:	☐ Check For Nearby Human Activity/ Dangerous
Wind:	☐ Verify Launch Pad Is Down-wind From Observers
Precipitation:	
☐ **Safety Briefing**	☐ Launch Pad/Barriers Placed

Equipment Checklist

☐ Airframe/Landing Gear Inspected	☐ Battery Installed
☐ Propellers Inspected/ Attached	☐ Gimbal/Lens Protector Removed
☐ Controller/Tablet Assembled	
☐ Memory Card Installed	☐ Camera Filters Installed

Pre-Flight Checklist

☐ Aircraft Placed on Lauch Pad	☐ Check The Aircraft Status LEDs	☐ Check Flight Mode Switch (P-Mode)
☐ Turn On Remote Controller/ Tablet/DJI Pilot App	☐ Verify the Gimbal is Level, Can Move Unobstructed	☐ Check Satellite and Compass Status
☐ Antennas Properly Positioned	☐ Check RC Battery Level	☐ Set RTH Location And Height
☐ Turn on Aircraft	☐ Check Aircraft Battery Level	☐ Check Camera Settings

Takeoff Checklist

☐ Check Launch site is Clear for Takeoff	☐ Takeoff and Hover	☐ Check Flight Controls, Make Sure They Respond As Expected
☐ Start the motors	☐ Make Sure The Aircraft Is Stable While Hovering	☐ Start Recording Video

Post Flight Checklist

☐ Remove Battery From Aircraft	☐ Repack All Equipment
☐ Install Gimbal Guard	☐ **Complete The Flight Log**

FLIGHT | 20

FLIGHT PLAN

PILOT NAME: ....   FAA ID: ....

ADDRESS: ....   PHONE: ....

VISUAL OBSERVER(S): ....

LOCATION: ....

DATE: ....   AIRCRAFT TYPE/NAME: ....

PLANNED TIME: ....   AIRCRAFT CERTIFICATE N°: ....

ESTIMATED FLIGHT DURATION: ....   FLIGHT TYPE: ....

AIRPORTS WITHIN 5 MILES: ....

WAIVERS APPLIED FOR: ....

FLIGHT DESCRIPTION/ROUTE: ....

....

....

FLIGHT RECORD

FLIGHT 1

TAKEOFF LOC.: ....   LAUNCH TIME: ....   FLIGHT NOTES: ....

LANDING LOC.: ....   LANDING TIME: ....

BATTERY VOLTAGE: ....   ELAPSED TIME: ....

FLIGHT 2

TAKEOFF LOC.: ....   LAUNCH TIME: ....   FLIGHT NOTES: ....

LANDING LOC.: ....   LANDING TIME: ....

BATTERY VOLTAGE: ....   ELAPSED TIME: ....

FLIGHT 3

TAKEOFF LOC.: ....   LAUNCH TIME: ....   FLIGHT NOTES: ....

LANDING LOC.: ....   LANDING TIME: ....

BATTERY VOLTAGE: ....   ELAPSED TIME: ....

FLIGHT 4

TAKEOFF LOC.: ....   LAUNCH TIME: ....   FLIGHT NOTES: ....

LANDING LOC.: ....   LANDING TIME: ....

BATTERY VOLTAGE: ....   ELAPSED TIME: ....

GENERAL NOTES: ....

....

....

Flight Checklist

☐ Airport(s) Notified	☐ UAV Batteries Charged	☐ Gimbal Protector Installed
☐ Location is OK To Fly	Battery 1 volts:	☐ Propellers Packed
☐ Weather Forecast OK	Battery 2 volts:	☐ Cables Packed
Temperature:	Battery 3 volts:	☐ Camera Filters Packed
Wind:	Battery 4 volts:	☐ Sun Shade Packed
Precipitation:	☐ Controller Charged	☐ Tools Packed
☐ Firmware up-to-date	☐ Tablet Charged	☐ Flight Plan designed/entered in Software
☐ Memory Card Formatted	☐ Mobile Phone Charged	☐ Logbook Packed

Launch Site Checklist

☐ Verify Weather is OK To Fly	☐ Check For Obstacles, Interferences
Temperature:	☐ Check For Nearby Human Activity/ Dangerous
Wind:	☐ Verify Launch Pad is Down-wind From Observers
Precipitation:	☐ Launch Pad/Barriers Placed
☐ **Safety Briefing**	

Equipment Checklist

☐ Airframe/Landing Gear Inspected	☐ Battery Installed
☐ Propellers Inspected/ Attached	☐ Gimbal/Lens Protector Removed
☐ Controller/Tablet Assembled	
☐ Memory Card Installed	☐ Camera Filters Installed

Pre-Flight Checklist

☐ Aircraft Placed on Lauch Pad	☐ Check The Aircraft Status LEDs	☐ Check Flight Mode Switch (P-Mode)
☐ Turn On Remote Controller/ Tablet/DJI Pilot App	☐ Verify the Gimbal is Level, Can Move Unobstructed	☐ Check Satellite and Compass Status
☐ Antennas Properly Positioned	☐ Check RC Battery Level	☐ Set RTH Location And Height
☐ Turn on Aircraft	☐ Check Aircraft Battery Level	☐ Check Camera Settings

Takeoff Checklist

☐ Check Launch site is Clear for Takeoff	☐ Takeoff and Hover	☐ Check Flight Controls, Make Sure They Respond As Expected
☐ Start the motors	☐ Make Sure The Aircraft Is Stable While Hovering	☐ Start Recording Video

Post Flight Checklist

☐ Remove Battery From Aircraft	☐ Repack All Equipment
☐ Install Gimbal Guard	☐ **Complete The Flight Log**

FLIGHT 21

Flight Plan

PILOT NAME: .... FAA ID: ....

ADDRESS: .... PHONE: ....

VISUAL OBSERVER(S): ....

LOCATION: ....

DATE: .... AIRCRAFT TYPE/NAME: ....

PLANNED TIME: .... AIRCRAFT CERTIFICATE N°: ....

ESTIMATED FLIGHT DURATION: .... FLIGHT TYPE: ....

AIRPORTS WITHIN 5 MILES: ....

WAIVERS APPLIED FOR: ....

FLIGHT DESCRIPTION/ROUTE: ....
....
....

Flight Record

FLIGHT 1

TAKEOFF LOC.: .... LAUNCH TIME: .... FLIGHT NOTES: ....

LANDING LOC.: .... LANDING TIME: ....

BATTERY VOLTAGE: .... ELAPSED TIME: ....

FLIGHT 2

TAKEOFF LOC.: .... LAUNCH TIME: .... FLIGHT NOTES: ....

LANDING LOC.: .... LANDING TIME: ....

BATTERY VOLTAGE: .... ELAPSED TIME: ....

FLIGHT 3

TAKEOFF LOC.: .... LAUNCH TIME: .... FLIGHT NOTES: ....

LANDING LOC.: .... LANDING TIME: ....

BATTERY VOLTAGE: .... ELAPSED TIME: ....

FLIGHT 4

TAKEOFF LOC.: .... LAUNCH TIME: .... FLIGHT NOTES: ....

LANDING LOC.: .... LANDING TIME: ....

BATTERY VOLTAGE: .... ELAPSED TIME: ....

GENERAL NOTES: ....
....
....

Flight Checklist

☐ Airport(s) Notified	☐ UAV Batteries Charged	☐ Gimbal Protector Installed
☐ Location is OK To Fly	Battery 1 volts:	☐ Propellers Packed
☐ Weather Forecast OK	Battery 2 volts:	☐ Cables Packed
Temperature:	Battery 3 volts:	☐ Camera Filters Packed
Wind:	Battery 4 volts:	☐ Sun Shade Packed
Precipitation:	☐ Controller Charged	☐ Tools Packed
☐ Firmware up-to-date	☐ Tablet Charged	☐ Flight Plan designed/entered in Software
☐ Memory Card Formatted	☐ Mobile Phone Charged	☐ Logbook Packed

Launch Site Checklist

☐ Verify Weather is OK To Fly	☐ Check For Obstacles, Interferences
Temperature:	☐ Check For Nearby Human Activity/ Dangerous
Wind:	☐ Verify Launch Pad Is Down-wind From Observers
Precipitation:	☐ Launch Pad/Barriers Placed
☐ **Safety Briefing**	

Equipment Checklist

☐ Airframe/Landing Gear Inspected	☐ Battery Installed
☐ Propellers Inspected/ Attached	☐ Gimbal/Lens Protector Removed
☐ Controller/Tablet Assembled	
☐ Memory Card Installed	☐ Camera Filters Installed

Pre-Flight Checklist

☐ Aircraft Placed on Lauch Pad	☐ Check The Aircraft Status LEDs	☐ Check Flight Mode Switch (P-Mode)
☐ Turn On Remote Controller/ Tablet/DJI Pilot App	☐ Verify the Gimbal is Level, Can Move Unobstructed	☐ Check Satellite and Compass Status
☐ Antennas Properly Positioned	☐ Check RC Battery Level	☐ Set RTH Location And Height
☐ Turn on Aircraft	☐ Check Aircraft Battery Level	☐ Check Camera Settings

Takeoff Checklist

☐ Check Launch site is Clear for Takeoff	☐ Takeoff and Hover	☐ Check Flight Controls, Make Sure They Respond As Expected
☐ Start the motors	☐ Make Sure The Aircraft Is Stable While Hovering	☐ Start Recording Video

Post Flight Checklist

☐ Remove Battery From Aircraft	☐ Repack All Equipment
☐ Install Gimbal Guard	☐ **Complete The Flight Log**

FLIGHT | 22

FLIGHT PLAN

PILOT NAME: .... FAA ID: ....

ADDRESS: .... PHONE: ....

VISUAL OBSERVER(S): ....

LOCATION: ....

DATE: .... AIRCRAFT TYPE/NAME: ....

PLANNED TIME: .... AIRCRAFT CERTIFICATE N°: ....

ESTIMATED FLIGHT DURATION: .... FLIGHT TYPE: ....

AIRPORTS WITHIN 5 MILES: ....

WAIVERS APPLIED FOR: ....

FLIGHT DESCRIPTION/ROUTE: ....

....

....

FLIGHT RECORD

FLIGHT 1

TAKEOFF LOC.: .... LAUNCH TIME: .... FLIGHT NOTES: ....

LANDING LOC.: .... LANDING TIME: ....

BATTERY VOLTAGE: .... ELAPSED TIME: ....

FLIGHT 2

TAKEOFF LOC.: .... LAUNCH TIME: .... FLIGHT NOTES: ....

LANDING LOC.: .... LANDING TIME: ....

BATTERY VOLTAGE: .... ELAPSED TIME: ....

FLIGHT 3

TAKEOFF LOC.: .... LAUNCH TIME: .... FLIGHT NOTES: ....

LANDING LOC.: .... LANDING TIME: ....

BATTERY VOLTAGE: .... ELAPSED TIME: ....

FLIGHT 4

TAKEOFF LOC.: .... LAUNCH TIME: .... FLIGHT NOTES: ....

LANDING LOC.: .... LANDING TIME: ....

BATTERY VOLTAGE: .... ELAPSED TIME: ....

GENERAL NOTES: ....

....

....

Flight Checklist

☐ Airport(s) Notified	☐ UAV Batteries Charged	☐ Gimbal Protector Installed
☐ Location is OK To Fly	Battery 1 volts:	☐ Propellers Packed
☐ Weather Forecast OK	Battery 2 volts:	☐ Cables Packed
Temperature:	Battery 3 volts:	☐ Camera Filters Packed
Wind:	Battery 4 volts:	☐ Sun Shade Packed
Precipitation:	☐ Controller Charged	☐ Tools Packed
☐ Firmware up-to-date	☐ Tablet Charged	☐ Flight Plan designed/entered in Software
☐ Memory Card Formatted	☐ Mobile Phone Charged	☐ Logbook Packed

Launch Site Checklist

☐ Verify Weather is OK To Fly	☐ Check For Obstacles, Interferences
Temperature:	☐ Check For Nearby Human Activity/ Dangerous
Wind:	☐ Verify Launch Pad Is Down-wind From Observers
Precipitation:	☐ Launch Pad/Barriers Placed
☐ **Safety Briefing**	

Equipment Checklist

☐ Airframe/Landing Gear Inspected	☐ Battery Installed
☐ Propellers Inspected/ Attached	☐ Gimbal/Lens Protector Removed
☐ Controller/Tablet Assembled	
☐ Memory Card Installed	☐ Camera Filters Installed

Pre-Flight Checklist

☐ Aircraft Placed on Lauch Pad	☐ Check The Aircraft Status LEDs	☐ Check Flight Mode Switch (P-Mode)
☐ Turn On Remote Controller/ Tablet/DJI Pilot App	☐ Verify the Gimbal is Level, Can Move Unobstructed	☐ Check Satellite and Compass Status
☐ Antennas Properly Positioned	☐ Check RC Battery Level	☐ Set RTH Location And Height
☐ Turn on Aircraft	☐ Check Aircraft Battery Level	☐ Check Camera Settings

Takeoff Checklist

☐ Check Launch site is Clear for Takeoff	☐ Takeoff and Hover	☐ Check Flight Controls, Make Sure They Respond As Expected
☐ Start the motors	☐ Make Sure The Aircraft Is Stable While Hovering	☐ Start Recording Video

Post Flight Checklist

☐ Remove Battery From Aircraft	☐ Repack All Equipment
☐ Install Gimbal Guard	☐ **Complete The Flight Log**

FLIGHT 23

FLIGHT PLAN

PILOT NAME: .... FAA ID: ....

ADDRESS: .... PHONE: ....

VISUAL OBSERVER(S): ....

LOCATION: ....

DATE: .... AIRCRAFT TYPE/NAME: ....

PLANNED TIME: .... AIRCRAFT CERTIFICATE N°: ....

ESTIMATED FLIGHT DURATION: .... FLIGHT TYPE: ....

AIRPORTS WITHIN 5 MILES: ....

WAIVERS APPLIED FOR: ....

FLIGHT DESCRIPTION/ROUTE: ....

....

....

FLIGHT RECORD

FLIGHT 1
TAKEOFF LOC.: .... LAUNCH TIME: .... FLIGHT NOTES: ....

LANDING LOC.: .... LANDING TIME: ....

BATTERY VOLTAGE: .... ELAPSED TIME: ....

FLIGHT 2
TAKEOFF LOC.: .... LAUNCH TIME: .... FLIGHT NOTES: ....

LANDING LOC.: .... LANDING TIME: ....

BATTERY VOLTAGE: .... ELAPSED TIME: ....

FLIGHT 3
TAKEOFF LOC.: .... LAUNCH TIME: .... FLIGHT NOTES: ....

LANDING LOC.: .... LANDING TIME: ....

BATTERY VOLTAGE: .... ELAPSED TIME: ....

FLIGHT 4
TAKEOFF LOC.: .... LAUNCH TIME: .... FLIGHT NOTES: ....

LANDING LOC.: .... LANDING TIME: ....

BATTERY VOLTAGE: .... ELAPSED TIME: ....

GENERAL NOTES: ....

....

....

Flight Checklist

☐ Airport(s) Notified	☐ UAV Batteries Charged	☐ Gimbal Protector Installed
☐ Location is OK To Fly	Battery 1 volts:	☐ Propellers Packed
☐ Weather Forecast OK	Battery 2 volts:	☐ Cables Packed
Temperature:	Battery 3 volts:	☐ Camera Filters Packed
Wind:	Battery 4 volts:	☐ Sun Shade Packed
Precipitation:	☐ Controller Charged	☐ Tools Packed
☐ Firmware up-to-date	☐ Tablet Charged	☐ Flight Plan designed/entered in Software
☐ Memory Card Formatted	☐ Mobile Phone Charged	☐ Logbook Packed

Launch Site Checklist

☐ Verify Weather is OK To Fly	☐ Check For Obstacles, Interferences
Temperature:	☐ Check For Nearby Human Activity/ Dangerous
Wind:	☐ Verify Launch Pad Is Down-wind From Observers
Precipitation:	
☐ **Safety Briefing**	☐ Launch Pad/Barriers Placed

Equipment Checklist

☐ Airframe/Landing Gear Inspected	☐ Battery Installed
☐ Propellers Inspected/ Attached	☐ Gimbal/Lens Protector Removed
☐ Controller/Tablet Assembled	
☐ Memory Card Installed	☐ Camera Filters Installed

Pre-Flight Checklist

☐ Aircraft Placed on Lauch Pad	☐ Check The Aircraft Status LEDs	☐ Check Flight Mode Switch (P-Mode)
☐ Turn On Remote Controller/ Tablet/DJI Pilot App	☐ Verify the Gimbal is Level, Can Move Unobstructed	☐ Check Satellite and Compass Status
☐ Antennas Properly Positioned	☐ Check RC Battery Level	☐ Set RTH Location And Height
☐ Turn on Aircraft	☐ Check Aircraft Battery Level	☐ Check Camera Settings

Takeoff Checklist

☐ Check Launch site is Clear for Takeoff	☐ Takeoff and Hover	☐ Check Flight Controls, Make Sure They Respond As Expected
☐ Start the motors	☐ Make Sure The Aircraft Is Stable While Hovering	☐ Start Recording Video

Post Flight Checklist

☐ Remove Battery From Aircraft	☐ Repack All Equipment
☐ Install Gimbal Guard	☐ **Complete The Flight Log**

FLIGHT PLAN

PILOT NAME: ....   FAA ID: ....

ADDRESS: ....   PHONE: ....

VISUAL OBSERVER(S): ....

LOCATION: ....

DATE: ....   AIRCRAFT TYPE/NAME: ....

PLANNED TIME: ....   AIRCRAFT CERTIFICATE n°: ....

ESTIMATED FLIGHT DURATION: ....   FLIGHT TYPE: ....

AIRPORTS WITHIN 5 MILES: ....

WAIVERS APPLIED FOR: ....

FLIGHT DESCRIPTION/ROUTE: ....

....

....

FLIGHT RECORD

FLIGHT 1

TAKEOFF LOC.: ....   LAUNCH TIME: ....   FLIGHT NOTES: ....

LANDING LOC.: ....   LANDING TIME: ....

BATTERY VOLTAGE: ....   ELAPSED TIME: ....

FLIGHT 2

TAKEOFF LOC.: ....   LAUNCH TIME: ....   FLIGHT NOTES: ....

LANDING LOC.: ....   LANDING TIME: ....

BATTERY VOLTAGE: ....   ELAPSED TIME: ....

FLIGHT 3

TAKEOFF LOC.: ....   LAUNCH TIME: ....   FLIGHT NOTES: ....

LANDING LOC.: ....   LANDING TIME: ....

BATTERY VOLTAGE: ....   ELAPSED TIME: ....

FLIGHT 4

TAKEOFF LOC.: ....   LAUNCH TIME: ....   FLIGHT NOTES: ....

LANDING LOC.: ....   LANDING TIME: ....

BATTERY VOLTAGE: ....   ELAPSED TIME: ....

GENERAL NOTES: ....

....

....

Flight Checklist

☐ Airport(s) Notified	☐ UAV Batteries Charged	☐ Gimbal Protector Installed
☐ Location is OK To Fly	Battery 1 volts:	☐ Propellers Packed
☐ Weather Forecast OK	Battery 2 volts:	☐ Cables Packed
Temperature:	Battery 3 volts:	☐ Camera Filters Packed
Wind:	Battery 4 volts:	☐ Sun Shade Packed
Precipitation:	☐ Controller Charged	☐ Tools Packed
☐ Firmware up-to-date	☐ Tablet Charged	☐ Flight Plan designed/entered in Software
☐ Memory Card Formatted	☐ Mobile Phone Charged	☐ Logbook Packed

Launch Site Checklist

☐ Verify Weather is OK To Fly	☐ Check For Obstacles, Interferences
Temperature:	☐ Check For Nearby Human Activity/ Dangerous
Wind:	☐ Verify Launch Pad Is Down-wind From Observers
Precipitation:	
☐ **Safety Briefing**	☐ Launch Pad/Barriers Placed

Equipment Checklist

☐ Airframe/Landing Gear Inspected	☐ Battery Installed
☐ Propellers Inspected/ Attached	☐ Gimbal/Lens Protector Removed
☐ Controller/Tablet Assembled	
☐ Memory Card Installed	☐ Camera Filters Installed

Pre-Flight Checklist

☐ Aircraft Placed on Lauch Pad	☐ Check The Aircraft Status LEDs	☐ Check Flight Mode Switch (P-Mode)
☐ Turn On Remote Controller/ Tablet/DJI Pilot App	☐ Verify the Gimbal is Level, Can Move Unobstructed	☐ Check Satellite and Compass Status
☐ Antennas Properly Positioned	☐ Check RC Battery Level	☐ Set RTH Location And Height
☐ Turn on Aircraft	☐ Check Aircraft Battery Level	☐ Check Camera Settings

Takeoff Checklist

☐ Check Launch site is Clear for Takeoff	☐ Takeoff and Hover	☐ Check Flight Controls, Make Sure They Respond As Expected
☐ Start the motors	☐ Make Sure The Aircraft Is Stable While Hovering	☐ Start Recording Video

Post Flight Checklist

☐ Remove Battery From Aircraft	☐ Repack All Equipment
☐ Install Gimbal Guard	☐ **Complete The Flight Log**

FLIGHT 25

FLIGHT PLAN

PILOT NAME: .... FAA ID: ....

ADDRESS: .... PHONE: ....

VISUAL OBSERVER(S): ....

LOCATION: ....

DATE: .... AIRCRAFT TYPE/NAME: ....

PLANNED TIME: .... AIRCRAFT CERTIFICATE N°: ....

ESTIMATED FLIGHT DURATION: .... FLIGHT TYPE: ....

AIRPORTS WITHIN 5 MILES: ....

....

WAIVERS APPLIED FOR: ....

FLIGHT DESCRIPTION/ROUTE: ....

....

....

FLIGHT RECORD

FLIGHT 1

TAKEOFF LOC.: .... LAUNCH TIME: .... FLIGHT NOTES: ....

LANDING LOC.: .... LANDING TIME: ....

BATTERY VOLTAGE: .... ELAPSED TIME: ....

FLIGHT 2

TAKEOFF LOC.: .... LAUNCH TIME: .... FLIGHT NOTES: ....

LANDING LOC.: .... LANDING TIME: ....

BATTERY VOLTAGE: .... ELAPSED TIME: ....

FLIGHT 3

TAKEOFF LOC.: .... LAUNCH TIME: .... FLIGHT NOTES: ....

LANDING LOC.: .... LANDING TIME: ....

BATTERY VOLTAGE: .... ELAPSED TIME: ....

FLIGHT 4

TAKEOFF LOC.: .... LAUNCH TIME: .... FLIGHT NOTES: ....

LANDING LOC.: .... LANDING TIME: ....

BATTERY VOLTAGE: .... ELAPSED TIME: ....

GENERAL NOTES: ....

....

....

LIGHT CHECKLIST

☐ Airport(s) Notified	☐ UAV Batteries Charged	☐ Gimbal Protector Installed
☐ Location is OK To Fly	Battery 1 volts:	☐ Propellers Packed
☐ Weather Forecast OK	Battery 2 volts:	☐ Cables Packed
Emperature:	Battery 3 volts:	☐ Camera Filters Packed
Vind:	Battery 4 volts:	☐ Sun Shade Packed
Recipitation:	☐ Controller Charged	☐ Tools Packed
☐ Firmware up-to-date	☐ Tablet Charged	☐ Flight Plan designed/entered in Software
☐ Memory Card Formatted	☐ Mobile Phone Charged	☐ Logbook Packed

AUNCH SITE CHECKLIST

☐ Verify Weather is OK To Fly	☐ Check For Obstacles, Interferences
Emperature:	☐ Check For Nearby Human Activity/ Dangerous
Vind:	☐ Verify Launch Pad Is Down-wind From Observers
Recipitation:	☐ Launch Pad/Barriers Placed
☐ **Safety Briefing**	

EQUIPMENT CHECKLIST

☐ Airframe/Landing Gear Inspected	☐ Battery Installed
☐ Propellers Inspected/ Attached	☐ Gimbal/Lens Protector Removed
☐ Controller/Tablet Assembled	
☐ Memory Card Installed	☐ Camera Filters Installed

RE-FLIGHT CHECKLIST

☐ Aircraft Placed on Lauch Pad	☐ Check The Aircraft Status LEDs	☐ Check Flight Mode Switch (P-Mode)
☐ Turn On Remote Controller/ Tablet/DJI Pilot App	☐ Verify the Gimbal is Level, Can Move Unobstructed	☐ Check Satellite and Compass Status
☐ Antennas Properly Positioned	☐ Check RC Battery Level	☐ Set RTH Location And Height
☐ Turn on Aircraft	☐ Check Aircraft Battery Level	☐ Check Camera Settings

AKEOFF CHECKLIST

☐ Check Launch site is Clear for Takeoff	☐ Takeoff and Hover	☐ Check Flight Controls, Make Sure They Respond As Expected
☐ Start the motors	☐ Make Sure The Aircraft Is Stable While Hovering	☐ Start Recording Video

OST FLIGHT CHECKLIST

☐ Remove Battery From Aircraft	☐ Repack All Equipment
☐ Install Gimbal Guard	☐ **Complete The Flight Log**

FLIGHT PLAN

PILOT NAME: .... FAA ID: ....

ADDRESS: .... PHONE: ....

VISUAL OBSERVER(S): ....

LOCATION: ....

DATE: .... AIRCRAFT TYPE/NAME: ....

PLANNED TIME: .... AIRCRAFT CERTIFICATE N°: ....

ESTIMATED FLIGHT DURATION: .... FLIGHT TYPE: ....

AIRPORTS WITHIN 5 MILES: ....

WAIVERS APPLIED FOR: ....

FLIGHT DESCRIPTION/ROUTE: ....

....

....

FLIGHT RECORD

FLIGHT 1

TAKEOFF LOC.: .... LAUNCH TIME: .... FLIGHT NOTES: ....

LANDING LOC.: .... LANDING TIME: ....

BATTERY VOLTAGE: .... ELAPSED TIME: ....

FLIGHT 2

TAKEOFF LOC.: .... LAUNCH TIME: .... FLIGHT NOTES: ....

LANDING LOC.: .... LANDING TIME: ....

BATTERY VOLTAGE: .... ELAPSED TIME: ....

FLIGHT 3

TAKEOFF LOC.: .... LAUNCH TIME: .... FLIGHT NOTES: ....

LANDING LOC.: .... LANDING TIME: ....

BATTERY VOLTAGE: .... ELAPSED TIME: ....

FLIGHT 4

TAKEOFF LOC.: .... LAUNCH TIME: .... FLIGHT NOTES: ....

LANDING LOC.: .... LANDING TIME: ....

BATTERY VOLTAGE: .... ELAPSED TIME: ....

GENERAL NOTES: ....

....

....

Flight Checklist

☐ Airport(s) Notified	☐ UAV Batteries Charged	☐ Gimbal Protector Installed
☐ Location is OK To Fly	Battery 1 volts:	☐ Propellers Packed
☐ Weather Forecast OK	Battery 2 volts:	☐ Cables Packed
Temperature:	Battery 3 volts:	☐ Camera Filters Packed
Wind:	Battery 4 volts:	☐ Sun Shade Packed
Precipitation:	☐ Controller Charged	☐ Tools Packed
☐ Firmware up-to-date	☐ Tablet Charged	☐ Flight Plan designed/entered in Software
☐ Memory Card Formatted	☐ Mobile Phone Charged	☐ Logbook Packed

Launch Site Checklist

☐ Verify Weather is OK To Fly	☐ Check For Obstacles, Interferences
Temperature:	☐ Check For Nearby Human Activity/ Dangerous
Wind:	☐ Verify Launch Pad Is Down-wind From Observers
Recipitation:	
☐ **Safety Briefing**	☐ Launch Pad/Barriers Placed

Equipment Checklist

☐ Airframe/Landing Gear Inspected	☐ Battery Installed
☐ Propellers Inspected/ Attached	☐ Gimbal/Lens Protector Removed
☐ Controller/Tablet Assembled	
☐ Memory Card Installed	☐ Camera Filters Installed

Pre-Flight Checklist

☐ Aircraft Placed on Lauch Pad	☐ Check The Aircraft Status LEDs	☐ Check Flight Mode Switch (P-Mode)
☐ Turn On Remote Controller/ Tablet/DJI Pilot App	☐ Verify the Gimbal is Level, Can Move Unobstructed	☐ Check Satellite and Compass Status
☐ Antennas Properly Positioned	☐ Check RC Battery Level	☐ Set RTH Location And Height
☐ Turn on Aircraft	☐ Check Aircraft Battery Level	☐ Check Camera Settings

Takeoff Checklist

☐ Check Launch site is Clear for Takeoff	☐ Takeoff and Hover	☐ Check Flight Controls, Make Sure They Respond As Expected
☐ Start the motors	☐ Make Sure The Aircraft Is Stable While Hovering	☐ Start Recording Video

Post Flight Checklist

☐ Remove Battery From Aircraft	☐ Repack All Equipment
☐ Install Gimbal Guard	☐ **Complete The Flight Log**

FLIGHT 27

Flight Plan

Pilot Name: .... FAA ID: ....

Address: .... Phone: ....

Visual Observer(s): ....

Location: ....

Date: .... Aircraft Type/Name: ....

Planned Time: .... Aircraft Certificate n°: ....

Estimated Flight Duration: .... Flight Type: ....

Airports Within 5 Miles: ....

Waivers Applied For: ....

Flight Description/Route: ....

....

....

Flight Record

FLIGHT 1

Takeoff Loc.: .... Launch Time: .... Flight Notes: ....

Landing Loc.: .... Landing Time: ....

Battery Voltage: .... Elapsed Time: ....

FLIGHT 2

Takeoff Loc.: .... Launch Time: .... Flight Notes: ....

Landing Loc.: .... Landing Time: ....

Battery Voltage: .... Elapsed Time: ....

FLIGHT 3

Takeoff Loc.: .... Launch Time: .... Flight Notes: ....

Landing Loc.: .... Landing Time: ....

Battery Voltage: .... Elapsed Time: ....

FLIGHT 4

Takeoff Loc.: .... Launch Time: .... Flight Notes: ....

Landing Loc.: .... Landing Time: ....

Battery Voltage: .... Elapsed Time: ....

General Notes: ....

....

....

FLIGHT CHECKLIST

Airport(s) Notified	UAV Batteries Charged	Gimbal Protector Installed
Location is OK To Fly	Battery 1 volts:	Propellers Packed
Weather Forecast OK	Battery 2 volts:	Cables Packed
Temperature:	Battery 3 volts:	Camera Filters Packed
Wind:	Battery 4 volts:	Sun Shade Packed
Precipitation:	Controller Charged	Tools Packed
Firmware up-to-date	Tablet Charged	Flight Plan designed/entered in Software
Memory Card Formatted	Mobile Phone Charged	Logbook Packed

LAUNCH SITE CHECKLIST

Verify Weather is OK To Fly	Check For Obstacles, Interferences
Temperature:	Check For Nearby Human Activity/ Dangerous
Wind:	Verify Launch Pad Is Down-wind From Observers
Precipitation:	
Safety Briefing	Launch Pad/Barriers Placed

EQUIPMENT CHECKLIST

Airframe/Landing Gear Inspected	Battery Installed
Propellers Inspected/ Attached	Gimbal/Lens Protector Removed
Controller/Tablet Assembled	
Memory Card Installed	Camera Filters Installed

PRE-FLIGHT CHECKLIST

Aircraft Placed on Lauch Pad	Check The Aircraft Status LEDs	Check Flight Mode Switch (P-Mode)
Turn On Remote Controller/ Tablet/DJI Pilot App	Verify the Gimbal is Level, Can Move Unobstructed	Check Satellite and Compass Status
Antennas Properly Positioned	Check RC Battery Level	Set RTH Location And Height
Turn on Aircraft	Check Aircraft Battery Level	Check Camera Settings

TAKEOFF CHECKLIST

Check Launch site is Clear for Takeoff	Takeoff and Hover	Check Flight Controls, Make Sure They Respond As Expected
Start the motors	Make Sure The Aircraft Is Stable While Hovering	Start Recording Video

POST FLIGHT CHECKLIST

Remove Battery From Aircraft	Repack All Equipment
Install Gimbal Guard	**Complete The Flight Log**

28

FLIGHT PLAN

PILOT NAME: .... FAA ID: ....

ADDRESS: .... PHONE: ....

VISUAL OBSERVER(S): ....

LOCATION: ....

DATE: .... AIRCRAFT TYPE/NAME: ....

PLANNED TIME: .... AIRCRAFT CERTIFICATE N°: ....

ESTIMATED FLIGHT DURATION: .... FLIGHT TYPE: ....

AIRPORTS WITHIN 5 MILES: ....

WAIVERS APPLIED FOR: ....

FLIGHT DESCRIPTION/ROUTE: ....

....

....

FLIGHT RECORD

FLIGHT 1

TAKEOFF LOC.: .... LAUNCH TIME: .... FLIGHT NOTES: ....

LANDING LOC.: .... LANDING TIME: ....

BATTERY VOLTAGE: .... ELAPSED TIME: ....

FLIGHT 2

TAKEOFF LOC.: .... LAUNCH TIME: .... FLIGHT NOTES: ....

LANDING LOC.: .... LANDING TIME: ....

BATTERY VOLTAGE: .... ELAPSED TIME: ....

FLIGHT 3

TAKEOFF LOC.: .... LAUNCH TIME: .... FLIGHT NOTES: ....

LANDING LOC.: .... LANDING TIME: ....

BATTERY VOLTAGE: .... ELAPSED TIME: ....

FLIGHT 4

TAKEOFF LOC.: .... LAUNCH TIME: .... FLIGHT NOTES: ....

LANDING LOC.: .... LANDING TIME: ....

BATTERY VOLTAGE: .... ELAPSED TIME: ....

GENERAL NOTES: ....

....

....

Flight Checklist

☐ Airport(s) Notified	☐ UAV Batteries Charged	☐ Gimbal Protector Installed
☐ Location is OK To Fly	Battery 1 volts:	☐ Propellers Packed
☐ Weather Forecast OK	Battery 2 volts:	☐ Cables Packed
Temperature:	Battery 3 volts:	☐ Camera Filters Packed
Wind:	Battery 4 volts:	☐ Sun Shade Packed
Precipitation:	☐ Controller Charged	☐ Tools Packed
☐ Firmware up-to-date	☐ Tablet Charged	☐ Flight Plan designed/entered in Software
☐ Memory Card Formatted	☐ Mobile Phone Charged	☐ Logbook Packed

Launch Site Checklist

☐ Verify Weather is OK To Fly	☐ Check For Obstacles, Interferences
Temperature:	☐ Check For Nearby Human Activity/ Dangerous
Wind:	☐ Verify Launch Pad is Down-wind From Observers
Precipitation:	
☐ **Safety Briefing**	☐ Launch Pad/Barriers Placed

Equipment Checklist

☐ Airframe/Landing Gear Inspected	☐ Battery Installed
☐ Propellers Inspected/ Attached	☐ Gimbal/Lens Protector Removed
☐ Controller/Tablet Assembled	
☐ Memory Card Installed	☐ Camera Filters Installed

Pre-Flight Checklist

☐ Aircraft Placed on Lauch Pad	☐ Check The Aircraft Status LEDs	☐ Check Flight Mode Switch (P-Mode)
☐ Turn On Remote Controller/ Tablet/DJI Pilot App	☐ Verify the Gimbal is Level, Can Move Unobstructed	☐ Check Satellite and Compass Status
☐ Antennas Properly Positioned	☐ Check RC Battery Level	☐ Set RTH Location And Height
☐ Turn on Aircraft	☐ Check Aircraft Battery Level	☐ Check Camera Settings

Takeoff Checklist

☐ Check Launch site is Clear for Takeoff	☐ Takeoff and Hover	☐ Check Flight Controls, Make Sure They Respond As Expected
☐ Start the motors	☐ Make Sure The Aircraft is Stable While Hovering	☐ Start Recording Video

Post Flight Checklist

☐ Remove Battery From Aircraft	☐ Repack All Equipment
☐ Install Gimbal Guard	☐ **Complete The Flight Log**

FLIGHT PLAN

PILOT NAME: .... FAA ID: ....

ADDRESS: .... PHONE: ....

VISUAL OBSERVER(S): ....

LOCATION: ....

DATE: .... AIRCRAFT TYPE/NAME: ....

PLANNED TIME: .... AIRCRAFT CERTIFICATE n°: ....

ESTIMATED FLIGHT DURATION: .... FLIGHT TYPE: ....

AIRPORTS WITHIN 5 MILES: ....

WAIVERS APPLIED FOR: ....

FLIGHT DESCRIPTION/ROUTE: ....

....

....

FLIGHT RECORD

FLIGHT 1

TAKEOFF LOC.: .... LAUNCH TIME: .... FLIGHT NOTES: ....

LANDING LOC.: .... LANDING TIME: ....

BATTERY VOLTAGE: .... ELAPSED TIME: ....

FLIGHT 2

TAKEOFF LOC.: .... LAUNCH TIME: .... FLIGHT NOTES: ....

LANDING LOC.: .... LANDING TIME: ....

BATTERY VOLTAGE: .... ELAPSED TIME: ....

FLIGHT 3

TAKEOFF LOC.: .... LAUNCH TIME: .... FLIGHT NOTES: ....

LANDING LOC.: .... LANDING TIME: ....

BATTERY VOLTAGE: .... ELAPSED TIME: ....

FLIGHT 4

TAKEOFF LOC.: .... LAUNCH TIME: .... FLIGHT NOTES: ....

LANDING LOC.: .... LANDING TIME: ....

BATTERY VOLTAGE: .... ELAPSED TIME: ....

GENERAL NOTES: ....

....

....

Flight Checklist

☐ Airport(s) Notified	☐ UAV Batteries Charged	☐ Gimbal Protector Installed
☐ Location is OK To Fly	Battery 1 volts:	☐ Propellers Packed
☐ Weather Forecast OK	Battery 2 volts:	☐ Cables Packed
Temperature:	Battery 3 volts:	☐ Camera Filters Packed
Wind:	Battery 4 volts:	☐ Sun Shade Packed
Precipitation:	☐ Controller Charged	☐ Tools Packed
☐ Firmware up-to-date	☐ Tablet Charged	☐ Flight Plan designed/entered in Software
☐ Memory Card Formatted	☐ Mobile Phone Charged	☐ Logbook Packed

Launch Site Checklist

☐ Verify Weather is OK To Fly	☐ Check For Obstacles, Interferences
Temperature:	☐ Check For Nearby Human Activity/ Dangerous
Wind:	☐ Verify Launch Pad Is Down-wind From Observers
Precipitation:	
☐ **Safety Briefing**	☐ Launch Pad/Barriers Placed

Equipment Checklist

☐ Airframe/Landing Gear Inspected	☐ Battery Installed
☐ Propellers Inspected/ Attached	☐ Gimbal/Lens Protector Removed
☐ Controller/Tablet Assembled	
☐ Memory Card Installed	☐ Camera Filters Installed

Pre-Flight Checklist

☐ Aircraft Placed on Lauch Pad	☐ Check The Aircraft Status LEDs	☐ Check Flight Mode Switch (P-Mode)
☐ Turn On Remote Controller/ Tablet/DJI Pilot App	☐ Verify the Gimbal is Level, Can Move Unobstructed	☐ Check Satellite and Compass Status
☐ Antennas Properly Positioned	☐ Check RC Battery Level	☐ Set RTH Location And Height
☐ Turn on Aircraft	☐ Check Aircraft Battery Level	☐ Check Camera Settings

Takeoff Checklist

☐ Check Launch site is Clear for Takeoff	☐ Takeoff and Hover	☐ Check Flight Controls, Make Sure They Respond As Expected
☐ Start the motors	☐ Make Sure The Aircraft Is Stable While Hovering	☐ Start Recording Video

Post Flight Checklist

☐ Remove Battery From Aircraft	☐ Repack All Equipment
☐ Install Gimbal Guard	☐ **Complete The Flight Log**

FLIGHT | 30

FLIGHT PLAN

PILOT NAME: .... FAA ID: ....

ADDRESS: .... PHONE: ....

VISUAL OBSERVER(S): ....

LOCATION: ....

DATE: .... AIRCRAFT TYPE/NAME: ....

PLANNED TIME: .... AIRCRAFT CERTIFICATE N°: ....

ESTIMATED FLIGHT DURATION: .... FLIGHT TYPE: ....

AIRPORTS WITHIN 5 MILES: ....

WAIVERS APPLIED FOR: ....

FLIGHT DESCRIPTION/ROUTE: ....

....

....

FLIGHT RECORD

FLIGHT 1
TAKEOFF LOC.: .... LAUNCH TIME: .... FLIGHT NOTES: ....

LANDING LOC.: .... LANDING TIME: ....

BATTERY VOLTAGE: .... ELAPSED TIME: ....

FLIGHT 2
TAKEOFF LOC.: .... LAUNCH TIME: .... FLIGHT NOTES: ....

LANDING LOC.: .... LANDING TIME: ....

BATTERY VOLTAGE: .... ELAPSED TIME: ....

FLIGHT 3
TAKEOFF LOC.: .... LAUNCH TIME: .... FLIGHT NOTES: ....

LANDING LOC.: .... LANDING TIME: ....

BATTERY VOLTAGE: .... ELAPSED TIME: ....

FLIGHT 4
TAKEOFF LOC.: .... LAUNCH TIME: .... FLIGHT NOTES: ....

LANDING LOC.: .... LANDING TIME: ....

BATTERY VOLTAGE: .... ELAPSED TIME: ....

GENERAL NOTES: ....

....

....

Flight Checklist

☐ Airport(s) Notified	☐ UAV Batteries Charged	☐ Gimbal Protector Installed
☐ Location is OK To Fly	Battery 1 volts:	☐ Propellers Packed
☐ Weather Forecast OK	Battery 2 volts:	☐ Cables Packed
Temperature:	Battery 3 volts:	☐ Camera Filters Packed
Wind:	Battery 4 volts:	☐ Sun Shade Packed
Precipitation:	☐ Controller Charged	☐ Tools Packed
☐ Firmware up-to-date	☐ Tablet Charged	☐ Flight Plan designed/entered in Software
☐ Memory Card Formatted	☐ Mobile Phone Charged	☐ Logbook Packed

Launch Site Checklist

☐ Verify Weather is OK To Fly	☐ Check For Obstacles, Interferences
Temperature:	☐ Check For Nearby Human Activity/ Dangerous
Wind:	☐ Verify Launch Pad Is Down-wind From Observers
Precipitation:	☐ Launch Pad/Barriers Placed
☐ **Safety Briefing**	

Equipment Checklist

☐ Airframe/Landing Gear Inspected	☐ Battery Installed
☐ Propellers Inspected/ Attached	☐ Gimbal/Lens Protector Removed
☐ Controller/Tablet Assembled	
☐ Memory Card Installed	☐ Camera Filters Installed

Pre-Flight Checklist

☐ Aircraft Placed on Lauch Pad	☐ Check The Aircraft Status LEDs	☐ Check Flight Mode Switch (P-Mode)
☐ Turn On Remote Controller/ Tablet/DJI Pilot App	☐ Verify the Gimbal is Level, Can Move Unobstructed	☐ Check Satellite and Compass Status
☐ Antennas Properly Positioned	☐ Check RC Battery Level	☐ Set RTH Location And Height
☐ Turn on Aircraft	☐ Check Aircraft Battery Level	☐ Check Camera Settings

Takeoff Checklist

☐ Check Launch site is Clear for Takeoff	☐ Takeoff and Hover	☐ Check Flight Controls, Make Sure They Respond As Expected
☐ Start the motors	☐ Make Sure The Aircraft Is Stable While Hovering	☐ Start Recording Video

Post Flight Checklist

☐ Remove Battery From Aircraft	☐ Repack All Equipment
☐ Install Gimbal Guard	☐ **Complete The Flight Log**

FLIGHT **31**

FLIGHT PLAN

PILOT NAME: .... FAA ID: ....

ADDRESS: .... PHONE: ....

VISUAL OBSERVER(S): ....

LOCATION: ....

DATE: .... AIRCRAFT TYPE/NAME: ....

PLANNED TIME: .... AIRCRAFT CERTIFICATE N°: ....

ESTIMATED FLIGHT DURATION: .... FLIGHT TYPE: ....

AIRPORTS WITHIN 5 MILES: ....

WAIVERS APPLIED FOR: ....

FLIGHT DESCRIPTION/ROUTE: ....

....

....

FLIGHT RECORD

FLIGHT 1
TAKEOFF LOC.: .... LAUNCH TIME: .... FLIGHT NOTES: ....
LANDING LOC.: .... LANDING TIME: ....
BATTERY VOLTAGE: .... ELAPSED TIME: ....

FLIGHT 2
TAKEOFF LOC.: .... LAUNCH TIME: .... FLIGHT NOTES: ....
LANDING LOC.: .... LANDING TIME: ....
BATTERY VOLTAGE: .... ELAPSED TIME: ....

FLIGHT 3
TAKEOFF LOC.: .... LAUNCH TIME: .... FLIGHT NOTES: ....
LANDING LOC.: .... LANDING TIME: ....
BATTERY VOLTAGE: .... ELAPSED TIME: ....

FLIGHT 4
TAKEOFF LOC.: .... LAUNCH TIME: .... FLIGHT NOTES: ....
LANDING LOC.: .... LANDING TIME: ....
BATTERY VOLTAGE: .... ELAPSED TIME: ....

GENERAL NOTES: ....

....

....

Flight Checklist

☐ Airport(s) Notified	☐ UAV Batteries Charged	☐ Gimbal Protector Installed
☐ Location is OK To Fly	Battery 1 volts:	☐ Propellers Packed
☐ Weather Forecast OK	Battery 2 volts:	☐ Cables Packed
Temperature:	Battery 3 volts:	☐ Camera Filters Packed
Wind:	Battery 4 volts:	☐ Sun Shade Packed
Precipitation:	☐ Controller Charged	☐ Tools Packed
☐ Firmware up-to-date	☐ Tablet Charged	☐ Flight Plan designed/entered in Software
☐ Memory Card Formatted	☐ Mobile Phone Charged	☐ Logbook Packed

Launch Site Checklist

☐ Verify Weather is OK To Fly	☐ Check For Obstacles, Interferences
Temperature:	☐ Check For Nearby Human Activity/ Dangerous
Wind:	☐ Verify Launch Pad Is Down-wind From Observers
☐ **Safety Briefing**	☐ Launch Pad/Barriers Placed

Equipment Checklist

☐ Airframe/Landing Gear Inspected	☐ Battery Installed
☐ Propellers Inspected/ Attached	☐ Gimbal/Lens Protector Removed
☐ Controller/Tablet Assembled	
☐ Memory Card Installed	☐ Camera Filters Installed

Pre-Flight Checklist

☐ Aircraft Placed on Lauch Pad	☐ Check The Aircraft Status LEDs	☐ Check Flight Mode Switch (P-Mode)
☐ Turn On Remote Controller/ Tablet/DJI Pilot App	☐ Verify the Gimbal is Level, Can Move Unobstructed	☐ Check Satellite and Compass Status
☐ Antennas Properly Positioned	☐ Check RC Battery Level	☐ Set RTH Location And Height
☐ Turn on Aircraft	☐ Check Aircraft Battery Level	☐ Check Camera Settings

Takeoff Checklist

☐ Check Launch site is Clear for Takeoff	☐ Takeoff and Hover	☐ Check Flight Controls, Make Sure They Respond As Expected
☐ Start the motors	☐ Make Sure The Aircraft Is Stable While Hovering	☐ Start Recording Video

Post Flight Checklist

☐ Remove Battery From Aircraft	☐ Repack All Equipment
☐ Install Gimbal Guard	☐ **Complete The Flight Log**

FLIGHT | **32**

FLIGHT PLAN

PILOT NAME: .... FAA ID: ....

ADDRESS: .... PHONE: ....

VISUAL OBSERVER(S): ....

LOCATION: ....

DATE: .... AIRCRAFT TYPE/NAME: ....

PLANNED TIME: .... AIRCRAFT CERTIFICATE N°: ....

ESTIMATED FLIGHT DURATION: .... FLIGHT TYPE: ....

AIRPORTS WITHIN 5 MILES: ....

....

WAIVERS APPLIED FOR: ....

FLIGHT DESCRIPTION/ROUTE: ....

....

....

FLIGHT RECORD

FLIGHT 1
TAKEOFF LOC.: .... LAUNCH TIME: .... FLIGHT NOTES: ....
LANDING LOC.: .... LANDING TIME: ....
BATTERY VOLTAGE: .... ELAPSED TIME: ....

FLIGHT 2
TAKEOFF LOC.: .... LAUNCH TIME: .... FLIGHT NOTES: ....
LANDING LOC.: .... LANDING TIME: ....
BATTERY VOLTAGE: .... ELAPSED TIME: ....

FLIGHT 3
TAKEOFF LOC.: .... LAUNCH TIME: .... FLIGHT NOTES: ....
LANDING LOC.: .... LANDING TIME: ....
BATTERY VOLTAGE: .... ELAPSED TIME: ....

FLIGHT 4
TAKEOFF LOC.: .... LAUNCH TIME: .... FLIGHT NOTES: ....
LANDING LOC.: .... LANDING TIME: ....
BATTERY VOLTAGE: .... ELAPSED TIME: ....

GENERAL NOTES: ....

....

....

Flight Checklist

☐ Airport(s) Notified	☐ UAV Batteries Charged	☐ Gimbal Protector Installed
☐ Location is OK To Fly	Battery 1 volts:	☐ Propellers Packed
☐ Weather Forecast OK	Battery 2 volts:	☐ Cables Packed
Temperature:	Battery 3 volts:	☐ Camera Filters Packed
Wind:	Battery 4 volts:	☐ Sun Shade Packed
Precipitation:	☐ Controller Charged	☐ Tools Packed
☐ Firmware up-to-date	☐ Tablet Charged	☐ Flight Plan designed/entered in Software
☐ Memory Card Formatted	☐ Mobile Phone Charged	☐ Logbook Packed

Launch Site Checklist

☐ Verify Weather is OK To Fly	☐ Check For Obstacles, Interferences
Temperature:	☐ Check For Nearby Human Activity/ Dangerous
Wind:	☐ Verify Launch Pad Is Down-wind From Observers
Precipitation:	☐ Launch Pad/Barriers Placed
☐ Safety Briefing	

Equipment Checklist

☐ Airframe/Landing Gear Inspected	☐ Battery Installed
☐ Propellers Inspected/ Attached	☐ Gimbal/Lens Protector Removed
☐ Controller/Tablet Assembled	
☐ Memory Card Installed	☐ Camera Filters Installed

Pre-Flight Checklist

☐ Aircraft Placed on Lauch Pad	☐ Check The Aircraft Status LEDs	☐ Check Flight Mode Switch (P-Mode)
☐ Turn On Remote Controller/ Tablet/DJI Pilot App	☐ Verify the Gimbal is Level, Can Move Unobstructed	☐ Check Satellite and Compass Status
☐ Antennas Properly Positioned	☐ Check RC Battery Level	☐ Set RTH Location And Height
☐ Turn on Aircraft	☐ Check Aircraft Battery Level	☐ Check Camera Settings

Takeoff Checklist

☐ Check Launch site is Clear for Takeoff	☐ Takeoff and Hover	☐ Check Flight Controls, Make Sure They Respond As Expected
☐ Start the motors	☐ Make Sure The Aircraft Is Stable While Hovering	☐ Start Recording Video

Post Flight Checklist

☐ Remove Battery From Aircraft	☐ Repack All Equipment
☐ Install Gimbal Guard	☐ Complete The Flight Log

FLIGHT | 33

Flight Plan

Pilot Name: ....   FAA ID: ....

Address: ....   Phone: ....

Visual Observer(s): ....

Location: ....

Date: ....   Aircraft Type/Name: ....

Planned Time: ....   Aircraft Certificate n°: ....

Estimated Flight Duration: ....   Flight Type: ....

Airports Within 5 Miles: ....

....

Waivers Applied For: ....

Flight Description/Route: ....

....

....

Flight Record

Flight 1
Takeoff Loc.: ....   Launch Time: ....   Flight Notes: ....

Landing Loc.: ....   Landing Time: ....

Battery Voltage: ....   Elapsed Time: ....

Flight 2
Takeoff Loc.: ....   Launch Time: ....   Flight Notes: ....

Landing Loc.: ....   Landing Time: ....

Battery Voltage: ....   Elapsed Time: ....

Flight 3
Takeoff Loc.: ....   Launch Time: ....   Flight Notes: ....

Landing Loc.: ....   Landing Time: ....

Battery Voltage: ....   Elapsed Time: ....

Flight 4
Takeoff Loc.: ....   Launch Time: ....   Flight Notes: ....

Landing Loc.: ....   Landing Time: ....

Battery Voltage: ....   Elapsed Time: ....

General Notes: ....

....

....

Flight Checklist

☐ Airport(s) Notified	☐ UAV Batteries Charged	☐ Gimbal Protector Installed
☐ Location is OK To Fly	Battery 1 volts:	☐ Propellers Packed
☐ Weather Forecast OK	Battery 2 volts:	☐ Cables Packed
Temperature:	Battery 3 volts:	☐ Camera Filters Packed
Wind:	Battery 4 volts:	☐ Sun Shade Packed
Precipitation:	☐ Controller Charged	☐ Tools Packed
☐ Firmware up-to-date	☐ Tablet Charged	☐ Flight Plan designed/entered in Software
☐ Memory Card Formatted	☐ Mobile Phone Charged	☐ Logbook Packed

Launch Site Checklist

☐ Verify Weather is OK To Fly	☐ Check For Obstacles, Interferences
Temperature:	☐ Check For Nearby Human Activity/ Dangerous
Wind:	☐ Verify Launch Pad Is Down-wind From Observers
Precipitation:	
☐ **Safety Briefing**	☐ Launch Pad/Barriers Placed

Equipment Checklist

☐ Airframe/Landing Gear Inspected	☐ Battery Installed
☐ Propellers Inspected/ Attached	☐ Gimbal/Lens Protector Removed
☐ Controller/Tablet Assembled	
☐ Memory Card Installed	☐ Camera Filters Installed

Pre-Flight Checklist

☐ Aircraft Placed on Lauch Pad	☐ Check The Aircraft Status LEDs	☐ Check Flight Mode Switch (P-Mode)
☐ Turn On Remote Controller/ Tablet/DJI Pilot App	☐ Verify the Gimbal is Level, Can Move Unobstructed	☐ Check Satellite and Compass Status
☐ Antennas Properly Positioned	☐ Check RC Battery Level	☐ Set RTH Location And Height
☐ Turn on Aircraft	☐ Check Aircraft Battery Level	☐ Check Camera Settings

Takeoff Checklist

☐ Check Launch site is Clear for Takeoff	☐ Takeoff and Hover	☐ Check Flight Controls, Make Sure They Respond As Expected
☐ Start the motors	☐ Make Sure The Aircraft Is Stable While Hovering	☐ Start Recording Video

Post Flight Checklist

☐ Remove Battery From Aircraft	☐ Repack All Equipment
☐ Install Gimbal Guard	☐ **Complete The Flight Log**

FLIGHT | 34

FLIGHT PLAN

PILOT NAME: .... FAA ID: ....

ADDRESS: .... PHONE: ....

VISUAL OBSERVER(S): ....

LOCATION: ....

DATE: .... AIRCRAFT TYPE/NAME: ....

PLANNED TIME: .... AIRCRAFT CERTIFICATE N°: ....

ESTIMATED FLIGHT DURATION: .... FLIGHT TYPE: ....

AIRPORTS WITHIN 5 MILES: ....

WAIVERS APPLIED FOR: ....

FLIGHT DESCRIPTION/ROUTE: ....

....

....

FLIGHT RECORD

FLIGHT 1

TAKEOFF LOC.: .... LAUNCH TIME: .... FLIGHT NOTES: ....

LANDING LOC.: .... LANDING TIME: ....

BATTERY VOLTAGE: .... ELAPSED TIME: ....

FLIGHT 2

TAKEOFF LOC.: .... LAUNCH TIME: .... FLIGHT NOTES: ....

LANDING LOC.: .... LANDING TIME: ....

BATTERY VOLTAGE: .... ELAPSED TIME: ....

FLIGHT 3

TAKEOFF LOC.: .... LAUNCH TIME: .... FLIGHT NOTES: ....

LANDING LOC.: .... LANDING TIME: ....

BATTERY VOLTAGE: .... ELAPSED TIME: ....

FLIGHT 4

TAKEOFF LOC.: .... LAUNCH TIME: .... FLIGHT NOTES: ....

LANDING LOC.: .... LANDING TIME: ....

BATTERY VOLTAGE: .... ELAPSED TIME: ....

GENERAL NOTES: ....

....

....

Flight Checklist

☐ Airport(s) Notified	☐ UAV Batteries Charged	☐ Gimbal Protector Installed
☐ Location is OK To Fly	Battery 1 volts:	☐ Propellers Packed
☐ Weather Forecast OK	Battery 2 volts:	☐ Cables Packed
Temperature:	Battery 3 volts:	☐ Camera Filters Packed
Wind:	Battery 4 volts:	☐ Sun Shade Packed
Precipitation:	☐ Controller Charged	☐ Tools Packed
☐ Firmware up-to-date	☐ Tablet Charged	☐ Flight Plan designed/entered in Software
☐ Memory Card Formatted	☐ Mobile Phone Charged	☐ Logbook Packed

Launch Site Checklist

☐ Verify Weather is OK To Fly	☐ Check For Obstacles, Interferences
Temperature:	☐ Check For Nearby Human Activity/ Dangerous
Wind:	☐ Verify Launch Pad Is Down-wind From Observers
Precipitation:	☐ Launch Pad/Barriers Placed
☐ **Safety Briefing**	

Equipment Checklist

☐ Airframe/Landing Gear Inspected	☐ Battery Installed
☐ Propellers Inspected/ Attached	☐ Gimbal/Lens Protector Removed
☐ Controller/Tablet Assembled	
☐ Memory Card Installed	☐ Camera Filters Installed

Pre-Flight Checklist

☐ Aircraft Placed on Lauch Pad	☐ Check The Aircraft Status LEDs	☐ Check Flight Mode Switch (P-Mode)
☐ Turn On Remote Controller/ Tablet/DJI Pilot App	☐ Verify the Gimbal is Level, Can Move Unobstructed	☐ Check Satellite and Compass Status
☐ Antennas Properly Positioned	☐ Check RC Battery Level	☐ Set RTH Location And Height
☐ Turn on Aircraft	☐ Check Aircraft Battery Level	☐ Check Camera Settings

Takeoff Checklist

☐ Check Launch site is Clear for Takeoff	☐ Takeoff and Hover	☐ Check Flight Controls, Make Sure They Respond As Expected
☐ Start the motors	☐ Make Sure The Aircraft Is Stable While Hovering	☐ Start Recording Video

Post Flight Checklist

☐ Remove Battery From Aircraft	☐ Repack All Equipment
☐ Install Gimbal Guard	☐ **Complete The Flight Log**

FLIGHT | **35**

FLIGHT PLAN

PILOT NAME: .... FAA ID: ....

ADDRESS: .... PHONE: ....

VISUAL OBSERVER(S): ....

LOCATION: ....

DATE: .... AIRCRAFT TYPE/NAME: ....

PLANNED TIME: .... AIRCRAFT CERTIFICATE N°: ....

ESTIMATED FLIGHT DURATION: .... FLIGHT TYPE: ....

AIRPORTS WITHIN 5 MILES: ....

WAIVERS APPLIED FOR: ....

FLIGHT DESCRIPTION/ROUTE: ....

....

....

FLIGHT RECORD

FLIGHT 1
TAKEOFF LOC.: .... LAUNCH TIME: .... FLIGHT NOTES: ....
LANDING LOC.: .... LANDING TIME: ....
BATTERY VOLTAGE: .... ELAPSED TIME: ....

FLIGHT 2
TAKEOFF LOC.: .... LAUNCH TIME: .... FLIGHT NOTES: ....
LANDING LOC.: .... LANDING TIME: ....
BATTERY VOLTAGE: .... ELAPSED TIME: ....

FLIGHT 3
TAKEOFF LOC.: .... LAUNCH TIME: .... FLIGHT NOTES: ....
LANDING LOC.: .... LANDING TIME: ....
BATTERY VOLTAGE: .... ELAPSED TIME: ....

FLIGHT 4
TAKEOFF LOC.: .... LAUNCH TIME: .... FLIGHT NOTES: ....
LANDING LOC.: .... LANDING TIME: ....
BATTERY VOLTAGE: .... ELAPSED TIME: ....

GENERAL NOTES: ....

....

....

FLIGHT CHECKLIST

☐ Airport(s) Notified	☐ UAV Batteries Charged	☐ Gimbal Protector Installed
☐ Location is OK To Fly	Battery 1 volts:	☐ Propellers Packed
☐ Weather Forecast OK	Battery 2 volts:	☐ Cables Packed
Temperature:	Battery 3 volts:	☐ Camera Filters Packed
Wind:	Battery 4 volts:	☐ Sun Shade Packed
Precipitation:	☐ Controller Charged	☐ Tools Packed
☐ Firmware up-to-date	☐ Tablet Charged	☐ Flight Plan designed/entered in Software
☐ Memory Card Formatted	☐ Mobile Phone Charged	☐ Logbook Packed

LAUNCH SITE CHECKLIST

☐ Verify Weather is OK To Fly	☐ Check For Obstacles, Interferences
Temperature:	☐ Check For Nearby Human Activity/ Dangerous
Wind:	☐ Verify Launch Pad is Down-wind From Observers
Precipitation:	
☐ **Safety Briefing**	☐ Launch Pad/Barriers Placed

EQUIPMENT CHECKLIST

☐ Airframe/Landing Gear Inspected	☐ Battery Installed
☐ Propellers Inspected/ Attached	☐ Gimbal/Lens Protector Removed
☐ Controller/Tablet Assembled	
☐ Memory Card Installed	☐ Camera Filters Installed

PRE-FLIGHT CHECKLIST

☐ Aircraft Placed on Lauch Pad	☐ Check The Aircraft Status LEDs	☐ Check Flight Mode Switch (P-Mode)
☐ Turn On Remote Controller/ Tablet/DJI Pilot App	☐ Verify the Gimbal is Level, Can Move Unobstructed	☐ Check Satellite and Compass Status
☐ Antennas Properly Positioned	☐ Check RC Battery Level	☐ Set RTH Location And Height
☐ Turn on Aircraft	☐ Check Aircraft Battery Level	☐ Check Camera Settings

TAKEOFF CHECKLIST

☐ Check Launch site is Clear for Takeoff	☐ Takeoff and Hover	☐ Check Flight Controls, Make Sure They Respond As Expected
☐ Start the motors	☐ Make Sure The Aircraft Is Stable While Hovering	☐ Start Recording Video

POST FLIGHT CHECKLIST

☐ Remove Battery From Aircraft	☐ Repack All Equipment
☐ Install Gimbal Guard	☐ **Complete The Flight Log**

FLIGHT | 36

FLIGHT PLAN

PILOT NAME: ....   FAA ID: ....

ADDRESS: ....   PHONE: ....

VISUAL OBSERVER(S): ....

LOCATION: ....

DATE: ....   AIRCRAFT TYPE/NAME: ....

PLANNED TIME: ....   AIRCRAFT CERTIFICATE N°: ....

ESTIMATED FLIGHT DURATION: ....   FLIGHT TYPE: ....

AIRPORTS WITHIN 5 MILES: ....

WAIVERS APPLIED FOR: ....

FLIGHT DESCRIPTION/ROUTE: ....
....
....

FLIGHT RECORD

FLIGHT 1
TAKEOFF LOC.: ....   LAUNCH TIME: ....   FLIGHT NOTES: ....

LANDING LOC.: ....   LANDING TIME: ....

BATTERY VOLTAGE: ....   ELAPSED TIME: ....

FLIGHT 2
TAKEOFF LOC.: ....   LAUNCH TIME: ....   FLIGHT NOTES: ....

LANDING LOC.: ....   LANDING TIME: ....

BATTERY VOLTAGE: ....   ELAPSED TIME: ....

FLIGHT 3
TAKEOFF LOC.: ....   LAUNCH TIME: ....   FLIGHT NOTES: ....

LANDING LOC.: ....   LANDING TIME: ....

BATTERY VOLTAGE: ....   ELAPSED TIME: ....

FLIGHT 4
TAKEOFF LOC.: ....   LAUNCH TIME: ....   FLIGHT NOTES: ....

LANDING LOC.: ....   LANDING TIME: ....

BATTERY VOLTAGE: ....   ELAPSED TIME: ....

GENERAL NOTES: ....
....
....

FLIGHT CHECKLIST

☐ Airport(s) Notified	☐ UAV Batteries Charged	☐ Gimbal Protector Installed
☐ Location is OK To Fly	Battery 1 volts:	☐ Propellers Packed
☐ Weather Forecast OK	Battery 2 volts:	☐ Cables Packed
Temperature:	Battery 3 volts:	☐ Camera Filters Packed
Wind:	Battery 4 volts:	☐ Sun Shade Packed
Precipitation:	☐ Controller Charged	☐ Tools Packed
☐ Firmware up-to-date	☐ Tablet Charged	☐ Flight Plan designed/entered in Software
☐ Memory Card Formatted	☐ Mobile Phone Charged	☐ Logbook Packed

LAUNCH SITE CHECKLIST

☐ Verify Weather is OK To Fly	☐ Check For Obstacles, Interferences
Temperature:	☐ Check For Nearby Human Activity/ Dangerous
Wind:	☐ Verify Launch Pad Is Down-wind From Observers
Precipitation:	
☐ **Safety Briefing**	☐ Launch Pad/Barriers Placed

EQUIPMENT CHECKLIST

☐ Airframe/Landing Gear Inspected	☐ Battery Installed
☐ Propellers Inspected/ Attached	☐ Gimbal/Lens Protector Removed
☐ Controller/Tablet Assembled	
☐ Memory Card Installed	☐ Camera Filters Installed

PRE-FLIGHT CHECKLIST

☐ Aircraft Placed on Lauch Pad	☐ Check The Aircraft Status LEDs	☐ Check Flight Mode Switch (P-Mode)
☐ Turn On Remote Controller/ Tablet/DJI Pilot App	☐ Verify the Gimbal is Level, Can Move Unobstructed	☐ Check Satellite and Compass Status
☐ Antennas Properly Positioned	☐ Check RC Battery Level	☐ Set RTH Location And Height
☐ Turn on Aircraft	☐ Check Aircraft Battery Level	☐ Check Camera Settings

TAKEOFF CHECKLIST

☐ Check Launch site is Clear for Takeoff	☐ Takeoff and Hover	☐ Check Flight Controls, Make Sure They Respond As Expected
☐ Start the motors	☐ Make Sure The Aircraft Is Stable While Hovering	☐ Start Recording Video

POST FLIGHT CHECKLIST

☐ Remove Battery From Aircraft	☐ Repack All Equipment
☐ Install Gimbal Guard	☐ **Complete The Flight Log**

Flight Plan

PILOT NAME: .... FAA ID: ....

ADDRESS: .... PHONE: ....

VISUAL OBSERVER(S): ....

LOCATION: ....

DATE: .... AIRCRAFT TYPE/NAME: ....

PLANNED TIME: .... AIRCRAFT CERTIFICATE N°: ....

ESTIMATED FLIGHT DURATION: .... FLIGHT TYPE: ....

AIRPORTS WITHIN 5 MILES: ....

WAIVERS APPLIED FOR: ....

FLIGHT DESCRIPTION/ROUTE: ....

....

....

Flight Record

FLIGHT 1
TAKEOFF LOC.: .... LAUNCH TIME: .... FLIGHT NOTES: ....

LANDING LOC.: .... LANDING TIME: ....

BATTERY VOLTAGE: .... ELAPSED TIME: ....

FLIGHT 2
TAKEOFF LOC.: .... LAUNCH TIME: .... FLIGHT NOTES: ....

LANDING LOC.: .... LANDING TIME: ....

BATTERY VOLTAGE: .... ELAPSED TIME: ....

FLIGHT 3
TAKEOFF LOC.: .... LAUNCH TIME: .... FLIGHT NOTES: ....

LANDING LOC.: .... LANDING TIME: ....

BATTERY VOLTAGE: .... ELAPSED TIME: ....

FLIGHT 4
TAKEOFF LOC.: .... LAUNCH TIME: .... FLIGHT NOTES: ....

LANDING LOC.: .... LANDING TIME: ....

BATTERY VOLTAGE: .... ELAPSED TIME: ....

GENERAL NOTES: ....

....

....

Flight Checklist

☐ Airport(s) Notified	☐ UAV Batteries Charged	☐ Gimbal Protector Installed
☐ Location is OK To Fly	Battery 1 volts:	☐ Propellers Packed
☐ Weather Forecast OK	Battery 2 volts:	☐ Cables Packed
Temperature:	Battery 3 volts:	☐ Camera Filters Packed
Wind:	Battery 4 volts:	☐ Sun Shade Packed
Precipitation:	☐ Controller Charged	☐ Tools Packed
☐ Firmware up-to-date	☐ Tablet Charged	☐ Flight Plan designed/entered in Software
☐ Memory Card Formatted	☐ Mobile Phone Charged	☐ Logbook Packed

Launch Site Checklist

☐ Verify Weather is OK To Fly	☐ Check For Obstacles, Interferences
Temperature:	☐ Check For Nearby Human Activity/ Dangerous
Wind:	☐ Verify Launch Pad Is Down-wind From Observers
Precipitation:	☐ Launch Pad/Barriers Placed
☐ **Safety Briefing**	

Equipment Checklist

☐ Airframe/Landing Gear Inspected	☐ Battery Installed
☐ Propellers Inspected/ Attached	☐ Gimbal/Lens Protector Removed
☐ Controller/Tablet Assembled	
☐ Memory Card Installed	☐ Camera Filters Installed

Pre-Flight Checklist

☐ Aircraft Placed on Lauch Pad	☐ Check The Aircraft Status LEDs	☐ Check Flight Mode Switch (P-Mode)
☐ Turn On Remote Controller/ Tablet/DJI Pilot App	☐ Verify the Gimbal is Level, Can Move Unobstructed	☐ Check Satellite and Compass Status
☐ Antennas Properly Positioned	☐ Check RC Battery Level	☐ Set RTH Location And Height
☐ Turn on Aircraft	☐ Check Aircraft Battery Level	☐ Check Camera Settings

Takeoff Checklist

☐ Check Launch site is Clear for Takeoff	☐ Takeoff and Hover	☐ Check Flight Controls, Make Sure They Respond As Expected
☐ Start the motors	☐ Make Sure The Aircraft Is Stable While Hovering	☐ Start Recording Video

Post Flight Checklist

☐ Remove Battery From Aircraft	☐ Repack All Equipment
☐ Install Gimbal Guard	☐ **Complete The Flight Log**

FLIGHT | 38

FLIGHT PLAN

PILOT NAME: .... FAA ID: ....

ADDRESS: .... PHONE: ....

VISUAL OBSERVER(S): ....

LOCATION: ....

DATE: .... AIRCRAFT TYPE/NAME: ....

PLANNED TIME: .... AIRCRAFT CERTIFICATE N°: ....

ESTIMATED FLIGHT DURATION: .... FLIGHT TYPE: ....

AIRPORTS WITHIN 5 MILES: ....

....

WAIVERS APPLIED FOR: ....

FLIGHT DESCRIPTION/ROUTE: ....

....

....

FLIGHT RECORD

FLIGHT 1

TAKEOFF LOC.: .... LAUNCH TIME: .... FLIGHT NOTES: ....

LANDING LOC.: .... LANDING TIME: ....

BATTERY VOLTAGE: .... ELAPSED TIME: ....

FLIGHT 2

TAKEOFF LOC.: .... LAUNCH TIME: .... FLIGHT NOTES: ....

LANDING LOC.: .... LANDING TIME: ....

BATTERY VOLTAGE: .... ELAPSED TIME: ....

FLIGHT 3

TAKEOFF LOC.: .... LAUNCH TIME: .... FLIGHT NOTES: ....

LANDING LOC.: .... LANDING TIME: ....

BATTERY VOLTAGE: .... ELAPSED TIME: ....

FLIGHT 4

TAKEOFF LOC.: .... LAUNCH TIME: .... FLIGHT NOTES: ....

LANDING LOC.: .... LANDING TIME: ....

BATTERY VOLTAGE: .... ELAPSED TIME: ....

GENERAL NOTES: ....

....

....

FLIGHT CHECKLIST

☐ Airport(s) Notified	☐ UAV Batteries Charged	☐ Gimbal Protector Installed
☐ Location is OK To Fly	Battery 1 volts:	☐ Propellers Packed
☐ Weather Forecast OK	Battery 2 volts:	☐ Cables Packed
Temperature:	Battery 3 volts:	☐ Camera Filters Packed
Wind:	Battery 4 volts:	☐ Sun Shade Packed
Precipitation:	☐ Controller Charged	☐ Tools Packed
☐ Firmware up-to-date	☐ Tablet Charged	☐ Flight Plan designed/entered in Software
☐ Memory Card Formatted	☐ Mobile Phone Charged	☐ Logbook Packed

LAUNCH SITE CHECKLIST

☐ Verify Weather is OK To Fly	☐ Check For Obstacles, Interferences
Temperature:	☐ Check For Nearby Human Activity/ Dangerous
Wind:	☐ Verify Launch Pad Is Down-wind From Observers
Precipitation:	
☐ Safety Briefing	☐ Launch Pad/Barriers Placed

EQUIPMENT CHECKLIST

☐ Airframe/Landing Gear Inspected	☐ Battery Installed
☐ Propellers Inspected/ Attached	☐ Gimbal/Lens Protector Removed
☐ Controller/Tablet Assembled	
☐ Memory Card Installed	☐ Camera Filters Installed

PRE-FLIGHT CHECKLIST

☐ Aircraft Placed on Lauch Pad	☐ Check The Aircraft Status LEDs	☐ Check Flight Mode Switch (P-Mode)
☐ Turn On Remote Controller/ Tablet/DJI Pilot App	☐ Verify the Gimbal is Level, Can Move Unobstructed	☐ Check Satellite and Compass Status
☐ Antennas Properly Positioned	☐ Check RC Battery Level	☐ Set RTH Location And Height
☐ Turn on Aircraft	☐ Check Aircraft Battery Level	☐ Check Camera Settings

TAKEOFF CHECKLIST

☐ Check Launch site is Clear for Takeoff	☐ Takeoff and Hover	☐ Check Flight Controls, Make Sure They Respond As Expected
☐ Start the motors	☐ Make Sure The Aircraft Is Stable While Hovering	☐ Start Recording Video

POST FLIGHT CHECKLIST

☐ Remove Battery From Aircraft	☐ Repack All Equipment
☐ Install Gimbal Guard	☐ Complete The Flight Log

FLIGHT 39

Flight Plan

Pilot Name: .... FAA ID: ....

Address: .... Phone: ....

Visual Observer(s): ....

Location: ....

Date: .... Aircraft Type/Name: ....

Planned Time: .... Aircraft Certificate n°: ....

Estimated Flight Duration: .... Flight Type: ....

Airports Within 5 Miles: ....

Waivers Applied For: ....

Flight Description/Route: ....

....

....

Flight Record

FLIGHT 1

Takeoff Loc.: .... Launch Time: .... Flight Notes: ....

Landing Loc.: .... Landing Time: ....

Battery Voltage: .... Elapsed Time: ....

FLIGHT 2

Takeoff Loc.: .... Launch Time: .... Flight Notes: ....

Landing Loc.: .... Landing Time: ....

Battery Voltage: .... Elapsed Time: ....

FLIGHT 3

Takeoff Loc.: .... Launch Time: .... Flight Notes: ....

Landing Loc.: .... Landing Time: ....

Battery Voltage: .... Elapsed Time: ....

FLIGHT 4

Takeoff Loc.: .... Launch Time: .... Flight Notes: ....

Landing Loc.: .... Landing Time: ....

Battery Voltage: .... Elapsed Time: ....

General Notes: ....

....

....

Flight Checklist

☐ Airport(s) Notified	☐ UAV Batteries Charged	☐ Gimbal Protector Installed
☐ Location is OK To Fly	Battery 1 volts:	☐ Propellers Packed
☐ Weather Forecast OK	Battery 2 volts:	☐ Cables Packed
Temperature:	Battery 3 volts:	☐ Camera Filters Packed
Wind:	Battery 4 volts:	☐ Sun Shade Packed
Precipitation:	☐ Controller Charged	☐ Tools Packed
☐ Firmware up-to-date	☐ Tablet Charged	☐ Flight Plan designed/entered in Software
☐ Memory Card Formatted	☐ Mobile Phone Charged	☐ Logbook Packed

Launch Site Checklist

☐ Verify Weather is OK To Fly	☐ Check For Obstacles, Interferences
Temperature:	☐ Check For Nearby Human Activity/ Dangerous
Wind:	☐ Verify Launch Pad Is Down-wind From Observers
Precipitation:	
☐ **Safety Briefing**	☐ Launch Pad/Barriers Placed

Equipment Checklist

☐ Airframe/Landing Gear Inspected	☐ Battery Installed
☐ Propellers Inspected/ Attached	☐ Gimbal/Lens Protector Removed
☐ Controller/Tablet Assembled	
☐ Memory Card Installed	☐ Camera Filters Installed

Pre-Flight Checklist

☐ Aircraft Placed on Lauch Pad	☐ Check The Aircraft Status LEDs	☐ Check Flight Mode Switch (P-Mode)
☐ Turn On Remote Controller/ Tablet/DJI Pilot App	☐ Verify the Gimbal is Level, Can Move Unobstructed	☐ Check Satellite and Compass Status
☐ Antennas Properly Positioned	☐ Check RC Battery Level	☐ Set RTH Location And Height
☐ Turn on Aircraft	☐ Check Aircraft Battery Level	☐ Check Camera Settings

Takeoff Checklist

☐ Check Launch site is Clear for Takeoff	☐ Takeoff and Hover	☐ Check Flight Controls, Make Sure They Respond As Expected
☐ Start the motors	☐ Make Sure The Aircraft Is Stable While Hovering	☐ Start Recording Video

Post Flight Checklist

☐ Remove Battery From Aircraft	☐ Repack All Equipment
☐ Install Gimbal Guard	☐ **Complete The Flight Log**

40

FLIGHT PLAN

PILOT NAME: .... FAA ID: ....

ADDRESS: .... PHONE: ....

VISUAL OBSERVER(S): ....

LOCATION: ....

DATE: .... AIRCRAFT TYPE/NAME: ....

PLANNED TIME: .... AIRCRAFT CERTIFICATE N°: ....

ESTIMATED FLIGHT DURATION: .... FLIGHT TYPE: ....

AIRPORTS WITHIN 5 MILES: ....

WAIVERS APPLIED FOR: ....

FLIGHT DESCRIPTION/ROUTE: ....

....

....

FLIGHT RECORD

FLIGHT 1

TAKEOFF LOC.: .... LAUNCH TIME: .... FLIGHT NOTES: ....

LANDING LOC.: .... LANDING TIME: ....

BATTERY VOLTAGE: .... ELAPSED TIME: ....

FLIGHT 2

TAKEOFF LOC.: .... LAUNCH TIME: .... FLIGHT NOTES: ....

LANDING LOC.: .... LANDING TIME: ....

BATTERY VOLTAGE: .... ELAPSED TIME: ....

FLIGHT 3

TAKEOFF LOC.: .... LAUNCH TIME: .... FLIGHT NOTES: ....

LANDING LOC.: .... LANDING TIME: ....

BATTERY VOLTAGE: .... ELAPSED TIME: ....

FLIGHT 4

TAKEOFF LOC.: .... LAUNCH TIME: .... FLIGHT NOTES: ....

LANDING LOC.: .... LANDING TIME: ....

BATTERY VOLTAGE: .... ELAPSED TIME: ....

GENERAL NOTES: ....

....

....

Flight Checklist

☐ Airport(s) Notified	☐ UAV Batteries Charged	☐ Gimbal Protector Installed
☐ Location is OK To Fly	Battery 1 volts:	☐ Propellers Packed
☐ Weather Forecast OK	Battery 2 volts:	☐ Cables Packed
Temperature:	Battery 3 volts:	☐ Camera Filters Packed
Wind:	Battery 4 volts:	☐ Sun Shade Packed
Precipitation:	☐ Controller Charged	☐ Tools Packed
☐ Firmware up-to-date	☐ Tablet Charged	☐ Flight Plan designed/entered in Software
☐ Memory Card Formatted	☐ Mobile Phone Charged	☐ Logbook Packed

Launch Site Checklist

☐ Verify Weather is OK To Fly	☐ Check For Obstacles, Interferences
Temperature:	☐ Check For Nearby Human Activity/ Dangerous
Wind:	☐ Verify Launch Pad Is Down-wind From Observers
Precipitation:	
☐ **Safety Briefing**	☐ Launch Pad/Barriers Placed

Equipment Checklist

☐ Airframe/Landing Gear Inspected	☐ Battery Installed
☐ Propellers Inspected/ Attached	☐ Gimbal/Lens Protector Removed
☐ Controller/Tablet Assembled	
☐ Memory Card Installed	☐ Camera Filters Installed

Pre-Flight Checklist

☐ Aircraft Placed on Lauch Pad	☐ Check The Aircraft Status LEDs	☐ Check Flight Mode Switch (P-Mode)
☐ Turn On Remote Controller/ Tablet/DJI Pilot App	☐ Verify the Gimbal is Level, Can Move Unobstructed	☐ Check Satellite and Compass Status
☐ Antennas Properly Positioned	☐ Check RC Battery Level	☐ Set RTH Location And Height
☐ Turn on Aircraft	☐ Check Aircraft Battery Level	☐ Check Camera Settings

Takeoff Checklist

☐ Check Launch site is Clear for Takeoff	☐ Takeoff and Hover	☐ Check Flight Controls, Make Sure They Respond As Expected
☐ Start the motors	☐ Make Sure The Aircraft Is Stable While Hovering	☐ Start Recording Video

Post Flight Checklist

☐ Remove Battery From Aircraft	☐ Repack All Equipment
☐ Install Gimbal Guard	☐ **Complete The Flight Log**

FLIGHT PLAN

PILOT NAME: .... FAA ID: ....

ADDRESS: .... PHONE: ....

VISUAL OBSERVER(S): ....

LOCATION: ....

DATE: .... AIRCRAFT TYPE/NAME: ....

PLANNED TIME: .... AIRCRAFT CERTIFICATE n°: ....

ESTIMATED FLIGHT DURATION: .... FLIGHT TYPE: ....

AIRPORTS WITHIN 5 MILES: ....

WAIVERS APPLIED FOR: ....

FLIGHT DESCRIPTION/ROUTE: ....

....

....

FLIGHT RECORD

FLIGHT 1
TAKEOFF LOC.: .... LAUNCH TIME: .... FLIGHT NOTES: ....

LANDING LOC.: .... LANDING TIME: ....

BATTERY VOLTAGE: .... ELAPSED TIME: ....

FLIGHT 2
TAKEOFF LOC.: .... LAUNCH TIME: .... FLIGHT NOTES: ....

LANDING LOC.: .... LANDING TIME: ....

BATTERY VOLTAGE: .... ELAPSED TIME: ....

FLIGHT 3
TAKEOFF LOC.: .... LAUNCH TIME: .... FLIGHT NOTES: ....

LANDING LOC.: .... LANDING TIME: ....

BATTERY VOLTAGE: .... ELAPSED TIME: ....

FLIGHT 4
TAKEOFF LOC.: .... LAUNCH TIME: .... FLIGHT NOTES: ....

LANDING LOC.: .... LANDING TIME: ....

BATTERY VOLTAGE: .... ELAPSED TIME: ....

GENERAL NOTES: ....

....

....

Flight Checklist

☐ Airport(s) Notified	☐ UAV Batteries Charged	☐ Gimbal Protector Installed
☐ Location is OK To Fly	Battery 1 volts:	☐ Propellers Packed
☐ Weather Forecast OK	Battery 2 volts:	☐ Cables Packed
Temperature:	Battery 3 volts:	☐ Camera Filters Packed
Wind:	Battery 4 volts:	☐ Sun Shade Packed
Precipitation:	☐ Controller Charged	☐ Tools Packed
☐ Firmware up-to-date	☐ Tablet Charged	☐ Flight Plan designed/entered in Software
☐ Memory Card Formatted	☐ Mobile Phone Charged	☐ Logbook Packed

Launch Site Checklist

☐ Verify Weather is OK To Fly	☐ Check For Obstacles, Interferences
Temperature:	☐ Check For Nearby Human Activity/ Dangerous
Wind:	☐ Verify Launch Pad Is Down-wind From Observers
Precipitation:	
☐ **Safety Briefing**	☐ Launch Pad/Barriers Placed

Equipment Checklist

☐ Airframe/Landing Gear Inspected	☐ Battery Installed
☐ Propellers Inspected/ Attached	☐ Gimbal/Lens Protector Removed
☐ Controller/Tablet Assembled	
☐ Memory Card Installed	☐ Camera Filters Installed

Pre-Flight Checklist

☐ Aircraft Placed on Lauch Pad	☐ Check The Aircraft Status LEDs	☐ Check Flight Mode Switch (P-Mode)
☐ Turn On Remote Controller/ Tablet/DJI Pilot App	☐ Verify the Gimbal is Level, Can Move Unobstructed	☐ Check Satellite and Compass Status
☐ Antennas Properly Positioned	☐ Check RC Battery Level	☐ Set RTH Location And Height
☐ Turn on Aircraft	☐ Check Aircraft Battery Level	☐ Check Camera Settings

Takeoff Checklist

☐ Check Launch site is Clear for Takeoff	☐ Takeoff and Hover	☐ Check Flight Controls, Make Sure They Respond As Expected
☐ Start the motors	☐ Make Sure The Aircraft Is Stable While Hovering	☐ Start Recording Video

Post Flight Checklist

☐ Remove Battery From Aircraft	☐ Repack All Equipment
☐ Install Gimbal Guard	☐ **Complete The Flight Log**

FLIGHT PLAN

PILOT NAME: .... FAA ID: ....

ADDRESS: .... PHONE: ....

VISUAL OBSERVER(S): ....

LOCATION: ....

DATE: .... AIRCRAFT TYPE/NAME: ....

PLANNED TIME: .... AIRCRAFT CERTIFICATE N°: ....

ESTIMATED FLIGHT DURATION: .... FLIGHT TYPE: ....

AIRPORTS WITHIN 5 MILES: ....

WAIVERS APPLIED FOR: ....

FLIGHT DESCRIPTION/ROUTE: ....

....

....

FLIGHT RECORD

FLIGHT 1

TAKEOFF LOC.: .... LAUNCH TIME: .... FLIGHT NOTES: ....

LANDING LOC.: .... LANDING TIME: ....

BATTERY VOLTAGE: .... ELAPSED TIME: ....

FLIGHT 2

TAKEOFF LOC.: .... LAUNCH TIME: .... FLIGHT NOTES: ....

LANDING LOC.: .... LANDING TIME: ....

BATTERY VOLTAGE: .... ELAPSED TIME: ....

FLIGHT 3

TAKEOFF LOC.: .... LAUNCH TIME: .... FLIGHT NOTES: ....

LANDING LOC.: .... LANDING TIME: ....

BATTERY VOLTAGE: .... ELAPSED TIME: ....

FLIGHT 4

TAKEOFF LOC.: .... LAUNCH TIME: .... FLIGHT NOTES: ....

LANDING LOC.: .... LANDING TIME: ....

BATTERY VOLTAGE: .... ELAPSED TIME: ....

GENERAL NOTES: ....

....

....

Flight Checklist

☐ Airport(s) Notified	☐ UAV Batteries Charged	☐ Gimbal Protector Installed
☐ Location is OK To Fly	Battery 1 volts:	☐ Propellers Packed
☐ Weather Forecast OK	Battery 2 volts:	☐ Cables Packed
Temperature:	Battery 3 volts:	☐ Camera Filters Packed
Wind:	Battery 4 volts:	☐ Sun Shade Packed
Precipitation:	☐ Controller Charged	☐ Tools Packed
☐ Firmware up-to-date	☐ Tablet Charged	☐ Flight Plan designed/entered in Software
☐ Memory Card Formatted	☐ Mobile Phone Charged	☐ Logbook Packed

Launch Site Checklist

☐ Verify Weather is OK To Fly	☐ Check For Obstacles, Interferences
Temperature:	☐ Check For Nearby Human Activity/ Dangerous
Wind:	☐ Verify Launch Pad Is Down-wind From Observers
Precipitation:	
☐ **Safety Briefing**	☐ Launch Pad/Barriers Placed

Equipment Checklist

☐ Airframe/Landing Gear Inspected	☐ Battery Installed
☐ Propellers Inspected/ Attached	☐ Gimbal/Lens Protector Removed
☐ Controller/Tablet Assembled	
☐ Memory Card Installed	☐ Camera Filters Installed

Pre-Flight Checklist

☐ Aircraft Placed on Lauch Pad	☐ Check The Aircraft Status LEDs	☐ Check Flight Mode Switch (P-Mode)
☐ Turn On Remote Controller/ Tablet/DJI Pilot App	☐ Verify the Gimbal is Level, Can Move Unobstructed	☐ Check Satellite and Compass Status
☐ Antennas Properly Positioned	☐ Check RC Battery Level	☐ Set RTH Location And Height
☐ Turn on Aircraft	☐ Check Aircraft Battery Level	☐ Check Camera Settings

Takeoff Checklist

☐ Check Launch site is Clear for Takeoff	☐ Takeoff and Hover	☐ Check Flight Controls, Make Sure They Respond As Expected
☐ Start the motors	☐ Make Sure The Aircraft Is Stable While Hovering	☐ Start Recording Video

Post Flight Checklist

☐ Remove Battery From Aircraft	☐ Repack All Equipment
☐ Install Gimbal Guard	☐ **Complete The Flight Log**

FLIGHT PLAN

PILOT NAME: .... FAA ID: ....

ADDRESS: .... PHONE: ....

VISUAL OBSERVER(S): ....

LOCATION: ....

DATE: .... AIRCRAFT TYPE/NAME: ....

PLANNED TIME: .... AIRCRAFT CERTIFICATE n°: ....

ESTIMATED FLIGHT DURATION: .... FLIGHT TYPE: ....

AIRPORTS WITHIN 5 MILES: ....

WAIVERS APPLIED FOR: ....

FLIGHT DESCRIPTION/ROUTE: ....

....

....

FLIGHT RECORD

FLIGHT 1
TAKEOFF LOC.: .... LAUNCH TIME: .... FLIGHT NOTES: ....

LANDING LOC.: .... LANDING TIME: ....

BATTERY VOLTAGE: .... ELAPSED TIME: ....

FLIGHT 2
TAKEOFF LOC.: .... LAUNCH TIME: .... FLIGHT NOTES: ....

LANDING LOC.: .... LANDING TIME: ....

BATTERY VOLTAGE: .... ELAPSED TIME: ....

FLIGHT 3
TAKEOFF LOC.: .... LAUNCH TIME: .... FLIGHT NOTES: ....

LANDING LOC.: .... LANDING TIME: ....

BATTERY VOLTAGE: .... ELAPSED TIME: ....

FLIGHT 4
TAKEOFF LOC.: .... LAUNCH TIME: .... FLIGHT NOTES: ....

LANDING LOC.: .... LANDING TIME: ....

BATTERY VOLTAGE: .... ELAPSED TIME: ....

GENERAL NOTES: ....

....

....

Flight Checklist

☐ Airport(s) Notified	☐ UAV Batteries Charged	☐ Gimbal Protector Installed
☐ Location is OK To Fly	Battery 1 volts:	☐ Propellers Packed
☐ Weather Forecast OK	Battery 2 volts:	☐ Cables Packed
Temperature:	Battery 3 volts:	☐ Camera Filters Packed
Wind:	Battery 4 volts:	☐ Sun Shade Packed
Precipitation:	☐ Controller Charged	☐ Tools Packed
☐ Firmware up-to-date	☐ Tablet Charged	☐ Flight Plan designed/entered in Software
☐ Memory Card Formatted	☐ Mobile Phone Charged	☐ Logbook Packed

Launch Site Checklist

☐ Verify Weather is OK To Fly	☐ Check For Obstacles, Interferences
Temperature:	☐ Check For Nearby Human Activity/ Dangerous
Wind:	☐ Verify Launch Pad Is Down-wind From Observers
Precipitation:	☐ Launch Pad/Barriers Placed
☐ **Safety Briefing**	

Equipment Checklist

☐ Airframe/Landing Gear Inspected	☐ Battery Installed
☐ Propellers Inspected/ Attached	☐ Gimbal/Lens Protector Removed
☐ Controller/Tablet Assembled	
☐ Memory Card Installed	☐ Camera Filters Installed

Pre-Flight Checklist

☐ Aircraft Placed on Lauch Pad	☐ Check The Aircraft Status LEDs	☐ Check Flight Mode Switch (P-Mode)
☐ Turn On Remote Controller/ Tablet/DJI Pilot App	☐ Verify the Gimbal is Level, Can Move Unobstructed	☐ Check Satellite and Compass Status
☐ Antennas Properly Positioned	☐ Check RC Battery Level	☐ Set RTH Location And Height
☐ Turn on Aircraft	☐ Check Aircraft Battery Level	☐ Check Camera Settings

Takeoff Checklist

☐ Check Launch site is Clear for Takeoff	☐ Takeoff and Hover	☐ Check Flight Controls, Make Sure They Respond As Expected
☐ Start the motors	☐ Make Sure The Aircraft Is Stable While Hovering	☐ Start Recording Video

Post Flight Checklist

☐ Remove Battery From Aircraft	☐ Repack All Equipment
☐ Install Gimbal Guard	☐ **Complete The Flight Log**

FLIGHT 44

Flight Plan

Pilot Name: .... FAA ID: ....

Address: .... Phone: ....

Visual Observer(s): ....

Location: ....

Date: .... Aircraft Type/Name: ....

Planned Time: .... Aircraft Certificate n°: ....

Estimated Flight Duration: .... Flight Type: ....

Airports Within 5 Miles: ....

Waivers Applied For: ....

Flight Description/Route: ....

....

....

Flight Record

Flight 1

Takeoff Loc.: .... Launch Time: .... Flight Notes: ....

Landing Loc.: .... Landing Time: ....

Battery Voltage: .... Elapsed Time: ....

Flight 2

Takeoff Loc.: .... Launch Time: .... Flight Notes: ....

Landing Loc.: .... Landing Time: ....

Battery Voltage: .... Elapsed Time: ....

Flight 3

Takeoff Loc.: .... Launch Time: .... Flight Notes: ....

Landing Loc.: .... Landing Time: ....

Battery Voltage: .... Elapsed Time: ....

Flight 4

Takeoff Loc.: .... Launch Time: .... Flight Notes: ....

Landing Loc.: .... Landing Time: ....

Battery Voltage: .... Elapsed Time: ....

General Notes: ....

....

....

Flight Checklist

☐ Airport(s) Notified	☐ UAV Batteries Charged	☐ Gimbal Protector Installed
☐ Location is OK To Fly	Battery 1 volts:	☐ Propellers Packed
☐ Weather Forecast OK	Battery 2 volts:	☐ Cables Packed
Temperature:	Battery 3 volts:	☐ Camera Filters Packed
Wind:	Battery 4 volts:	☐ Sun Shade Packed
Precipitation:	☐ Controller Charged	☐ Tools Packed
☐ Firmware up-to-date	☐ Tablet Charged	☐ Flight Plan designed/entered in Software
☐ Memory Card Formatted	☐ Mobile Phone Charged	☐ Logbook Packed

Launch Site Checklist

☐ Verify Weather is OK To Fly	☐ Check For Obstacles, Interferences
Temperature:	☐ Check For Nearby Human Activity/ Dangerous
Wind:	☐ Verify Launch Pad Is Down-wind From Observers
Precipitation:	
☐ **Safety Briefing**	☐ Launch Pad/Barriers Placed

Equipment Checklist

☐ Airframe/Landing Gear Inspected	☐ Battery Installed
☐ Propellers Inspected/ Attached	☐ Gimbal/Lens Protector Removed
☐ Controller/Tablet Assembled	
☐ Memory Card Installed	☐ Camera Filters Installed

Pre-Flight Checklist

☐ Aircraft Placed on Lauch Pad	☐ Check The Aircraft Status LEDs	☐ Check Flight Mode Switch (P-Mode)
☐ Turn On Remote Controller/ Tablet/DJI Pilot App	☐ Verify the Gimbal is Level, Can Move Unobstructed	☐ Check Satellite and Compass Status
☐ Antennas Properly Positioned	☐ Check RC Battery Level	☐ Set RTH Location And Height
☐ Turn on Aircraft	☐ Check Aircraft Battery Level	☐ Check Camera Settings

Takeoff Checklist

☐ Check Launch site is Clear for Takeoff	☐ Takeoff and Hover	☐ Check Flight Controls, Make Sure They Respond As Expected
☐ Start the motors	☐ Make Sure The Aircraft Is Stable While Hovering	☐ Start Recording Video

Post Flight Checklist

☐ Remove Battery From Aircraft	☐ Repack All Equipment
☐ Install Gimbal Guard	☐ **Complete The Flight Log**

FLIGHT 45

FLIGHT PLAN

PILOT NAME: .... FAA ID: ....

ADDRESS: .... PHONE: ....

VISUAL OBSERVER(S): ....

LOCATION: ....

DATE: .... AIRCRAFT TYPE/NAME: ....

PLANNED TIME: .... AIRCRAFT CERTIFICATE N°: ....

ESTIMATED FLIGHT DURATION: .... FLIGHT TYPE: ....

AIRPORTS WITHIN 5 MILES: ....

WAIVERS APPLIED FOR: ....

FLIGHT DESCRIPTION/ROUTE: ....

....

....

FLIGHT RECORD

FLIGHT 1

TAKEOFF LOC.: .... LAUNCH TIME: .... FLIGHT NOTES: ....

LANDING LOC.: .... LANDING TIME: ....

BATTERY VOLTAGE: .... ELAPSED TIME: ....

FLIGHT 2

TAKEOFF LOC.: .... LAUNCH TIME: .... FLIGHT NOTES: ....

LANDING LOC.: .... LANDING TIME: ....

BATTERY VOLTAGE: .... ELAPSED TIME: ....

FLIGHT 3

TAKEOFF LOC.: .... LAUNCH TIME: .... FLIGHT NOTES: ....

LANDING LOC.: .... LANDING TIME: ....

BATTERY VOLTAGE: .... ELAPSED TIME: ....

FLIGHT 4

TAKEOFF LOC.: .... LAUNCH TIME: .... FLIGHT NOTES: ....

LANDING LOC.: .... LANDING TIME: ....

BATTERY VOLTAGE: .... ELAPSED TIME: ....

GENERAL NOTES: ....

....

....

Flight Checklist

☐ Airport(s) Notified	☐ UAV Batteries Charged	☐ Gimbal Protector Installed
☐ Location is OK To Fly	Battery 1 volts:	☐ Propellers Packed
☐ Weather Forecast OK	Battery 2 volts:	☐ Cables Packed
Temperature:	Battery 3 volts:	☐ Camera Filters Packed
Wind:	Battery 4 volts:	☐ Sun Shade Packed
Precipitation:	☐ Controller Charged	☐ Tools Packed
☐ Firmware up-to-date	☐ Tablet Charged	☐ Flight Plan designed/entered in Software
☐ Memory Card Formatted	☐ Mobile Phone Charged	☐ Logbook Packed

Launch Site Checklist

☐ Verify Weather is OK To Fly	☐ Check For Obstacles, Interferences
Temperature:	☐ Check For Nearby Human Activity/ Dangerous
Wind:	☐ Verify Launch Pad Is Down-wind From Observers
Precipitation:	
☐ **Safety Briefing**	☐ Launch Pad/Barriers Placed

Equipment Checklist

☐ Airframe/Landing Gear Inspected	☐ Battery Installed
☐ Propellers Inspected/ Attached	☐ Gimbal/Lens Protector Removed
☐ Controller/Tablet Assembled	
☐ Memory Card Installed	☐ Camera Filters Installed

Pre-Flight Checklist

☐ Aircraft Placed on Lauch Pad	☐ Check The Aircraft Status LEDs	☐ Check Flight Mode Switch (P-Mode)
☐ Turn On Remote Controller/ Tablet/DJI Pilot App	☐ Verify the Gimbal is Level, Can Move Unobstructed	☐ Check Satellite and Compass Status
☐ Antennas Properly Positioned	☐ Check RC Battery Level	☐ Set RTH Location And Height
☐ Turn on Aircraft	☐ Check Aircraft Battery Level	☐ Check Camera Settings

Takeoff Checklist

☐ Check Launch site is Clear for Takeoff	☐ Takeoff and Hover	☐ Check Flight Controls, Make Sure They Respond As Expected
☐ Start the motors	☐ Make Sure The Aircraft Is Stable While Hovering	☐ Start Recording Video

Post Flight Checklist

☐ Remove Battery From Aircraft	☐ Repack All Equipment
☐ Install Gimbal Guard	☐ **Complete The Flight Log**

FLIGHT 46

FLIGHT PLAN

PILOT NAME: .... FAA ID: ....

ADDRESS: .... PHONE: ....

VISUAL OBSERVER(S): ....

LOCATION: ....

DATE: .... AIRCRAFT TYPE/NAME: ....

PLANNED TIME: .... AIRCRAFT CERTIFICATE N°: ....

ESTIMATED FLIGHT DURATION: .... FLIGHT TYPE: ....

AIRPORTS WITHIN 5 MILES: ....

WAIVERS APPLIED FOR: ....

FLIGHT DESCRIPTION/ROUTE: ....

....

....

FLIGHT RECORD

FLIGHT 1
TAKEOFF LOC.: .... LAUNCH TIME: .... FLIGHT NOTES: ....

LANDING LOC.: .... LANDING TIME: ....

BATTERY VOLTAGE: .... ELAPSED TIME: ....

FLIGHT 2
TAKEOFF LOC.: .... LAUNCH TIME: .... FLIGHT NOTES: ....

LANDING LOC.: .... LANDING TIME: ....

BATTERY VOLTAGE: .... ELAPSED TIME: ....

FLIGHT 3
TAKEOFF LOC.: .... LAUNCH TIME: .... FLIGHT NOTES: ....

LANDING LOC.: .... LANDING TIME: ....

BATTERY VOLTAGE: .... ELAPSED TIME: ....

FLIGHT 4
TAKEOFF LOC.: .... LAUNCH TIME: .... FLIGHT NOTES: ....

LANDING LOC.: .... LANDING TIME: ....

BATTERY VOLTAGE: .... ELAPSED TIME: ....

GENERAL NOTES: ....

....

....

Flight Checklist

☐ Airport(s) Notified	☐ UAV Batteries Charged	☐ Gimbal Protector Installed
☐ Location is OK To Fly	Battery 1 volts:	☐ Propellers Packed
☐ Weather Forecast OK	Battery 2 volts:	☐ Cables Packed
Temperature:	Battery 3 volts:	☐ Camera Filters Packed
Wind:	Battery 4 volts:	☐ Sun Shade Packed
Precipitation:	☐ Controller Charged	☐ Tools Packed
☐ Firmware up-to-date	☐ Tablet Charged	☐ Flight Plan designed/entered in Software
☐ Memory Card Formatted	☐ Mobile Phone Charged	☐ Logbook Packed

Launch Site Checklist

☐ Verify Weather is OK To Fly	☐ Check For Obstacles, Interferences
Temperature:	☐ Check For Nearby Human Activity/ Dangerous
Wind:	☐ Verify Launch Pad Is Down-wind From Observers
Precipitation:	☐ Launch Pad/Barriers Placed
☐ **Safety Briefing**	

Equipment Checklist

☐ Airframe/Landing Gear Inspected	☐ Battery Installed
☐ Propellers Inspected/ Attached	☐ Gimbal/Lens Protector Removed
☐ Controller/Tablet Assembled	
☐ Memory Card Installed	☐ Camera Filters Installed

Pre-Flight Checklist

☐ Aircraft Placed on Lauch Pad	☐ Check The Aircraft Status LEDs	☐ Check Flight Mode Switch (P-Mode)
☐ Turn On Remote Controller/ Tablet/DJI Pilot App	☐ Verify the Gimbal is Level, Can Move Unobstructed	☐ Check Satellite and Compass Status
☐ Antennas Properly Positioned	☐ Check RC Battery Level	☐ Set RTH Location And Height
☐ Turn on Aircraft	☐ Check Aircraft Battery Level	☐ Check Camera Settings

Takeoff Checklist

☐ Check Launch site is Clear for Takeoff	☐ Takeoff and Hover	☐ Check Flight Controls, Make Sure They Respond As Expected
☐ Start the motors	☐ Make Sure The Aircraft Is Stable While Hovering	☐ Start Recording Video

Post Flight Checklist

☐ Remove Battery From Aircraft	☐ Repack All Equipment
☐ Install Gimbal Guard	☐ **Complete The Flight Log**

FLIGHT PLAN

PILOT NAME: .... FAA ID: ....

ADDRESS: .... PHONE: ....

VISUAL OBSERVER(S): ....

LOCATION: ....

DATE: .... AIRCRAFT TYPE/NAME: ....

PLANNED TIME: .... AIRCRAFT CERTIFICATE N°: ....

ESTIMATED FLIGHT DURATION: .... FLIGHT TYPE: ....

AIRPORTS WITHIN 5 MILES: ....

WAIVERS APPLIED FOR: ....

FLIGHT DESCRIPTION/ROUTE: ....

....

....

FLIGHT RECORD

FLIGHT 1

TAKEOFF LOC.: .... LAUNCH TIME: .... FLIGHT NOTES: ....

LANDING LOC.: .... LANDING TIME: ....

BATTERY VOLTAGE: .... ELAPSED TIME: ....

FLIGHT 2

TAKEOFF LOC.: .... LAUNCH TIME: .... FLIGHT NOTES: ....

LANDING LOC.: .... LANDING TIME: ....

BATTERY VOLTAGE: .... ELAPSED TIME: ....

FLIGHT 3

TAKEOFF LOC.: .... LAUNCH TIME: .... FLIGHT NOTES: ....

LANDING LOC.: .... LANDING TIME: ....

BATTERY VOLTAGE: .... ELAPSED TIME: ....

FLIGHT 4

TAKEOFF LOC.: .... LAUNCH TIME: .... FLIGHT NOTES: ....

LANDING LOC.: .... LANDING TIME: ....

BATTERY VOLTAGE: .... ELAPSED TIME: ....

GENERAL NOTES: ....

....

....

Flight Checklist

☐ Airport(s) Notified	☐ UAV Batteries Charged	☐ Gimbal Protector Installed
☐ Location is OK To Fly	Battery 1 volts:	☐ Propellers Packed
☐ Weather Forecast OK	Battery 2 volts:	☐ Cables Packed
Temperature:	Battery 3 volts:	☐ Camera Filters Packed
Wind:	Battery 4 volts:	☐ Sun Shade Packed
Precipitation:	☐ Controller Charged	☐ Tools Packed
☐ Firmware up-to-date	☐ Tablet Charged	☐ Flight Plan designed/entered in Software
☐ Memory Card Formatted	☐ Mobile Phone Charged	☐ Logbook Packed

Launch Site Checklist

☐ Verify Weather is OK To Fly	☐ Check For Obstacles, Interferences
Temperature:	☐ Check For Nearby Human Activity/ Dangerous
Wind:	☐ Verify Launch Pad Is Down-wind From Observers
Precipitation:	
☐ **Safety Briefing**	☐ Launch Pad/Barriers Placed

Equipment Checklist

☐ Airframe/Landing Gear Inspected	☐ Battery Installed
☐ Propellers Inspected/ Attached	☐ Gimbal/Lens Protector Removed
☐ Controller/Tablet Assembled	
☐ Memory Card Installed	☐ Camera Filters Installed

Pre-Flight Checklist

☐ Aircraft Placed on Lauch Pad	☐ Check The Aircraft Status LEDs	☐ Check Flight Mode Switch (P-Mode)
☐ Turn On Remote Controller/ Tablet/DJI Pilot App	☐ Verify the Gimbal is Level, Can Move Unobstructed	☐ Check Satellite and Compass Status
☐ Antennas Properly Positioned	☐ Check RC Battery Level	☐ Set RTH Location And Height
☐ Turn on Aircraft	☐ Check Aircraft Battery Level	☐ Check Camera Settings

Takeoff Checklist

☐ Check Launch site is Clear for Takeoff	☐ Takeoff and Hover	☐ Check Flight Controls, Make Sure They Respond As Expected
☐ Start the motors	☐ Make Sure The Aircraft Is Stable While Hovering	☐ Start Recording Video

Post Flight Checklist

☐ Remove Battery From Aircraft	☐ Repack All Equipment
☐ Install Gimbal Guard	☐ **Complete The Flight Log**

FLIGHT | 48

FLIGHT PLAN

PILOT NAME: .... FAA ID: ....

ADDRESS: .... PHONE: ....

VISUAL OBSERVER(S): ....

LOCATION: ....

DATE: .... AIRCRAFT TYPE/NAME: ....

PLANNED TIME: .... AIRCRAFT CERTIFICATE N°: ....

ESTIMATED FLIGHT DURATION: .... FLIGHT TYPE: ....

AIRPORTS WITHIN 5 MILES: ....

WAIVERS APPLIED FOR: ....

FLIGHT DESCRIPTION/ROUTE: ....

....

....

FLIGHT RECORD

FLIGHT 1

TAKEOFF LOC.: .... LAUNCH TIME: .... FLIGHT NOTES: ....

LANDING LOC.: .... LANDING TIME: ....

BATTERY VOLTAGE: .... ELAPSED TIME: ....

FLIGHT 2

TAKEOFF LOC.: .... LAUNCH TIME: .... FLIGHT NOTES: ....

LANDING LOC.: .... LANDING TIME: ....

BATTERY VOLTAGE: .... ELAPSED TIME: ....

FLIGHT 3

TAKEOFF LOC.: .... LAUNCH TIME: .... FLIGHT NOTES: ....

LANDING LOC.: .... LANDING TIME: ....

BATTERY VOLTAGE: .... ELAPSED TIME: ....

FLIGHT 4

TAKEOFF LOC.: .... LAUNCH TIME: .... FLIGHT NOTES: ....

LANDING LOC.: .... LANDING TIME: ....

BATTERY VOLTAGE: .... ELAPSED TIME: ....

GENERAL NOTES: ....

....

....

Flight Checklist

☐ Airport(s) Notified	☐ UAV Batteries Charged	☐ Gimbal Protector Installed
☐ Location is OK To Fly	Battery 1 volts:	☐ Propellers Packed
☐ Weather Forecast OK	Battery 2 volts:	☐ Cables Packed
Temperature:	Battery 3 volts:	☐ Camera Filters Packed
Wind:	Battery 4 volts:	☐ Sun Shade Packed
Precipitation:	☐ Controller Charged	☐ Tools Packed
☐ Firmware up-to-date	☐ Tablet Charged	☐ Flight Plan designed/entered in Software
☐ Memory Card Formatted	☐ Mobile Phone Charged	☐ Logbook Packed

Launch Site Checklist

☐ Verify Weather is OK To Fly	☐ Check For Obstacles, Interferences
Temperature:	☐ Check For Nearby Human Activity/ Dangerous
Wind:	☐ Verify Launch Pad Is Down-wind From Observers
Precipitation:	
☐ **Safety Briefing**	☐ Launch Pad/Barriers Placed

Equipment Checklist

☐ Airframe/Landing Gear Inspected	☐ Battery Installed
☐ Propellers Inspected/ Attached	☐ Gimbal/Lens Protector Removed
☐ Controller/Tablet Assembled	
☐ Memory Card Installed	☐ Camera Filters Installed

Pre-Flight Checklist

☐ Aircraft Placed on Lauch Pad	☐ Check The Aircraft Status LEDs	☐ Check Flight Mode Switch (P-Mode)
☐ Turn On Remote Controller/ Tablet/DJI Pilot App	☐ Verify the Gimbal is Level, Can Move Unobstructed	☐ Check Satellite and Compass Status
☐ Antennas Properly Positioned	☐ Check RC Battery Level	☐ Set RTH Location And Height
☐ Turn on Aircraft	☐ Check Aircraft Battery Level	☐ Check Camera Settings

Takeoff Checklist

☐ Check Launch site is Clear for Takeoff	☐ Takeoff and Hover	☐ Check Flight Controls, Make Sure They Respond As Expected
☐ Start the motors	☐ Make Sure The Aircraft Is Stable While Hovering	☐ Start Recording Video

Post Flight Checklist

☐ Remove Battery From Aircraft	☐ Repack All Equipment
☐ Install Gimbal Guard	☐ **Complete The Flight Log**

FLIGHT | 49

FLIGHT PLAN

PILOT NAME: ....   FAA ID: ....

ADDRESS: ....   PHONE: ....

VISUAL OBSERVER(S): ....

LOCATION: ....

DATE: ....   AIRCRAFT TYPE/NAME: ....

PLANNED TIME: ....   AIRCRAFT CERTIFICATE N°: ....

ESTIMATED FLIGHT DURATION: ....   FLIGHT TYPE: ....

AIRPORTS WITHIN 5 MILES: ....

WAIVERS APPLIED FOR: ....

FLIGHT DESCRIPTION/ROUTE: ....
....
....

FLIGHT RECORD

FLIGHT 1
TAKEOFF LOC.: ....   LAUNCH TIME: ....   FLIGHT NOTES: ....
LANDING LOC.: ....   LANDING TIME: ....
BATTERY VOLTAGE: ....   ELAPSED TIME: ....

FLIGHT 2
TAKEOFF LOC.: ....   LAUNCH TIME: ....   FLIGHT NOTES: ....
LANDING LOC.: ....   LANDING TIME: ....
BATTERY VOLTAGE: ....   ELAPSED TIME: ....

FLIGHT 3
TAKEOFF LOC.: ....   LAUNCH TIME: ....   FLIGHT NOTES: ....
LANDING LOC.: ....   LANDING TIME: ....
BATTERY VOLTAGE: ....   ELAPSED TIME: ....

FLIGHT 4
TAKEOFF LOC.: ....   LAUNCH TIME: ....   FLIGHT NOTES: ....
LANDING LOC.: ....   LANDING TIME: ....
BATTERY VOLTAGE: ....   ELAPSED TIME: ....

GENERAL NOTES: ....
....
....

Flight Checklist

☐ Airport(s) Notified	☐ UAV Batteries Charged	☐ Gimbal Protector Installed
☐ Location is OK To Fly	Battery 1 volts:	☐ Propellers Packed
☐ Weather Forecast OK	Battery 2 volts:	☐ Cables Packed
Temperature:	Battery 3 volts:	☐ Camera Filters Packed
Wind:	Battery 4 volts:	☐ Sun Shade Packed
Precipitation:	☐ Controller Charged	☐ Tools Packed
☐ Firmware up-to-date	☐ Tablet Charged	☐ Flight Plan designed/entered in Software
☐ Memory Card Formatted	☐ Mobile Phone Charged	☐ Logbook Packed

Launch Site Checklist

☐ Verify Weather is OK To Fly	☐ Check For Obstacles, Interferences
Temperature:	☐ Check For Nearby Human Activity/ Dangerous
Wind:	☐ Verify Launch Pad Is Down-wind From Observers
Precipitation:	☐ Launch Pad/Barriers Placed
☐ **Safety Briefing**	

Equipment Checklist

☐ Airframe/Landing Gear Inspected	☐ Battery Installed
☐ Propellers Inspected/ Attached	☐ Gimbal/Lens Protector Removed
☐ Controller/Tablet Assembled	
☐ Memory Card Installed	☐ Camera Filters Installed

Pre-Flight Checklist

☐ Aircraft Placed on Lauch Pad	☐ Check The Aircraft Status LEDs	☐ Check Flight Mode Switch (P-Mode)
☐ Turn On Remote Controller/ Tablet/DJI Pilot App	☐ Verify the Gimbal is Level, Can Move Unobstructed	☐ Check Satellite and Compass Status
☐ Antennas Properly Positioned	☐ Check RC Battery Level	☐ Set RTH Location And Height
☐ Turn on Aircraft	☐ Check Aircraft Battery Level	☐ Check Camera Settings

Takeoff Checklist

☐ Check Launch site is Clear for Takeoff	☐ Takeoff and Hover	☐ Check Flight Controls, Make Sure They Respond As Expected
☐ Start the motors	☐ Make Sure The Aircraft Is Stable While Hovering	☐ Start Recording Video

Post Flight Checklist

☐ Remove Battery From Aircraft	☐ Repack All Equipment
☐ Install Gimbal Guard	☐ **Complete The Flight Log**

Flight Plan

Pilot Name: .... FAA ID: ....

Address: .... Phone: ....

Visual Observer(s): ....

Location: ....

Date: .... Aircraft Type/Name: ....

Planned Time: .... Aircraft Certificate n°: ....

Estimated Flight Duration: .... Flight Type: ....

Airports Within 5 Miles: ....

Waivers Applied For: ....

Flight Description/Route: ....

....

....

Flight Record

FLIGHT 1

Takeoff Loc.: .... Launch Time: .... Flight Notes: ....

Landing Loc.: .... Landing Time: ....

Battery Voltage: .... Elapsed Time: ....

FLIGHT 2

Takeoff Loc.: .... Launch Time: .... Flight Notes: ....

Landing Loc.: .... Landing Time: ....

Battery Voltage: .... Elapsed Time: ....

FLIGHT 3

Takeoff Loc.: .... Launch Time: .... Flight Notes: ....

Landing Loc.: .... Landing Time: ....

Battery Voltage: .... Elapsed Time: ....

FLIGHT 4

Takeoff Loc.: .... Launch Time: .... Flight Notes: ....

Landing Loc.: .... Landing Time: ....

Battery Voltage: .... Elapsed Time: ....

General Notes: ....

....

....

Flight Checklist

☐ Airport(s) Notified	☐ UAV Batteries Charged	☐ Gimbal Protector Installed
☐ Location is OK To Fly	Battery 1 volts:	☐ Propellers Packed
☐ Weather Forecast OK	Battery 2 volts:	☐ Cables Packed
Temperature:	Battery 3 volts:	☐ Camera Filters Packed
Wind:	Battery 4 volts:	☐ Sun Shade Packed
Precipitation:	☐ Controller Charged	☐ Tools Packed
☐ Firmware up-to-date	☐ Tablet Charged	☐ Flight Plan designed/entered in Software
☐ Memory Card Formatted	☐ Mobile Phone Charged	☐ Logbook Packed

Launch Site Checklist

☐ Verify Weather is OK To Fly	☐ Check For Obstacles, Interferences
Temperature:	☐ Check For Nearby Human Activity/ Dangerous
Wind:	☐ Verify Launch Pad Is Down-wind From Observers
Precipitation:	☐ Launch Pad/Barriers Placed
☐ **Safety Briefing**	

Equipment Checklist

☐ Airframe/Landing Gear Inspected	☐ Battery Installed
☐ Propellers Inspected/ Attached	☐ Gimbal/Lens Protector Removed
☐ Controller/Tablet Assembled	
☐ Memory Card Installed	☐ Camera Filters Installed

Pre-Flight Checklist

☐ Aircraft Placed on Lauch Pad	☐ Check The Aircraft Status LEDs	☐ Check Flight Mode Switch (P-Mode)
☐ Turn On Remote Controller/ Tablet/DJI Pilot App	☐ Verify the Gimbal is Level, Can Move Unobstructed	☐ Check Satellite and Compass Status
☐ Antennas Properly Positioned	☐ Check RC Battery Level	☐ Set RTH Location And Height
☐ Turn on Aircraft	☐ Check Aircraft Battery Level	☐ Check Camera Settings

Takeoff Checklist

☐ Check Launch site is Clear for Takeoff	☐ Takeoff and Hover	☐ Check Flight Controls, Make Sure They Respond As Expected
☐ Start the motors	☐ Make Sure The Aircraft Is Stable While Hovering	☐ Start Recording Video

Post Flight Checklist

☐ Remove Battery From Aircraft	☐ Repack All Equipment
☐ Install Gimbal Guard	☐ **Complete The Flight Log**

FLIGHT 51

FLIGHT PLAN

PILOT NAME: .... FAA ID: ....

ADDRESS: .... PHONE: ....

VISUAL OBSERVER(S): ....

LOCATION: ....

DATE: .... AIRCRAFT TYPE/NAME: ....

PLANNED TIME: .... AIRCRAFT CERTIFICATE N°: ....

ESTIMATED FLIGHT DURATION: .... FLIGHT TYPE: ....

AIRPORTS WITHIN 5 MILES: ....

WAIVERS APPLIED FOR: ....

FLIGHT DESCRIPTION/ROUTE: ....

....

....

FLIGHT RECORD

FLIGHT 1

TAKEOFF LOC.: .... LAUNCH TIME: .... FLIGHT NOTES: ....

LANDING LOC.: .... LANDING TIME: ....

BATTERY VOLTAGE: .... ELAPSED TIME: ....

FLIGHT 2

TAKEOFF LOC.: .... LAUNCH TIME: .... FLIGHT NOTES: ....

LANDING LOC.: .... LANDING TIME: ....

BATTERY VOLTAGE: .... ELAPSED TIME: ....

FLIGHT 3

TAKEOFF LOC.: .... LAUNCH TIME: .... FLIGHT NOTES: ....

LANDING LOC.: .... LANDING TIME: ....

BATTERY VOLTAGE: .... ELAPSED TIME: ....

FLIGHT 4

TAKEOFF LOC.: .... LAUNCH TIME: .... FLIGHT NOTES: ....

LANDING LOC.: .... LANDING TIME: ....

BATTERY VOLTAGE: .... ELAPSED TIME: ....

GENERAL NOTES: ....

....

....

Flight Checklist

☐ Airport(s) Notified	☐ UAV Batteries Charged	☐ Gimbal Protector Installed
☐ Location is OK To Fly	Battery 1 volts:	☐ Propellers Packed
☐ Weather Forecast OK	Battery 2 volts:	☐ Cables Packed
Temperature:	Battery 3 volts:	☐ Camera Filters Packed
Wind:	Battery 4 volts:	☐ Sun Shade Packed
Precipitation:	☐ Controller Charged	☐ Tools Packed
☐ Firmware up-to-date	☐ Tablet Charged	☐ Flight Plan designed/entered in Software
☐ Memory Card Formatted	☐ Mobile Phone Charged	☐ Logbook Packed

Launch Site Checklist

☐ Verify Weather is OK To Fly	☐ Check For Obstacles, Interferences
Temperature:	☐ Check For Nearby Human Activity/ Dangerous
Wind:	☐ Verify Launch Pad Is Down-wind From Observers
Precipitation:	☐ Launch Pad/Barriers Placed
☐ **Safety Briefing**	

Equipment Checklist

☐ Airframe/Landing Gear Inspected	☐ Battery Installed
☐ Propellers Inspected/ Attached	☐ Gimbal/Lens Protector Removed
☐ Controller/Tablet Assembled	
☐ Memory Card Installed	☐ Camera Filters Installed

Pre-Flight Checklist

☐ Aircraft Placed on Lauch Pad	☐ Check The Aircraft Status LEDs	☐ Check Flight Mode Switch (P-Mode)
☐ Turn On Remote Controller/ Tablet/DJI Pilot App	☐ Verify the Gimbal is Level, Can Move Unobstructed	☐ Check Satellite and Compass Status
☐ Antennas Properly Positioned	☐ Check RC Battery Level	☐ Set RTH Location And Height
☐ Turn on Aircraft	☐ Check Aircraft Battery Level	☐ Check Camera Settings

Takeoff Checklist

☐ Check Launch site is Clear for Takeoff	☐ Takeoff and Hover	☐ Check Flight Controls, Make Sure They Respond As Expected
☐ Start the motors	☐ Make Sure The Aircraft Is Stable While Hovering	☐ Start Recording Video

Post Flight Checklist

☐ Remove Battery From Aircraft	☐ Repack All Equipment
☐ Install Gimbal Guard	☐ **Complete The Flight Log**

Flight Plan

Pilot Name: .... FAA ID: ....

Address: .... Phone: ....

Visual Observer(s): ....

Location: ....

Date: .... Aircraft Type/Name: ....

Planned Time: .... Aircraft Certificate n°: ....

Estimated Flight Duration: .... Flight Type: ....

Airports Within 5 Miles: ....

Waivers Applied For: ....

Flight Description/Route: ....

....

....

Flight Record

FLIGHT 1

Takeoff Loc.: .... Launch Time: .... Flight Notes: ....

Landing Loc.: .... Landing Time: ....

Battery Voltage: .... Elapsed Time: ....

FLIGHT 2

Takeoff Loc.: .... Launch Time: .... Flight Notes: ....

Landing Loc.: .... Landing Time: ....

Battery Voltage: .... Elapsed Time: ....

FLIGHT 3

Takeoff Loc.: .... Launch Time: .... Flight Notes: ....

Landing Loc.: .... Landing Time: ....

Battery Voltage: .... Elapsed Time: ....

FLIGHT 4

Takeoff Loc.: .... Launch Time: .... Flight Notes: ....

Landing Loc.: .... Landing Time: ....

Battery Voltage: .... Elapsed Time: ....

General Notes: ....

....

....

Flight Checklist

☐ Airport(s) Notified	☐ UAV Batteries Charged	☐ Gimbal Protector Installed
☐ Location is OK To Fly	Battery 1 volts:	☐ Propellers Packed
☐ Weather Forecast OK	Battery 2 volts:	☐ Cables Packed
Temperature:	Battery 3 volts:	☐ Camera Filters Packed
Wind:	Battery 4 volts:	☐ Sun Shade Packed
Precipitation:	☐ Controller Charged	☐ Tools Packed
☐ Firmware up-to-date	☐ Tablet Charged	☐ Flight Plan designed/entered in Software
☐ Memory Card Formatted	☐ Mobile Phone Charged	☐ Logbook Packed

Launch Site Checklist

☐ Verify Weather is OK To Fly	☐ Check For Obstacles, Interferences
Temperature:	☐ Check For Nearby Human Activity/ Dangerous
Wind:	☐ Verify Launch Pad Is Down-wind From Observers
Precipitation:	
☐ **Safety Briefing**	☐ Launch Pad/Barriers Placed

Equipment Checklist

☐ Airframe/Landing Gear Inspected	☐ Battery Installed
☐ Propellers Inspected/ Attached	☐ Gimbal/Lens Protector Removed
☐ Controller/Tablet Assembled	
☐ Memory Card Installed	☐ Camera Filters Installed

Pre-Flight Checklist

☐ Aircraft Placed on Lauch Pad	☐ Check The Aircraft Status LEDs	☐ Check Flight Mode Switch (P-Mode)
☐ Turn On Remote Controller/ Tablet/DJI Pilot App	☐ Verify the Gimbal is Level, Can Move Unobstructed	☐ Check Satellite and Compass Status
☐ Antennas Properly Positioned	☐ Check RC Battery Level	☐ Set RTH Location And Height
☐ Turn on Aircraft	☐ Check Aircraft Battery Level	☐ Check Camera Settings

Takeoff Checklist

☐ Check Launch site is Clear for Takeoff	☐ Takeoff and Hover	☐ Check Flight Controls, Make Sure They Respond As Expected
☐ Start the motors	☐ Make Sure The Aircraft Is Stable While Hovering	☐ Start Recording Video

Post Flight Checklist

☐ Remove Battery From Aircraft	☐ Repack All Equipment
☐ Install Gimbal Guard	☐ **Complete The Flight Log**

FLIGHT 53

FLIGHT PLAN

PILOT NAME: .... FAA ID: ....

ADDRESS: .... PHONE: ....

VISUAL OBSERVER(S): ....

LOCATION: ....

DATE: .... AIRCRAFT TYPE/NAME: ....

PLANNED TIME: .... AIRCRAFT CERTIFICATE N°: ....

ESTIMATED FLIGHT DURATION: .... FLIGHT TYPE: ....

AIRPORTS WITHIN 5 MILES: ....

WAIVERS APPLIED FOR: ....

FLIGHT DESCRIPTION/ROUTE: ....

....

....

FLIGHT RECORD

FLIGHT 1

TAKEOFF LOC.: .... LAUNCH TIME: .... FLIGHT NOTES: ....

LANDING LOC.: .... LANDING TIME: ....

BATTERY VOLTAGE: .... ELAPSED TIME: ....

FLIGHT 2

TAKEOFF LOC.: .... LAUNCH TIME: .... FLIGHT NOTES: ....

LANDING LOC.: .... LANDING TIME: ....

BATTERY VOLTAGE: .... ELAPSED TIME: ....

FLIGHT 3

TAKEOFF LOC.: .... LAUNCH TIME: .... FLIGHT NOTES: ....

LANDING LOC.: .... LANDING TIME: ....

BATTERY VOLTAGE: .... ELAPSED TIME: ....

FLIGHT 4

TAKEOFF LOC.: .... LAUNCH TIME: .... FLIGHT NOTES: ....

LANDING LOC.: .... LANDING TIME: ....

BATTERY VOLTAGE: .... ELAPSED TIME: ....

GENERAL NOTES: ....

....

....

FLIGHT CHECKLIST

☐ Airport(s) Notified	☐ UAV Batteries Charged	☐ Gimbal Protector Installed
☐ Location is OK To Fly	Battery 1 volts:	☐ Propellers Packed
☐ Weather Forecast OK	Battery 2 volts:	☐ Cables Packed
Temperature:	Battery 3 volts:	☐ Camera Filters Packed
Wind:	Battery 4 volts:	☐ Sun Shade Packed
Precipitation:	☐ Controller Charged	☐ Tools Packed
☐ Firmware up-to-date	☐ Tablet Charged	☐ Flight Plan designed/entered in Software
☐ Memory Card Formatted	☐ Mobile Phone Charged	☐ Logbook Packed

LAUNCH SITE CHECKLIST

☐ Verify Weather is OK To Fly	☐ Check For Obstacles, Interferences
Temperature:	☐ Check For Nearby Human Activity/ Dangerous
Wind:	☐ Verify Launch Pad Is Down-wind From Observers
Precipitation:	☐ Launch Pad/Barriers Placed
☐ **Safety Briefing**	

EQUIPMENT CHECKLIST

☐ Airframe/Landing Gear Inspected	☐ Battery Installed
☐ Propellers Inspected/ Attached	☐ Gimbal/Lens Protector Removed
☐ Controller/Tablet Assembled	
☐ Memory Card Installed	☐ Camera Filters Installed

PRE-FLIGHT CHECKLIST

☐ Aircraft Placed on Lauch Pad	☐ Check The Aircraft Status LEDs	☐ Check Flight Mode Switch (P-Mode)
☐ Turn On Remote Controller/ Tablet/DJI Pilot App	☐ Verify the Gimbal is Level, Can Move Unobstructed	☐ Check Satellite and Compass Status
☐ Antennas Properly Positioned	☐ Check RC Battery Level	☐ Set RTH Location And Height
☐ Turn on Aircraft	☐ Check Aircraft Battery Level	☐ Check Camera Settings

TAKEOFF CHECKLIST

☐ Check Launch site is Clear for Takeoff	☐ Takeoff and Hover	☐ Check Flight Controls, Make Sure They Respond As Expected
☐ Start the motors	☐ Make Sure The Aircraft Is Stable While Hovering	☐ Start Recording Video

POST FLIGHT CHECKLIST

☐ Remove Battery From Aircraft	☐ Repack All Equipment
☐ Install Gimbal Guard	☐ **Complete The Flight Log**

FLIGHT PLAN

PILOT NAME: ....   FAA ID: ....

ADDRESS: ....   PHONE: ....

VISUAL OBSERVER(S): ....

LOCATION: ....

DATE: ....   AIRCRAFT TYPE/NAME: ....

PLANNED TIME: ....   AIRCRAFT CERTIFICATE N°: ....

ESTIMATED FLIGHT DURATION: ....   FLIGHT TYPE: ....

AIRPORTS WITHIN 5 MILES: ....

WAIVERS APPLIED FOR: ....

FLIGHT DESCRIPTION/ROUTE: ....

....

....

FLIGHT RECORD

FLIGHT 1

TAKEOFF LOC.: ....   LAUNCH TIME: ....   FLIGHT NOTES: ....

LANDING LOC.: ....   LANDING TIME: ....

BATTERY VOLTAGE: ....   ELAPSED TIME: ....

FLIGHT 2

TAKEOFF LOC.: ....   LAUNCH TIME: ....   FLIGHT NOTES: ....

LANDING LOC.: ....   LANDING TIME: ....

BATTERY VOLTAGE: ....   ELAPSED TIME: ....

FLIGHT 3

TAKEOFF LOC.: ....   LAUNCH TIME: ....   FLIGHT NOTES: ....

LANDING LOC.: ....   LANDING TIME: ....

BATTERY VOLTAGE: ....   ELAPSED TIME: ....

FLIGHT 4

TAKEOFF LOC.: ....   LAUNCH TIME: ....   FLIGHT NOTES: ....

LANDING LOC.: ....   LANDING TIME: ....

BATTERY VOLTAGE: ....   ELAPSED TIME: ....

GENERAL NOTES: ....

....

....

Flight Checklist

☐ Airport(s) Notified	☐ UAV Batteries Charged	☐ Gimbal Protector Installed
☐ Location is OK To Fly	Battery 1 volts:	☐ Propellers Packed
☐ Weather Forecast OK	Battery 2 volts:	☐ Cables Packed
Temperature:	Battery 3 volts:	☐ Camera Filters Packed
Wind:	Battery 4 volts:	☐ Sun Shade Packed
Precipitation:	☐ Controller Charged	☐ Tools Packed
☐ Firmware up-to-date	☐ Tablet Charged	☐ Flight Plan designed/entered in Software
☐ Memory Card Formatted	☐ Mobile Phone Charged	☐ Logbook Packed

Launch Site Checklist

☐ Verify Weather is OK To Fly	☐ Check For Obstacles, Interferences
Temperature:	☐ Check For Nearby Human Activity/ Dangerous
Wind:	☐ Verify Launch Pad Is Down-wind From Observers
Precipitation:	☐ Launch Pad/Barriers Placed
☐ **Safety Briefing**	

Equipment Checklist

☐ Airframe/Landing Gear Inspected	☐ Battery Installed
☐ Propellers Inspected/ Attached	☐ Gimbal/Lens Protector Removed
☐ Controller/Tablet Assembled	
☐ Memory Card Installed	☐ Camera Filters Installed

Pre-Flight Checklist

☐ Aircraft Placed on Lauch Pad	☐ Check The Aircraft Status LEDs	☐ Check Flight Mode Switch (P-Mode)
☐ Turn On Remote Controller/ Tablet/DJI Pilot App	☐ Verify the Gimbal is Level, Can Move Unobstructed	☐ Check Satellite and Compass Status
☐ Antennas Properly Positioned	☐ Check RC Battery Level	☐ Set RTH Location And Height
☐ Turn on Aircraft	☐ Check Aircraft Battery Level	☐ Check Camera Settings

Takeoff Checklist

☐ Check Launch site is Clear for Takeoff	☐ Takeoff and Hover	☐ Check Flight Controls, Make Sure They Respond As Expected
☐ Start the motors	☐ Make Sure The Aircraft Is Stable While Hovering	☐ Start Recording Video

Post Flight Checklist

☐ Remove Battery From Aircraft	☐ Repack All Equipment
☐ Install Gimbal Guard	☐ **Complete The Flight Log**

FLIGHT 55

FLIGHT PLAN

PILOT NAME: .... FAA ID: ....

ADDRESS: .... PHONE: ....

VISUAL OBSERVER(S): ....

LOCATION: ....

DATE: .... AIRCRAFT TYPE/NAME: ....

PLANNED TIME: .... AIRCRAFT CERTIFICATE N°: ....

ESTIMATED FLIGHT DURATION: .... FLIGHT TYPE: ....

AIRPORTS WITHIN 5 MILES: ....

WAIVERS APPLIED FOR: ....

FLIGHT DESCRIPTION/ROUTE: ....

....

....

FLIGHT RECORD

FLIGHT 1
TAKEOFF LOC.: .... LAUNCH TIME: .... FLIGHT NOTES: ....

LANDING LOC.: .... LANDING TIME: ....

BATTERY VOLTAGE: .... ELAPSED TIME: ....

FLIGHT 2
TAKEOFF LOC.: .... LAUNCH TIME: .... FLIGHT NOTES: ....

LANDING LOC.: .... LANDING TIME: ....

BATTERY VOLTAGE: .... ELAPSED TIME: ....

FLIGHT 3
TAKEOFF LOC.: .... LAUNCH TIME: .... FLIGHT NOTES: ....

LANDING LOC.: .... LANDING TIME: ....

BATTERY VOLTAGE: .... ELAPSED TIME: ....

FLIGHT 4
TAKEOFF LOC.: .... LAUNCH TIME: .... FLIGHT NOTES: ....

LANDING LOC.: .... LANDING TIME: ....

BATTERY VOLTAGE: .... ELAPSED TIME: ....

GENERAL NOTES: ....

....

....

FLIGHT CHECKLIST

☐ Airport(s) Notified	☐ UAV Batteries Charged	☐ Gimbal Protector Installed
☐ Location is OK To Fly	Battery 1 volts:	☐ Propellers Packed
☐ Weather Forecast OK	Battery 2 volts:	☐ Cables Packed
Temperature:	Battery 3 volts:	☐ Camera Filters Packed
Wind:	Battery 4 volts:	☐ Sun Shade Packed
Precipitation:	☐ Controller Charged	☐ Tools Packed
☐ Firmware up-to-date	☐ Tablet Charged	☐ Flight Plan designed/entered in Software
☐ Memory Card Formatted	☐ Mobile Phone Charged	☐ Logbook Packed

LAUNCH SITE CHECKLIST

☐ Verify Weather is OK To Fly	☐ Check For Obstacles, Interferences
Temperature:	☐ Check For Nearby Human Activity/ Dangerous
Wind:	☐ Verify Launch Pad Is Down-wind From Observers
Precipitation:	☐ Launch Pad/Barriers Placed
☐ **Safety Briefing**	

EQUIPMENT CHECKLIST

☐ Airframe/Landing Gear Inspected	☐ Battery Installed
☐ Propellers Inspected/ Attached	☐ Gimbal/Lens Protector Removed
☐ Controller/Tablet Assembled	
☐ Memory Card Installed	☐ Camera Filters Installed

PRE-FLIGHT CHECKLIST

☐ Aircraft Placed on Lauch Pad	☐ Check The Aircraft Status LEDs	☐ Check Flight Mode Switch (P-Mode)
☐ Turn On Remote Controller/ Tablet/DJI Pilot App	☐ Verify the Gimbal is Level, Can Move Unobstructed	☐ Check Satellite and Compass Status
☐ Antennas Properly Positioned	☐ Check RC Battery Level	☐ Set RTH Location And Height
☐ Turn on Aircraft	☐ Check Aircraft Battery Level	☐ Check Camera Settings

TAKEOFF CHECKLIST

☐ Check Launch site is Clear for Takeoff	☐ Takeoff and Hover	☐ Check Flight Controls, Make Sure They Respond As Expected
☐ Start the motors	☐ Make Sure The Aircraft Is Stable While Hovering	☐ Start Recording Video

POST FLIGHT CHECKLIST

☐ Remove Battery From Aircraft	☐ Repack All Equipment
☐ Install Gimbal Guard	☐ **Complete The Flight Log**

FLIGHT PLAN

PILOT NAME: .... FAA ID: ....

ADDRESS: .... PHONE: ....

VISUAL OBSERVER(S): ....

LOCATION: ....

DATE: .... AIRCRAFT TYPE/NAME: ....

PLANNED TIME: .... AIRCRAFT CERTIFICATE N°: ....

ESTIMATED FLIGHT DURATION: .... FLIGHT TYPE: ....

AIRPORTS WITHIN 5 MILES: ....

WAIVERS APPLIED FOR: ....

FLIGHT DESCRIPTION/ROUTE: ....

....

....

FLIGHT RECORD

FLIGHT 1
TAKEOFF LOC.: .... LAUNCH TIME: .... FLIGHT NOTES: ....
LANDING LOC.: .... LANDING TIME: ....
BATTERY VOLTAGE: .... ELAPSED TIME: ....

FLIGHT 2
TAKEOFF LOC.: .... LAUNCH TIME: .... FLIGHT NOTES: ....
LANDING LOC.: .... LANDING TIME: ....
BATTERY VOLTAGE: .... ELAPSED TIME: ....

FLIGHT 3
TAKEOFF LOC.: .... LAUNCH TIME: .... FLIGHT NOTES: ....
LANDING LOC.: .... LANDING TIME: ....
BATTERY VOLTAGE: .... ELAPSED TIME: ....

FLIGHT 4
TAKEOFF LOC.: .... LAUNCH TIME: .... FLIGHT NOTES: ....
LANDING LOC.: .... LANDING TIME: ....
BATTERY VOLTAGE: .... ELAPSED TIME: ....

GENERAL NOTES: ....

....

....

FLIGHT CHECKLIST

☐ Airport(s) Notified	☐ UAV Batteries Charged	☐ Gimbal Protector Installed
☐ Location is OK To Fly	Battery 1 volts:	☐ Propellers Packed
☐ Weather Forecast OK	Battery 2 volts:	☐ Cables Packed
Temperature:	Battery 3 volts:	☐ Camera Filters Packed
Wind:	Battery 4 volts:	☐ Sun Shade Packed
Precipitation:	☐ Controller Charged	☐ Tools Packed
☐ Firmware up-to-date	☐ Tablet Charged	☐ Flight Plan designed/entered in Software
☐ Memory Card Formatted	☐ Mobile Phone Charged	☐ Logbook Packed

LAUNCH SITE CHECKLIST

☐ Verify Weather is OK To Fly	☐ Check For Obstacles, Interferences
Temperature:	☐ Check For Nearby Human Activity/ Dangerous
Wind:	☐ Verify Launch Pad Is Down-wind From Observers
Precipitation:	
☐ **Safety Briefing**	☐ Launch Pad/Barriers Placed

EQUIPMENT CHECKLIST

☐ Airframe/Landing Gear Inspected	☐ Battery Installed
☐ Propellers Inspected/ Attached	☐ Gimbal/Lens Protector Removed
☐ Controller/Tablet Assembled	
☐ Memory Card Installed	☐ Camera Filters Installed

PRE-FLIGHT CHECKLIST

☐ Aircraft Placed on Lauch Pad	☐ Check The Aircraft Status LEDs	☐ Check Flight Mode Switch (P-Mode)
☐ Turn On Remote Controller/Tablet/DJI Pilot App	☐ Verify the Gimbal is Level, Can Move Unobstructed	☐ Check Satellite and Compass Status
☐ Antennas Properly Positioned	☐ Check RC Battery Level	☐ Set RTH Location And Height
☐ Turn on Aircraft	☐ Check Aircraft Battery Level	☐ Check Camera Settings

TAKEOFF CHECKLIST

☐ Check Launch site is Clear for Takeoff	☐ Takeoff and Hover	☐ Check Flight Controls, Make Sure They Respond As Expected
☐ Start the motors	☐ Make Sure The Aircraft Is Stable While Hovering	☐ Start Recording Video

POST FLIGHT CHECKLIST

☐ Remove Battery From Aircraft	☐ Repack All Equipment
☐ Install Gimbal Guard	☐ **Complete The Flight Log**

FLIGHT | 57

FLIGHT PLAN

PILOT NAME: .... FAA ID: ....

ADDRESS: .... PHONE: ....

VISUAL OBSERVER(S): ....

LOCATION: ....

DATE: .... AIRCRAFT TYPE/NAME: ....

PLANNED TIME: .... AIRCRAFT CERTIFICATE N°: ....

ESTIMATED FLIGHT DURATION: .... FLIGHT TYPE: ....

AIRPORTS WITHIN 5 MILES: ....

WAIVERS APPLIED FOR: ....

FLIGHT DESCRIPTION/ROUTE: ....

....

....

FLIGHT RECORD

FLIGHT 1
TAKEOFF LOC.: .... LAUNCH TIME: .... FLIGHT NOTES: ....
LANDING LOC.: .... LANDING TIME: ....
BATTERY VOLTAGE: .... ELAPSED TIME: ....

FLIGHT 2
TAKEOFF LOC.: .... LAUNCH TIME: .... FLIGHT NOTES: ....
LANDING LOC.: .... LANDING TIME: ....
BATTERY VOLTAGE: .... ELAPSED TIME: ....

FLIGHT 3
TAKEOFF LOC.: .... LAUNCH TIME: .... FLIGHT NOTES: ....
LANDING LOC.: .... LANDING TIME: ....
BATTERY VOLTAGE: .... ELAPSED TIME: ....

FLIGHT 4
TAKEOFF LOC.: .... LAUNCH TIME: .... FLIGHT NOTES: ....
LANDING LOC.: .... LANDING TIME: ....
BATTERY VOLTAGE: .... ELAPSED TIME: ....

GENERAL NOTES: ....

....

....

FLIGHT CHECKLIST

☐ Airport(s) Notified	☐ UAV Batteries Charged	☐ Gimbal Protector Installed
☐ Location is OK To Fly	Battery 1 volts:	☐ Propellers Packed
☐ Weather Forecast OK	Battery 2 volts:	☐ Cables Packed
Temperature:	Battery 3 volts:	☐ Camera Filters Packed
Wind:	Battery 4 volts:	☐ Sun Shade Packed
Precipitation:	☐ Controller Charged	☐ Tools Packed
☐ Firmware up-to-date	☐ Tablet Charged	☐ Flight Plan designed/entered in Software
☐ Memory Card Formatted	☐ Mobile Phone Charged	☐ Logbook Packed

LAUNCH SITE CHECKLIST

☐ Verify Weather is OK To Fly	☐ Check For Obstacles, Interferences
Temperature:	☐ Check For Nearby Human Activity/ Dangerous
Wind:	☐ Verify Launch Pad Is Down-wind From Observers
Precipitation:	☐ Launch Pad/Barriers Placed
☐ **Safety Briefing**	

EQUIPMENT CHECKLIST

☐ Airframe/Landing Gear Inspected	☐ Battery Installed
☐ Propellers Inspected/ Attached	☐ Gimbal/Lens Protector Removed
☐ Controller/Tablet Assembled	
☐ Memory Card Installed	☐ Camera Filters Installed

PRE-FLIGHT CHECKLIST

☐ Aircraft Placed on Lauch Pad	☐ Check The Aircraft Status LEDs	☐ Check Flight Mode Switch (P-Mode)
☐ Turn On Remote Controller/ Tablet/DJI Pilot App	☐ Verify the Gimbal is Level, Can Move Unobstructed	☐ Check Satellite and Compass Status
☐ Antennas Properly Positioned	☐ Check RC Battery Level	☐ Set RTH Location And Height
☐ Turn on Aircraft	☐ Check Aircraft Battery Level	☐ Check Camera Settings

TAKEOFF CHECKLIST

☐ Check Launch site is Clear for Takeoff	☐ Takeoff and Hover	☐ Check Flight Controls, Make Sure They Respond As Expected
☐ Start the motors	☐ Make Sure The Aircraft Is Stable While Hovering	☐ Start Recording Video

POST FLIGHT CHECKLIST

☐ Remove Battery From Aircraft	☐ Repack All Equipment
☐ Install Gimbal Guard	☐ **Complete The Flight Log**

Flight Plan

PILOT NAME: .... FAA ID: ....

ADDRESS: .... PHONE: ....

VISUAL OBSERVER(S): ....

LOCATION: ....

DATE: .... AIRCRAFT TYPE/NAME: ....

PLANNED TIME: .... AIRCRAFT CERTIFICATE N°: ....

ESTIMATED FLIGHT DURATION: .... FLIGHT TYPE: ....

AIRPORTS WITHIN 5 MILES: ....

WAIVERS APPLIED FOR: ....

FLIGHT DESCRIPTION/ROUTE: ....

....

....

Flight Record

FLIGHT 1
TAKEOFF LOC.: .... LAUNCH TIME: .... FLIGHT NOTES: ....
LANDING LOC.: .... LANDING TIME: ....
BATTERY VOLTAGE: .... ELAPSED TIME: ....

FLIGHT 2
TAKEOFF LOC.: .... LAUNCH TIME: .... FLIGHT NOTES: ....
LANDING LOC.: .... LANDING TIME: ....
BATTERY VOLTAGE: .... ELAPSED TIME: ....

FLIGHT 3
TAKEOFF LOC.: .... LAUNCH TIME: .... FLIGHT NOTES: ....
LANDING LOC.: .... LANDING TIME: ....
BATTERY VOLTAGE: .... ELAPSED TIME: ....

FLIGHT 4
TAKEOFF LOC.: .... LAUNCH TIME: .... FLIGHT NOTES: ....
LANDING LOC.: .... LANDING TIME: ....
BATTERY VOLTAGE: .... ELAPSED TIME: ....

GENERAL NOTES: ....

....

....

FLIGHT CHECKLIST

☐ Airport(s) Notified	☐ UAV Batteries Charged	☐ Gimbal Protector Installed
☐ Location is OK To Fly	Battery 1 volts:	☐ Propellers Packed
☐ Weather Forecast OK	Battery 2 volts:	☐ Cables Packed
Temperature:	Battery 3 volts:	☐ Camera Filters Packed
Wind:	Battery 4 volts:	☐ Sun Shade Packed
Precipitation:	☐ Controller Charged	☐ Tools Packed
☐ Firmware up-to-date	☐ Tablet Charged	☐ Flight Plan designed/entered in Software
☐ Memory Card Formatted	☐ Mobile Phone Charged	☐ Logbook Packed

LAUNCH SITE CHECKLIST

☐ Verify Weather is OK To Fly	☐ Check For Obstacles, Interferences
Temperature:	☐ Check For Nearby Human Activity/ Dangerous
Wind:	☐ Verify Launch Pad Is Down-wind From Observers
Precipitation:	
☐ Safety Briefing	☐ Launch Pad/Barriers Placed

EQUIPMENT CHECKLIST

☐ Airframe/Landing Gear Inspected	☐ Battery Installed
☐ Propellers Inspected/ Attached	☐ Gimbal/Lens Protector Removed
☐ Controller/Tablet Assembled	
☐ Memory Card Installed	☐ Camera Filters Installed

PRE-FLIGHT CHECKLIST

☐ Aircraft Placed on Lauch Pad	☐ Check The Aircraft Status LEDs	☐ Check Flight Mode Switch (P-Mode)
☐ Turn On Remote Controller/ Tablet/DJI Pilot App	☐ Verify the Gimbal is Level, Can Move Unobstructed	☐ Check Satellite and Compass Status
☐ Antennas Properly Positioned	☐ Check RC Battery Level	☐ Set RTH Location And Height
☐ Turn on Aircraft	☐ Check Aircraft Battery Level	☐ Check Camera Settings

TAKEOFF CHECKLIST

☐ Check Launch site is Clear for Takeoff	☐ Takeoff and Hover	☐ Check Flight Controls, Make Sure They Respond As Expected
☐ Start the motors	☐ Make Sure The Aircraft Is Stable While Hovering	☐ Start Recording Video

POST FLIGHT CHECKLIST

☐ Remove Battery From Aircraft	☐ Repack All Equipment
☐ Install Gimbal Guard	☐ Complete The Flight Log

Flight Plan

PILOT NAME: .... FAA ID: ....

ADDRESS: .... PHONE: ....

VISUAL OBSERVER(S): ....

LOCATION: ....

DATE: .... AIRCRAFT TYPE/NAME: ....

PLANNED TIME: .... AIRCRAFT CERTIFICATE N°: ....

ESTIMATED FLIGHT DURATION: .... FLIGHT TYPE: ....

AIRPORTS WITHIN 5 MILES: ....

WAIVERS APPLIED FOR: ....

FLIGHT DESCRIPTION/ROUTE: ....

....

....

Flight Record

FLIGHT 1

TAKEOFF LOC.: .... LAUNCH TIME: .... FLIGHT NOTES: ....

LANDING LOC.: .... LANDING TIME: ....

BATTERY VOLTAGE: .... ELAPSED TIME: ....

FLIGHT 2

TAKEOFF LOC.: .... LAUNCH TIME: .... FLIGHT NOTES: ....

LANDING LOC.: .... LANDING TIME: ....

BATTERY VOLTAGE: .... ELAPSED TIME: ....

FLIGHT 3

TAKEOFF LOC.: .... LAUNCH TIME: .... FLIGHT NOTES: ....

LANDING LOC.: .... LANDING TIME: ....

BATTERY VOLTAGE: .... ELAPSED TIME: ....

FLIGHT 4

TAKEOFF LOC.: .... LAUNCH TIME: .... FLIGHT NOTES: ....

LANDING LOC.: .... LANDING TIME: ....

BATTERY VOLTAGE: .... ELAPSED TIME: ....

GENERAL NOTES: ....

....

....

Flight Checklist

☐ Airport(s) Notified	☐ UAV Batteries Charged	☐ Gimbal Protector Installed
☐ Location is OK To Fly	Battery 1 volts:	☐ Propellers Packed
☐ Weather Forecast OK	Battery 2 volts:	☐ Cables Packed
Temperature:	Battery 3 volts:	☐ Camera Filters Packed
Wind:	Battery 4 volts:	☐ Sun Shade Packed
Precipitation:	☐ Controller Charged	☐ Tools Packed
☐ Firmware up-to-date	☐ Tablet Charged	☐ Flight Plan designed/entered in Software
☐ Memory Card Formatted	☐ Mobile Phone Charged	☐ Logbook Packed

Launch Site Checklist

☐ Verify Weather is OK To Fly	☐ Check For Obstacles, Interferences
Temperature:	☐ Check For Nearby Human Activity/ Dangerous
Wind:	☐ Verify Launch Pad Is Down-wind From Observers
Precipitation:	
☐ **Safety Briefing**	☐ Launch Pad/Barriers Placed

Equipment Checklist

☐ Airframe/Landing Gear Inspected	☐ Battery Installed
☐ Propellers Inspected/ Attached	☐ Gimbal/Lens Protector Removed
☐ Controller/Tablet Assembled	
☐ Memory Card Installed	☐ Camera Filters Installed

Pre-Flight Checklist

☐ Aircraft Placed on Lauch Pad	☐ Check The Aircraft Status LEDs	☐ Check Flight Mode Switch (P-Mode)
☐ Turn On Remote Controller/ Tablet/DJI Pilot App	☐ Verify the Gimbal is Level, Can Move Unobstructed	☐ Check Satellite and Compass Status
☐ Antennas Properly Positioned	☐ Check RC Battery Level	☐ Set RTH Location And Height
☐ Turn on Aircraft	☐ Check Aircraft Battery Level	☐ Check Camera Settings

Takeoff Checklist

☐ Check Launch site is Clear for Takeoff	☐ Takeoff and Hover	☐ Check Flight Controls, Make Sure They Respond As Expected
☐ Start the motors	☐ Make Sure The Aircraft Is Stable While Hovering	☐ Start Recording Video

Post Flight Checklist

☐ Remove Battery From Aircraft	☐ Repack All Equipment
☐ Install Gimbal Guard	☐ **Complete The Flight Log**

FLIGHT | 60

FLIGHT PLAN

PILOT NAME: .... FAA ID: ....

ADDRESS: .... PHONE: ....

VISUAL OBSERVER(S): ....

LOCATION: ....

DATE: .... AIRCRAFT TYPE/NAME: ....

PLANNED TIME: .... AIRCRAFT CERTIFICATE N°: ....

ESTIMATED FLIGHT DURATION: .... FLIGHT TYPE: ....

AIRPORTS WITHIN 5 MILES: ....

WAIVERS APPLIED FOR: ....

FLIGHT DESCRIPTION/ROUTE: ....

....

....

FLIGHT RECORD

FLIGHT 1

TAKEOFF LOC.: .... LAUNCH TIME: .... FLIGHT NOTES: ....

LANDING LOC.: .... LANDING TIME: ....

BATTERY VOLTAGE: .... ELAPSED TIME: ....

FLIGHT 2

TAKEOFF LOC.: .... LAUNCH TIME: .... FLIGHT NOTES: ....

LANDING LOC.: .... LANDING TIME: ....

BATTERY VOLTAGE: .... ELAPSED TIME: ....

FLIGHT 3

TAKEOFF LOC.: .... LAUNCH TIME: .... FLIGHT NOTES: ....

LANDING LOC.: .... LANDING TIME: ....

BATTERY VOLTAGE: .... ELAPSED TIME: ....

FLIGHT 4

TAKEOFF LOC.: .... LAUNCH TIME: .... FLIGHT NOTES: ....

LANDING LOC.: .... LANDING TIME: ....

BATTERY VOLTAGE: .... ELAPSED TIME: ....

GENERAL NOTES: ....

....

....

Flight Checklist

☐ Airport(s) Notified	☐ UAV Batteries Charged	☐ Gimbal Protector Installed
☐ Location is OK To Fly	Battery 1 volts:	☐ Propellers Packed
☐ Weather Forecast OK	Battery 2 volts:	☐ Cables Packed
Temperature:	Battery 3 volts:	☐ Camera Filters Packed
Wind:	Battery 4 volts:	☐ Sun Shade Packed
Precipitation:	☐ Controller Charged	☐ Tools Packed
☐ Firmware up-to-date	☐ Tablet Charged	☐ Flight Plan designed/entered in Software
☐ Memory Card Formatted	☐ Mobile Phone Charged	☐ Logbook Packed

Launch Site Checklist

☐ Verify Weather is OK To Fly	☐ Check For Obstacles, Interferences
Temperature:	☐ Check For Nearby Human Activity/ Dangerous
Wind:	☐ Verify Launch Pad Is Down-wind From Observers
Precipitation:	☐ Launch Pad/Barriers Placed
☐ **Safety Briefing**	

Equipment Checklist

☐ Airframe/Landing Gear Inspected	☐ Battery Installed
☐ Propellers Inspected/ Attached	☐ Gimbal/Lens Protector Removed
☐ Controller/Tablet Assembled	
☐ Memory Card Installed	☐ Camera Filters Installed

Pre-Flight Checklist

☐ Aircraft Placed on Lauch Pad	☐ Check The Aircraft Status LEDs	☐ Check Flight Mode Switch (P-Mode)
☐ Turn On Remote Controller/ Tablet/DJI Pilot App	☐ Verify the Gimbal is Level, Can Move Unobstructed	☐ Check Satellite and Compass Status
☐ Antennas Properly Positioned	☐ Check RC Battery Level	☐ Set RTH Location And Height
☐ Turn on Aircraft	☐ Check Aircraft Battery Level	☐ Check Camera Settings

Takeoff Checklist

☐ Check Launch site is Clear for Takeoff	☐ Takeoff and Hover	☐ Check Flight Controls, Make Sure They Respond As Expected
☐ Start the Motors	☐ Make Sure The Aircraft Is Stable While Hovering	☐ Start Recording Video

Post Flight Checklist

☐ Remove Battery From Aircraft	☐ Repack All Equipment
☐ Install Gimbal Guard	☐ **Complete The Flight Log**

Flight Plan

PILOT NAME: .... FAA ID: ....

ADDRESS: .... PHONE: ....

VISUAL OBSERVER(S): ....

LOCATION: ....

DATE: .... AIRCRAFT TYPE/NAME: ....

PLANNED TIME: .... AIRCRAFT CERTIFICATE N°: ....

ESTIMATED FLIGHT DURATION: .... FLIGHT TYPE: ....

AIRPORTS WITHIN 5 MILES: ....

WAIVERS APPLIED FOR: ....

FLIGHT DESCRIPTION/ROUTE: ....

....

....

Flight Record

FLIGHT 1

TAKEOFF LOC.: .... LAUNCH TIME: .... FLIGHT NOTES: ....

LANDING LOC.: .... LANDING TIME: ....

BATTERY VOLTAGE: .... ELAPSED TIME: ....

FLIGHT 2

TAKEOFF LOC.: .... LAUNCH TIME: .... FLIGHT NOTES: ....

LANDING LOC.: .... LANDING TIME: ....

BATTERY VOLTAGE: .... ELAPSED TIME: ....

FLIGHT 3

TAKEOFF LOC.: .... LAUNCH TIME: .... FLIGHT NOTES: ....

LANDING LOC.: .... LANDING TIME: ....

BATTERY VOLTAGE: .... ELAPSED TIME: ....

FLIGHT 4

TAKEOFF LOC.: .... LAUNCH TIME: .... FLIGHT NOTES: ....

LANDING LOC.: .... LANDING TIME: ....

BATTERY VOLTAGE: .... ELAPSED TIME: ....

GENERAL NOTES: ....

....

....

Flight Checklist

☐ Airport(s) Notified	☐ UAV Batteries Charged	☐ Gimbal Protector Installed
☐ Location is OK To Fly	Battery 1 volts:	☐ Propellers Packed
☐ Weather Forecast OK	Battery 2 volts:	☐ Cables Packed
Temperature:	Battery 3 volts:	☐ Camera Filters Packed
Wind:	Battery 4 volts:	☐ Sun Shade Packed
Precipitation:	☐ Controller Charged	☐ Tools Packed
☐ Firmware up-to-date	☐ Tablet Charged	☐ Flight Plan designed/entered in Software
☐ Memory Card Formatted	☐ Mobile Phone Charged	☐ Logbook Packed

Launch Site Checklist

☐ Verify Weather is OK To Fly	☐ Check For Obstacles, Interferences
Temperature:	☐ Check For Nearby Human Activity/ Dangerous
Wind:	☐ Verify Launch Pad Is Down-wind From Observers
Precipitation:	☐ Launch Pad/Barriers Placed
☐ **Safety Briefing**	

Equipment Checklist

☐ Airframe/Landing Gear Inspected	☐ Battery Installed
☐ Propellers Inspected/ Attached	☐ Gimbal/Lens Protector Removed
☐ Controller/Tablet Assembled	
☐ Memory Card Installed	☐ Camera Filters Installed

Pre-Flight Checklist

☐ Aircraft Placed on Lauch Pad	☐ Check The Aircraft Status LEDs	☐ Check Flight Mode Switch (P-Mode)
☐ Turn On Remote Controller/ Tablet/DJI Pilot App	☐ Verify the Gimbal is Level, Can Move Unobstructed	☐ Check Satellite and Compass Status
☐ Antennas Properly Positioned	☐ Check RC Battery Level	☐ Set RTH Location And Height
☐ Turn on Aircraft	☐ Check Aircraft Battery Level	☐ Check Camera Settings

Takeoff Checklist

☐ Check Launch site is Clear for Takeoff	☐ Takeoff and Hover	☐ Check Flight Controls, Make Sure They Respond As Expected
☐ Start the motors	☐ Make Sure The Aircraft Is Stable While Hovering	☐ Start Recording Video

Post Flight Checklist

☐ Remove Battery From Aircraft	☐ Repack All Equipment
☐ Install Gimbal Guard	☐ **Complete The Flight Log**

FLIGHT PLAN

PILOT NAME: ....   FAA ID: ....

ADDRESS: ....   PHONE: ....

VISUAL OBSERVER(S): ....

LOCATION: ....

DATE: ....   AIRCRAFT TYPE/NAME: ....

PLANNED TIME: ....   AIRCRAFT CERTIFICATE N°: ....

ESTIMATED FLIGHT DURATION: ....   FLIGHT TYPE: ....

AIRPORTS WITHIN 5 MILES: ....

WAIVERS APPLIED FOR: ....

FLIGHT DESCRIPTION/ROUTE: ....

....

....

FLIGHT RECORD

FLIGHT 1

TAKEOFF LOC.: ....   LAUNCH TIME: ....   FLIGHT NOTES: ....

LANDING LOC.: ....   LANDING TIME: ....

BATTERY VOLTAGE: ....   ELAPSED TIME: ....

FLIGHT 2

TAKEOFF LOC.: ....   LAUNCH TIME: ....   FLIGHT NOTES: ....

LANDING LOC.: ....   LANDING TIME: ....

BATTERY VOLTAGE: ....   ELAPSED TIME: ....

FLIGHT 3

TAKEOFF LOC.: ....   LAUNCH TIME: ....   FLIGHT NOTES: ....

LANDING LOC.: ....   LANDING TIME: ....

BATTERY VOLTAGE: ....   ELAPSED TIME: ....

FLIGHT 4

TAKEOFF LOC.: ....   LAUNCH TIME: ....   FLIGHT NOTES: ....

LANDING LOC.: ....   LANDING TIME: ....

BATTERY VOLTAGE: ....   ELAPSED TIME: ....

GENERAL NOTES: ....

....

....

Flight Checklist

☐ Airport(s) Notified	☐ UAV Batteries Charged	☐ Gimbal Protector Installed
☐ Location is OK To Fly	Battery 1 volts:	☐ Propellers Packed
☐ Weather Forecast OK	Battery 2 volts:	☐ Cables Packed
Temperature:	Battery 3 volts:	☐ Camera Filters Packed
Wind:	Battery 4 volts:	☐ Sun Shade Packed
Precipitation:	☐ Controller Charged	☐ Tools Packed
☐ Firmware up-to-date	☐ Tablet Charged	☐ Flight Plan designed/entered in Software
☐ Memory Card Formatted	☐ Mobile Phone Charged	☐ Logbook Packed

Launch Site Checklist

☐ Verify Weather is OK To Fly	☐ Check For Obstacles, Interferences
Temperature:	☐ Check For Nearby Human Activity/ Dangerous
Wind:	☐ Verify Launch Pad Is Down-wind From Observers
Precipitation:	☐ Launch Pad/Barriers Placed
☐ **Safety Briefing**	

Equipment Checklist

☐ Airframe/Landing Gear Inspected	☐ Battery Installed
☐ Propellers Inspected/ Attached	☐ Gimbal/Lens Protector Removed
☐ Controller/Tablet Assembled	
☐ Memory Card Installed	☐ Camera Filters Installed

Pre-Flight Checklist

☐ Aircraft Placed on Lauch Pad	☐ Check The Aircraft Status LEDs	☐ Check Flight Mode Switch (P-Mode)
☐ Turn On Remote Controller/ Tablet/DJI Pilot App	☐ Verify the Gimbal is Level, Can Move Unobstructed	☐ Check Satellite and Compass Status
☐ Antennas Properly Positioned	☐ Check RC Battery Level	☐ Set RTH Location And Height
☐ Turn on Aircraft	☐ Check Aircraft Battery Level	☐ Check Camera Settings

Takeoff Checklist

☐ Check Launch site is Clear for Takeoff	☐ Takeoff and Hover	☐ Check Flight Controls, Make Sure They Respond As Expected
☐ Start the motors	☐ Make Sure The Aircraft Is Stable While Hovering	☐ Start Recording Video

Post Flight Checklist

☐ Remove Battery From Aircraft	☐ Repack All Equipment
☐ Install Gimbal Guard	☐ **Complete The Flight Log**

FLIGHT PLAN

PILOT NAME: .... FAA ID: ....

ADDRESS: .... PHONE: ....

VISUAL OBSERVER(S): ....

LOCATION: ....

DATE: .... AIRCRAFT TYPE/NAME: ....

PLANNED TIME: .... AIRCRAFT CERTIFICATE N°: ....

ESTIMATED FLIGHT DURATION: .... FLIGHT TYPE: ....

AIRPORTS WITHIN 5 MILES: ....

WAIVERS APPLIED FOR: ....

FLIGHT DESCRIPTION/ROUTE: ....

....

....

FLIGHT RECORD

FLIGHT 1

TAKEOFF LOC.:	LAUNCH TIME:	FLIGHT NOTES: ....
LANDING LOC.:	LANDING TIME:	....
BATTERY VOLTAGE:	ELAPSED TIME:	

FLIGHT 2

TAKEOFF LOC.:	LAUNCH TIME:	FLIGHT NOTES: ....
LANDING LOC.:	LANDING TIME:	....
BATTERY VOLTAGE:	ELAPSED TIME:	

FLIGHT 3

TAKEOFF LOC.:	LAUNCH TIME:	FLIGHT NOTES: ....
LANDING LOC.:	LANDING TIME:	....
BATTERY VOLTAGE:	ELAPSED TIME:	

FLIGHT 4

TAKEOFF LOC.:	LAUNCH TIME:	FLIGHT NOTES: ....
LANDING LOC.:	LANDING TIME:	....
BATTERY VOLTAGE:	ELAPSED TIME:	

GENERAL NOTES: ....

....

....

Flight Checklist

☐ Airport(s) Notified	☐ UAV Batteries Charged	☐ Gimbal Protector Installed
☐ Location is OK To Fly	Battery 1 volts:	☐ Propellers Packed
☐ Weather Forecast OK	Battery 2 volts:	☐ Cables Packed
Temperature:	Battery 3 volts:	☐ Camera Filters Packed
Wind:	Battery 4 volts:	☐ Sun Shade Packed
Precipitation:	☐ Controller Charged	☐ Tools Packed
☐ Firmware up-to-date	☐ Tablet Charged	☐ Flight Plan designed/entered in Software
☐ Memory Card Formatted	☐ Mobile Phone Charged	☐ Logbook Packed

Launch Site Checklist

☐ Verify Weather is OK To Fly	☐ Check For Obstacles, Interferences
Temperature:	☐ Check For Nearby Human Activity/ Dangerous
Wind:	☐ Verify Launch Pad Is Down-wind From Observers
Precipitation:	
☐ **Safety Briefing**	☐ Launch Pad/Barriers Placed

Equipment Checklist

☐ Airframe/Landing Gear Inspected	☐ Battery Installed
☐ Propellers Inspected/ Attached	☐ Gimbal/Lens Protector Removed
☐ Controller/Tablet Assembled	
☐ Memory Card Installed	☐ Camera Filters Installed

Pre-Flight Checklist

☐ Aircraft Placed on Lauch Pad	☐ Check The Aircraft Status LEDs	☐ Check Flight Mode Switch (P-Mode)
☐ Turn On Remote Controller/ Tablet/DJI Pilot App	☐ Verify the Gimbal is Level, Can Move Unobstructed	☐ Check Satellite and Compass Status
☐ Antennas Properly Positioned	☐ Check RC Battery Level	☐ Set RTH Location And Height
☐ Turn on Aircraft	☐ Check Aircraft Battery Level	☐ Check Camera Settings

Takeoff Checklist

☐ Check Launch site is Clear for Takeoff	☐ Takeoff and Hover	☐ Check Flight Controls, Make Sure They Respond As Expected
☐ Start the motors	☐ Make Sure The Aircraft Is Stable While Hovering	☐ Start Recording Video

Post Flight Checklist

☐ Remove Battery From Aircraft	☐ Repack All Equipment
☐ Install Gimbal Guard	☐ **Complete The Flight Log**

FLIGHT PLAN

PILOT NAME: .... FAA ID: ....

ADDRESS: .... PHONE: ....

VISUAL OBSERVER(S): ....

LOCATION: ....

DATE: .... AIRCRAFT TYPE/NAME: ....

PLANNED TIME: .... AIRCRAFT CERTIFICATE N°: ....

ESTIMATED FLIGHT DURATION: .... FLIGHT TYPE: ....

AIRPORTS WITHIN 5 MILES: ....

....

WAIVERS APPLIED FOR: ....

FLIGHT DESCRIPTION/ROUTE: ....

....

....

FLIGHT RECORD

FLIGHT 1
TAKEOFF LOC.: .... LAUNCH TIME: .... FLIGHT NOTES: ....
LANDING LOC.: .... LANDING TIME: ....
BATTERY VOLTAGE: .... ELAPSED TIME: ....

FLIGHT 2
TAKEOFF LOC.: .... LAUNCH TIME: .... FLIGHT NOTES: ....
LANDING LOC.: .... LANDING TIME: ....
BATTERY VOLTAGE: .... ELAPSED TIME: ....

FLIGHT 3
TAKEOFF LOC.: .... LAUNCH TIME: .... FLIGHT NOTES: ....
LANDING LOC.: .... LANDING TIME: ....
BATTERY VOLTAGE: .... ELAPSED TIME: ....

FLIGHT 4
TAKEOFF LOC.: .... LAUNCH TIME: .... FLIGHT NOTES: ....
LANDING LOC.: .... LANDING TIME: ....
BATTERY VOLTAGE: .... ELAPSED TIME: ....

GENERAL NOTES: ....

....

....

FLIGHT CHECKLIST

☐ Airport(s) Notified	☐ UAV Batteries Charged	☐ Gimbal Protector Installed
☐ Location is OK To Fly	Battery 1 volts:	☐ Propellers Packed
☐ Weather Forecast OK	Battery 2 volts:	☐ Cables Packed
Temperature:	Battery 3 volts:	☐ Camera Filters Packed
Wind:	Battery 4 volts:	☐ Sun Shade Packed
Precipitation:	☐ Controller Charged	☐ Tools Packed
☐ Firmware up-to-date	☐ Tablet Charged	☐ Flight Plan designed/entered in Software
☐ Memory Card Formatted	☐ Mobile Phone Charged	☐ Logbook Packed

LAUNCH SITE CHECKLIST

☐ Verify Weather is OK To Fly	☐ Check For Obstacles, Interferences
Temperature:	☐ Check For Nearby Human Activity/ Dangerous
Wind:	☐ Verify Launch Pad Is Down-wind From Observers
Precipitation:	☐ Launch Pad/Barriers Placed
☐ **Safety Briefing**	

EQUIPMENT CHECKLIST

☐ Airframe/Landing Gear Inspected	☐ Battery Installed
☐ Propellers Inspected/ Attached	☐ Gimbal/Lens Protector Removed
☐ Controller/Tablet Assembled	
☐ Memory Card Installed	☐ Camera Filters Installed

PRE-FLIGHT CHECKLIST

☐ Aircraft Placed on Lauch Pad	☐ Check The Aircraft Status LEDs	☐ Check Flight Mode Switch (P-Mode)
☐ Turn On Remote Controller/ Tablet/DJI Pilot App	☐ Verify the Gimbal is Level, Can Move Unobstructed	☐ Check Satellite and Compass Status
☐ Antennas Properly Positioned	☐ Check RC Battery Level	☐ Set RTH Location And Height
☐ Turn on Aircraft	☐ Check Aircraft Battery Level	☐ Check Camera Settings

TAKEOFF CHECKLIST

☐ Check Launch site is Clear for Takeoff	☐ Takeoff and Hover	☐ Check Flight Controls, Make Sure They Respond As Expected
☐ Start the motors	☐ Make Sure The Aircraft Is Stable While Hovering	☐ Start Recording Video

POST FLIGHT CHECKLIST

☐ Remove Battery From Aircraft	☐ Repack All Equipment
☐ Install Gimbal Guard	☐ **Complete The Flight Log**

FLIGHT 65

FLIGHT PLAN

PILOT NAME: .... FAA ID: ....

ADDRESS: .... PHONE: ....

VISUAL OBSERVER(S): ....

LOCATION: ....

DATE: .... AIRCRAFT TYPE/NAME: ....

PLANNED TIME: .... AIRCRAFT CERTIFICATE N°: ....

ESTIMATED FLIGHT DURATION: .... FLIGHT TYPE: ....

AIRPORTS WITHIN 5 MILES: ....

WAIVERS APPLIED FOR: ....

FLIGHT DESCRIPTION/ROUTE: ....

....

....

FLIGHT RECORD

FLIGHT 1
TAKEOFF LOC.: .... LAUNCH TIME: .... FLIGHT NOTES: ....
LANDING LOC.: .... LANDING TIME: ....
BATTERY VOLTAGE: .... ELAPSED TIME: ....

FLIGHT 2
TAKEOFF LOC.: .... LAUNCH TIME: .... FLIGHT NOTES: ....
LANDING LOC.: .... LANDING TIME: ....
BATTERY VOLTAGE: .... ELAPSED TIME: ....

FLIGHT 3
TAKEOFF LOC.: .... LAUNCH TIME: .... FLIGHT NOTES: ....
LANDING LOC.: .... LANDING TIME: ....
BATTERY VOLTAGE: .... ELAPSED TIME: ....

FLIGHT 4
TAKEOFF LOC.: .... LAUNCH TIME: .... FLIGHT NOTES: ....
LANDING LOC.: .... LANDING TIME: ....
BATTERY VOLTAGE: .... ELAPSED TIME: ....

GENERAL NOTES: ....

....

....

Flight Checklist

☐ Airport(s) Notified	☐ UAV Batteries Charged	☐ Gimbal Protector Installed
☐ Location is OK To Fly	Battery 1 volts:	☐ Propellers Packed
☐ Weather Forecast OK	Battery 2 volts:	☐ Cables Packed
Temperature:	Battery 3 volts:	☐ Camera Filters Packed
Wind:	Battery 4 volts:	☐ Sun Shade Packed
Precipitation:	☐ Controller Charged	☐ Tools Packed
☐ Firmware up-to-date	☐ Tablet Charged	☐ Flight Plan designed/entered in Software
☐ Memory Card Formatted	☐ Mobile Phone Charged	☐ Logbook Packed

Launch Site Checklist

☐ Verify Weather is OK To Fly	☐ Check For Obstacles, Interferences
Temperature:	☐ Check For Nearby Human Activity/ Dangerous
Wind:	☐ Verify Launch Pad is Down-wind From Observers
Precipitation:	☐ Launch Pad/Barriers Placed
☐ **Safety Briefing**	

Equipment Checklist

☐ Airframe/Landing Gear Inspected	☐ Battery Installed
☐ Propellers Inspected/ Attached	☐ Gimbal/Lens Protector Removed
☐ Controller/Tablet Assembled	
☐ Memory Card Installed	☐ Camera Filters Installed

Pre-Flight Checklist

☐ Aircraft Placed on Lauch Pad	☐ Check The Aircraft Status LEDs	☐ Check Flight Mode Switch (P-Mode)
☐ Turn On Remote Controller/ Tablet/DJI Pilot App	☐ Verify the Gimbal is Level, Can Move Unobstructed	☐ Check Satellite and Compass Status
☐ Antennas Properly Positioned	☐ Check RC Battery Level	☐ Set RTH Location And Height
☐ Turn on Aircraft	☐ Check Aircraft Battery Level	☐ Check Camera Settings

Takeoff Checklist

☐ Check Launch site is Clear for Takeoff	☐ Takeoff and Hover	☐ Check Flight Controls, Make Sure They Respond As Expected
☐ Start the motors	☐ Make Sure The Aircraft Is Stable While Hovering	☐ Start Recording Video

Post Flight Checklist

☐ Remove Battery From Aircraft	☐ Repack All Equipment
☐ Install Gimbal Guard	☐ **Complete The Flight Log**

FLIGHT PLAN

PILOT NAME: .... FAA ID: ....

ADDRESS: .... PHONE: ....

VISUAL OBSERVER(S): ....

LOCATION: ....

DATE: .... AIRCRAFT TYPE/NAME: ....

PLANNED TIME: .... AIRCRAFT CERTIFICATE N°: ....

ESTIMATED FLIGHT DURATION: .... FLIGHT TYPE: ....

AIRPORTS WITHIN 5 MILES: ....

WAIVERS APPLIED FOR: ....

FLIGHT DESCRIPTION/ROUTE: ....

....

....

FLIGHT RECORD

FLIGHT 1
TAKEOFF LOC.: .... LAUNCH TIME: .... FLIGHT NOTES: ....

LANDING LOC.: .... LANDING TIME: ....

BATTERY VOLTAGE: .... ELAPSED TIME: ....

FLIGHT 2
TAKEOFF LOC.: .... LAUNCH TIME: .... FLIGHT NOTES: ....

LANDING LOC.: .... LANDING TIME: ....

BATTERY VOLTAGE: .... ELAPSED TIME: ....

FLIGHT 3
TAKEOFF LOC.: .... LAUNCH TIME: .... FLIGHT NOTES: ....

LANDING LOC.: .... LANDING TIME: ....

BATTERY VOLTAGE: .... ELAPSED TIME: ....

FLIGHT 4
TAKEOFF LOC.: .... LAUNCH TIME: .... FLIGHT NOTES: ....

LANDING LOC.: .... LANDING TIME: ....

BATTERY VOLTAGE: .... ELAPSED TIME: ....

GENERAL NOTES: ....

....

....

Flight Checklist

☐ Airport(s) Notified	☐ UAV Batteries Charged	☐ Gimbal Protector Installed
☐ Location is OK To Fly	Battery 1 volts:	☐ Propellers Packed
☐ Weather Forecast OK	Battery 2 volts:	☐ Cables Packed
Temperature:	Battery 3 volts:	☐ Camera Filters Packed
Wind:	Battery 4 volts:	☐ Sun Shade Packed
Precipitation:	☐ Controller Charged	☐ Tools Packed
☐ Firmware up-to-date	☐ Tablet Charged	☐ Flight Plan designed/entered in Software
☐ Memory Card Formatted	☐ Mobile Phone Charged	☐ Logbook Packed

Launch Site Checklist

☐ Verify Weather is OK To Fly	☐ Check For Obstacles, Interferences
Temperature:	☐ Check For Nearby Human Activity/ Dangerous
Wind:	☐ Verify Launch Pad Is Down-wind From Observers
Precipitation:	
☐ **Safety Briefing**	☐ Launch Pad/Barriers Placed

Equipment Checklist

☐ Airframe/Landing Gear Inspected	☐ Battery Installed
☐ Propellers Inspected/ Attached	☐ Gimbal/Lens Protector Removed
☐ Controller/Tablet Assembled	
☐ Memory Card Installed	☐ Camera Filters Installed

Pre-Flight Checklist

☐ Aircraft Placed on Lauch Pad	☐ Check The Aircraft Status LEDs	☐ Check Flight Mode Switch (P-Mode)
☐ Turn On Remote Controller/ Tablet/DJI Pilot App	☐ Verify the Gimbal is Level, Can Move Unobstructed	☐ Check Satellite and Compass Status
☐ Antennas Properly Positioned	☐ Check RC Battery Level	☐ Set RTH Location And Height
☐ Turn on Aircraft	☐ Check Aircraft Battery Level	☐ Check Camera Settings

Takeoff Checklist

☐ Check Launch site is Clear for Takeoff	☐ Takeoff and Hover	☐ Check Flight Controls, Make Sure They Respond As Expected
☐ Start the motors	☐ Make Sure The Aircraft Is Stable While Hovering	☐ Start Recording Video

Post Flight Checklist

☐ Remove Battery From Aircraft	☐ Repack All Equipment
☐ Install Gimbal Guard	☐ **Complete The Flight Log**

FLIGHT PLAN

PILOT NAME: .... FAA ID: ....

ADDRESS: .... PHONE: ....

VISUAL OBSERVER(S): ....

LOCATION: ....

DATE: .... AIRCRAFT TYPE/NAME: ....

PLANNED TIME: .... AIRCRAFT CERTIFICATE N°: ....

ESTIMATED FLIGHT DURATION: .... FLIGHT TYPE: ....

AIRPORTS WITHIN 5 MILES: ....

WAIVERS APPLIED FOR: ....

FLIGHT DESCRIPTION/ROUTE: ....

....

....

FLIGHT RECORD

FLIGHT 1
TAKEOFF LOC.: .... LAUNCH TIME: .... FLIGHT NOTES: ....
LANDING LOC.: .... LANDING TIME: ....
BATTERY VOLTAGE: .... ELAPSED TIME: ....

FLIGHT 2
TAKEOFF LOC.: .... LAUNCH TIME: .... FLIGHT NOTES: ....
LANDING LOC.: .... LANDING TIME: ....
BATTERY VOLTAGE: .... ELAPSED TIME: ....

FLIGHT 3
TAKEOFF LOC.: .... LAUNCH TIME: .... FLIGHT NOTES: ....
LANDING LOC.: .... LANDING TIME: ....
BATTERY VOLTAGE: .... ELAPSED TIME: ....

FLIGHT 4
TAKEOFF LOC.: .... LAUNCH TIME: .... FLIGHT NOTES: ....
LANDING LOC.: .... LANDING TIME: ....
BATTERY VOLTAGE: .... ELAPSED TIME: ....

GENERAL NOTES: ....

....

....

Flight Checklist

☐ Airport(s) Notified	☐ UAV Batteries Charged	☐ Gimbal Protector Installed
☐ Location is OK To Fly	Battery 1 volts:	☐ Propellers Packed
☐ Weather Forecast OK	Battery 2 volts:	☐ Cables Packed
Temperature:	Battery 3 volts:	☐ Camera Filters Packed
Wind:	Battery 4 volts:	☐ Sun Shade Packed
Precipitation:	☐ Controller Charged	☐ Tools Packed
☐ Firmware up-to-date	☐ Tablet Charged	☐ Flight Plan designed/entered in Software
☐ Memory Card Formatted	☐ Mobile Phone Charged	☐ Logbook Packed

Launch Site Checklist

☐ Verify Weather is OK To Fly	☐ Check For Obstacles, Interferences
Temperature:	☐ Check For Nearby Human Activity/ Dangerous
Wind:	☐ Verify Launch Pad Is Down-wind From Observers
Precipitation:	☐ Launch Pad/Barriers Placed
☐ **Safety Briefing**	

Equipment Checklist

☐ Airframe/Landing Gear Inspected	☐ Battery Installed
☐ Propellers Inspected/ Attached	☐ Gimbal/Lens Protector Removed
☐ Controller/Tablet Assembled	
☐ Memory Card Installed	☐ Camera Filters Installed

Pre-Flight Checklist

☐ Aircraft Placed on Lauch Pad	☐ Check The Aircraft Status LEDs	☐ Check Flight Mode Switch (P-Mode)
☐ Turn On Remote Controller/ Tablet/DJI Pilot App	☐ Verify the Gimbal is Level, Can Move Unobstructed	☐ Check Satellite and Compass Status
☐ Antennas Properly Positioned	☐ Check RC Battery Level	☐ Set RTH Location And Height
☐ Turn on Aircraft	☐ Check Aircraft Battery Level	☐ Check Camera Settings

Takeoff Checklist

☐ Check Launch site is Clear for Takeoff	☐ Takeoff and Hover	☐ Check Flight Controls, Make Sure They Respond As Expected
☐ Start the motors	☐ Make Sure The Aircraft Is Stable While Hovering	☐ Start Recording Video

Post Flight Checklist

☐ Remove Battery From Aircraft	☐ Repack All Equipment
☐ Install Gimbal Guard	☐ **Complete The Flight Log**

FLIGHT | 68

FLIGHT PLAN

PILOT NAME: .... FAA ID: ....

ADDRESS: .... PHONE: ....

VISUAL OBSERVER(S): ....

LOCATION: ....

DATE: .... AIRCRAFT TYPE/NAME: ....

PLANNED TIME: .... AIRCRAFT CERTIFICATE N°: ....

ESTIMATED FLIGHT DURATION: .... FLIGHT TYPE: ....

AIRPORTS WITHIN 5 MILES: ....

WAIVERS APPLIED FOR: ....

FLIGHT DESCRIPTION/ROUTE: ....

....

....

FLIGHT RECORD

FLIGHT 1
TAKEOFF LOC.: .... LAUNCH TIME: .... FLIGHT NOTES: ....

LANDING LOC.: .... LANDING TIME: ....

BATTERY VOLTAGE: .... ELAPSED TIME: ....

FLIGHT 2
TAKEOFF LOC.: .... LAUNCH TIME: .... FLIGHT NOTES: ....

LANDING LOC.: .... LANDING TIME: ....

BATTERY VOLTAGE: .... ELAPSED TIME: ....

FLIGHT 3
TAKEOFF LOC.: .... LAUNCH TIME: .... FLIGHT NOTES: ....

LANDING LOC.: .... LANDING TIME: ....

BATTERY VOLTAGE: .... ELAPSED TIME: ....

FLIGHT 4
TAKEOFF LOC.: .... LAUNCH TIME: .... FLIGHT NOTES: ....

LANDING LOC.: .... LANDING TIME: ....

BATTERY VOLTAGE: .... ELAPSED TIME: ....

GENERAL NOTES: ....

....

....

Flight Checklist

☐ Airport(s) Notified	☐ UAV Batteries Charged	☐ Gimbal Protector Installed
☐ Location is OK To Fly	Battery 1 volts:	☐ Propellers Packed
☐ Weather Forecast OK	Battery 2 volts:	☐ Cables Packed
Temperature:	Battery 3 volts:	☐ Camera Filters Packed
Wind:	Battery 4 volts:	☐ Sun Shade Packed
Precipitation:	☐ Controller Charged	☐ Tools Packed
☐ Firmware up-to-date	☐ Tablet Charged	☐ Flight Plan designed/entered in Software
☐ Memory Card Formatted	☐ Mobile Phone Charged	☐ Logbook Packed

Launch Site Checklist

☐ Verify Weather is OK To Fly	☐ Check For Obstacles, Interferences
Temperature:	☐ Check For Nearby Human Activity/ Dangerous
Wind:	☐ Verify Launch Pad Is Down-wind From Observers
Precipitation:	☐ Launch Pad/Barriers Placed
☐ **Safety Briefing**	

Equipment Checklist

☐ Airframe/Landing Gear Inspected	☐ Battery Installed
☐ Propellers Inspected/ Attached	☐ Gimbal/Lens Protector Removed
☐ Controller/Tablet Assembled	
☐ Memory Card Installed	☐ Camera Filters Installed

Pre-Flight Checklist

☐ Aircraft Placed on Lauch Pad	☐ Check The Aircraft Status LEDs	☐ Check Flight Mode Switch (P-Mode)
☐ Turn On Remote Controller/ Tablet/DJI Pilot App	☐ Verify the Gimbal is Level, Can Move Unobstructed	☐ Check Satellite and Compass Status
☐ Antennas Properly Positioned	☐ Check RC Battery Level	☐ Set RTH Location And Height
☐ Turn on Aircraft	☐ Check Aircraft Battery Level	☐ Check Camera Settings

Takeoff Checklist

☐ Check Launch site is Clear for Takeoff	☐ Takeoff and Hover	☐ Check Flight Controls, Make Sure They Respond As Expected
☐ Start the motors	☐ Make Sure The Aircraft Is Stable While Hovering	☐ Start Recording Video

Post Flight Checklist

☐ Remove Battery From Aircraft	☐ Repack All Equipment
☐ Install Gimbal Guard	☐ **Complete The Flight Log**

FLIGHT PLAN

PILOT NAME: .... FAA ID: ....

ADDRESS: .... PHONE: ....

VISUAL OBSERVER(S): ....

LOCATION: ....

DATE: .... AIRCRAFT TYPE/NAME: ....

PLANNED TIME: .... AIRCRAFT CERTIFICATE N°: ....

ESTIMATED FLIGHT DURATION: .... FLIGHT TYPE: ....

AIRPORTS WITHIN 5 MILES: ....

WAIVERS APPLIED FOR: ....

FLIGHT DESCRIPTION/ROUTE: ....

....

....

FLIGHT RECORD

FLIGHT 1

TAKEOFF LOC.: .... LAUNCH TIME: .... FLIGHT NOTES: ....

LANDING LOC.: .... LANDING TIME: ....

BATTERY VOLTAGE: .... ELAPSED TIME: ....

FLIGHT 2

TAKEOFF LOC.: .... LAUNCH TIME: .... FLIGHT NOTES: ....

LANDING LOC.: .... LANDING TIME: ....

BATTERY VOLTAGE: .... ELAPSED TIME: ....

FLIGHT 3

TAKEOFF LOC.: .... LAUNCH TIME: .... FLIGHT NOTES: ....

LANDING LOC.: .... LANDING TIME: ....

BATTERY VOLTAGE: .... ELAPSED TIME: ....

FLIGHT 4

TAKEOFF LOC.: .... LAUNCH TIME: .... FLIGHT NOTES: ....

LANDING LOC.: .... LANDING TIME: ....

BATTERY VOLTAGE: .... ELAPSED TIME: ....

GENERAL NOTES: ....

....

....

FLIGHT CHECKLIST

☐ Airport(s) Notified	☐ UAV Batteries Charged	☐ Gimbal Protector Installed
☐ Location is OK To Fly	Battery 1 volts:	☐ Propellers Packed
☐ Weather Forecast OK	Battery 2 volts:	☐ Cables Packed
Temperature:	Battery 3 volts:	☐ Camera Filters Packed
Wind:	Battery 4 volts:	☐ Sun Shade Packed
Precipitation:	☐ Controller Charged	☐ Tools Packed
☐ Firmware up-to-date	☐ Tablet Charged	☐ Flight Plan designed/entered in Software
☐ Memory Card Formatted	☐ Mobile Phone Charged	☐ Logbook Packed

LAUNCH SITE CHECKLIST

☐ Verify Weather is OK To Fly	☐ Check For Obstacles, Interferences
Temperature:	☐ Check For Nearby Human Activity/ Dangerous
Wind:	☐ Verify Launch Pad Is Down-wind From Observers
Precipitation:	
☐ **Safety Briefing**	☐ Launch Pad/Barriers Placed

EQUIPMENT CHECKLIST

☐ Airframe/Landing Gear Inspected	☐ Battery Installed
☐ Propellers Inspected/ Attached	☐ Gimbal/Lens Protector Removed
☐ Controller/Tablet Assembled	
☐ Memory Card Installed	☐ Camera Filters Installed

PRE-FLIGHT CHECKLIST

☐ Aircraft Placed on Lauch Pad	☐ Check The Aircraft Status LEDs	☐ Check Flight Mode Switch (P-Mode)
☐ Turn On Remote Controller/ Tablet/DJI Pilot App	☐ Verify the Gimbal is Level, Can Move Unobstructed	☐ Check Satellite and Compass Status
☐ Antennas Properly Positioned	☐ Check RC Battery Level	☐ Set RTH Location And Height
☐ Turn on Aircraft	☐ Check Aircraft Battery Level	☐ Check Camera Settings

TAKEOFF CHECKLIST

☐ Check Launch site is Clear for Takeoff	☐ Takeoff and Hover	☐ Check Flight Controls, Make Sure They Respond As Expected
☐ Start the motors	☐ Make Sure The Aircraft Is Stable While Hovering	☐ Start Recording Video

POST FLIGHT CHECKLIST

☐ Remove Battery From Aircraft	☐ Repack All Equipment
☐ Install Gimbal Guard	☐ **Complete The Flight Log**

FLIGHT | **70**

FLIGHT PLAN

PILOT NAME: .... FAA ID: ....

ADDRESS: .... PHONE: ....

VISUAL OBSERVER(S): ....

LOCATION: ....

DATE: .... AIRCRAFT TYPE/NAME: ....

PLANNED TIME: .... AIRCRAFT CERTIFICATE N°: ....

ESTIMATED FLIGHT DURATION: .... FLIGHT TYPE: ....

AIRPORTS WITHIN 5 MILES: ....

WAIVERS APPLIED FOR: ....

FLIGHT DESCRIPTION/ROUTE: ....

....

....

FLIGHT RECORD

<table>
<tr><td rowspan="3">FLIGHT 1</td><td>TAKEOFF LOC.: ....</td><td>LAUNCH TIME: ....</td><td>FLIGHT NOTES: ....</td></tr>
<tr><td>LANDING LOC.: ....</td><td>LANDING TIME: ....</td><td></td></tr>
<tr><td>BATTERY VOLTAGE: ....</td><td>ELAPSED TIME: ....</td><td></td></tr>
<tr><td rowspan="3">FLIGHT 2</td><td>TAKEOFF LOC.: ....</td><td>LAUNCH TIME: ....</td><td>FLIGHT NOTES: ....</td></tr>
<tr><td>LANDING LOC.: ....</td><td>LANDING TIME: ....</td><td></td></tr>
<tr><td>BATTERY VOLTAGE: ....</td><td>ELAPSED TIME: ....</td><td></td></tr>
<tr><td rowspan="3">FLIGHT 3</td><td>TAKEOFF LOC.: ....</td><td>LAUNCH TIME: ....</td><td>FLIGHT NOTES: ....</td></tr>
<tr><td>LANDING LOC.: ....</td><td>LANDING TIME: ....</td><td></td></tr>
<tr><td>BATTERY VOLTAGE: ....</td><td>ELAPSED TIME: ....</td><td></td></tr>
<tr><td rowspan="3">FLIGHT 4</td><td>TAKEOFF LOC.: ....</td><td>LAUNCH TIME: ....</td><td>FLIGHT NOTES: ....</td></tr>
<tr><td>LANDING LOC.: ....</td><td>LANDING TIME: ....</td><td></td></tr>
<tr><td>BATTERY VOLTAGE: ....</td><td>ELAPSED TIME: ....</td><td></td></tr>
</table>

GENERAL NOTES: ....

....

....

Flight Checklist

☐ Airport(s) Notified	☐ UAV Batteries Charged	☐ Gimbal Protector Installed
☐ Location is OK To Fly	Battery 1 volts:	☐ Propellers Packed
☐ Weather Forecast OK	Battery 2 volts:	☐ Cables Packed
Temperature:	Battery 3 volts:	☐ Camera Filters Packed
Wind:	Battery 4 volts:	☐ Sun Shade Packed
Precipitation:	☐ Controller Charged	☐ Tools Packed
☐ Firmware up-to-date	☐ Tablet Charged	☐ Flight Plan designed/entered in Software
☐ Memory Card Formatted	☐ Mobile Phone Charged	☐ Logbook Packed

Launch Site Checklist

☐ Verify Weather is OK To Fly	☐ Check For Obstacles, Interferences
Temperature:	☐ Check For Nearby Human Activity/ Dangerous
Wind:	☐ Verify Launch Pad Is Down-wind From Observers
Precipitation:	
☐ **Safety Briefing**	☐ Launch Pad/Barriers Placed

Equipment Checklist

☐ Airframe/Landing Gear Inspected	☐ Battery Installed
☐ Propellers Inspected/ Attached	☐ Gimbal/Lens Protector Removed
☐ Controller/Tablet Assembled	
☐ Memory Card Installed	☐ Camera Filters Installed

Pre-Flight Checklist

☐ Aircraft Placed on Lauch Pad	☐ Check The Aircraft Status LEDs	☐ Check Flight Mode Switch (P-Mode)
☐ Turn On Remote Controller/ Tablet/DJI Pilot App	☐ Verify the Gimbal is Level, Can Move Unobstructed	☐ Check Satellite and Compass Status
☐ Antennas Properly Positioned	☐ Check RC Battery Level	☐ Set RTH Location And Height
☐ Turn on Aircraft	☐ Check Aircraft Battery Level	☐ Check Camera Settings

Takeoff Checklist

☐ Check Launch site is Clear for Takeoff	☐ Takeoff and Hover	☐ Check Flight Controls, Make Sure They Respond As Expected
☐ Start the motors	☐ Make Sure The Aircraft Is Stable While Hovering	☐ Start Recording Video

Post Flight Checklist

☐ Remove Battery From Aircraft	☐ Repack All Equipment
☐ Install Gimbal Guard	☐ **Complete The Flight Log**

FLIGHT | 71

FLIGHT PLAN

PILOT NAME: .... FAA ID: ....

ADDRESS: .... PHONE: ....

VISUAL OBSERVER(S): ....

LOCATION: ....

DATE: .... AIRCRAFT TYPE/NAME: ....

PLANNED TIME: .... AIRCRAFT CERTIFICATE N°: ....

ESTIMATED FLIGHT DURATION: .... FLIGHT TYPE: ....

AIRPORTS WITHIN 5 MILES: ....

WAIVERS APPLIED FOR: ....

FLIGHT DESCRIPTION/ROUTE: ....
....
....

FLIGHT RECORD

FLIGHT 1
TAKEOFF LOC.: .... LAUNCH TIME: .... FLIGHT NOTES: ....
LANDING LOC.: .... LANDING TIME: ....
BATTERY VOLTAGE: .... ELAPSED TIME: ....

FLIGHT 2
TAKEOFF LOC.: .... LAUNCH TIME: .... FLIGHT NOTES: ....
LANDING LOC.: .... LANDING TIME: ....
BATTERY VOLTAGE: .... ELAPSED TIME: ....

FLIGHT 3
TAKEOFF LOC.: .... LAUNCH TIME: .... FLIGHT NOTES: ....
LANDING LOC.: .... LANDING TIME: ....
BATTERY VOLTAGE: .... ELAPSED TIME: ....

FLIGHT 4
TAKEOFF LOC.: .... LAUNCH TIME: .... FLIGHT NOTES: ....
LANDING LOC.: .... LANDING TIME: ....
BATTERY VOLTAGE: .... ELAPSED TIME: ....

GENERAL NOTES: ....
....
....

Flight Checklist

☐ Airport(s) Notified	☐ UAV Batteries Charged	☐ Gimbal Protector Installed
☐ Location is OK To Fly	Battery 1 volts:	☐ Propellers Packed
☐ Weather Forecast OK	Battery 2 volts:	☐ Cables Packed
Temperature:	Battery 3 volts:	☐ Camera Filters Packed
Wind:	Battery 4 volts:	☐ Sun Shade Packed
Precipitation:	☐ Controller Charged	☐ Tools Packed
☐ Firmware up-to-date	☐ Tablet Charged	☐ Flight Plan designed/entered in Software
☐ Memory Card Formatted	☐ Mobile Phone Charged	☐ Logbook Packed

Launch Site Checklist

☐ Verify Weather is OK To Fly	☐ Check For Obstacles, Interferences
Temperature:	☐ Check For Nearby Human Activity/ Dangerous
Wind:	☐ Verify Launch Pad Is Down-wind From Observers
Precipitation:	☐ Launch Pad/Barriers Placed
☐ **Safety Briefing**	

Equipment Checklist

☐ Airframe/Landing Gear Inspected	☐ Battery Installed
☐ Propellers Inspected/ Attached	☐ Gimbal/Lens Protector Removed
☐ Controller/Tablet Assembled	
☐ Memory Card Installed	☐ Camera Filters Installed

Pre-Flight Checklist

☐ Aircraft Placed on Lauch Pad	☐ Check The Aircraft Status LEDs	☐ Check Flight Mode Switch (P-Mode)
☐ Turn On Remote Controller/ Tablet/DJI Pilot App	☐ Verify the Gimbal is Level, Can Move Unobstructed	☐ Check Satellite and Compass Status
☐ Antennas Properly Positioned	☐ Check RC Battery Level	☐ Set RTH Location And Height
☐ Turn on Aircraft	☐ Check Aircraft Battery Level	☐ Check Camera Settings

Takeoff Checklist

☐ Check Launch site is Clear for Takeoff	☐ Takeoff and Hover	☐ Check Flight Controls, Make Sure They Respond As Expected
☐ Start the motors	☐ Make Sure The Aircraft Is Stable While Hovering	☐ Start Recording Video

Post Flight Checklist

☐ Remove Battery From Aircraft	☐ Repack All Equipment
☐ Install Gimbal Guard	☐ **Complete The Flight Log**

FLIGHT PLAN

PILOT NAME: .... FAA ID: ....

ADDRESS: .... PHONE: ....

VISUAL OBSERVER(S): ....

LOCATION: ....

DATE: .... AIRCRAFT TYPE/NAME: ....

PLANNED TIME: .... AIRCRAFT CERTIFICATE N°: ....

ESTIMATED FLIGHT DURATION: .... FLIGHT TYPE: ....

AIRPORTS WITHIN 5 MILES: ....

WAIVERS APPLIED FOR: ....

FLIGHT DESCRIPTION/ROUTE: ....

....

....

FLIGHT RECORD

FLIGHT 1

TAKEOFF LOC.: .... LAUNCH TIME: .... FLIGHT NOTES: ....

LANDING LOC.: .... LANDING TIME: ....

BATTERY VOLTAGE: .... ELAPSED TIME: ....

FLIGHT 2

TAKEOFF LOC.: .... LAUNCH TIME: .... FLIGHT NOTES: ....

LANDING LOC.: .... LANDING TIME: ....

BATTERY VOLTAGE: .... ELAPSED TIME: ....

FLIGHT 3

TAKEOFF LOC.: .... LAUNCH TIME: .... FLIGHT NOTES: ....

LANDING LOC.: .... LANDING TIME: ....

BATTERY VOLTAGE: .... ELAPSED TIME: ....

FLIGHT 4

TAKEOFF LOC.: .... LAUNCH TIME: .... FLIGHT NOTES: ....

LANDING LOC.: .... LANDING TIME: ....

BATTERY VOLTAGE: .... ELAPSED TIME: ....

GENERAL NOTES: ....

....

....

Flight Checklist

☐ Airport(s) Notified	☐ UAV Batteries Charged	☐ Gimbal Protector Installed
☐ Location is OK To Fly	Battery 1 volts:	☐ Propellers Packed
☐ Weather Forecast OK	Battery 2 volts:	☐ Cables Packed
Temperature:	Battery 3 volts:	☐ Camera Filters Packed
Wind:	Battery 4 volts:	☐ Sun Shade Packed
Precipitation:	☐ Controller Charged	☐ Tools Packed
☐ Firmware up-to-date	☐ Tablet Charged	☐ Flight Plan designed/entered in Software
☐ Memory Card Formatted	☐ Mobile Phone Charged	☐ Logbook Packed

Launch Site Checklist

☐ Verify Weather is OK To Fly	☐ Check For Obstacles, Interferences
Temperature:	☐ Check For Nearby Human Activity/ Dangerous
Wind:	☐ Verify Launch Pad Is Down-wind From Observers
Precipitation:	
☐ **Safety Briefing**	☐ Launch Pad/Barriers Placed

Equipment Checklist

☐ Airframe/Landing Gear Inspected	☐ Battery Installed
☐ Propellers Inspected/ Attached	☐ Gimbal/Lens Protector Removed
☐ Controller/Tablet Assembled	
☐ Memory Card Installed	☐ Camera Filters Installed

Pre-Flight Checklist

☐ Aircraft Placed on Lauch Pad	☐ Check The Aircraft Status LEDs	☐ Check Flight Mode Switch (P-Mode)
☐ Turn On Remote Controller/ Tablet/DJI Pilot App	☐ Verify the Gimbal is Level, Can Move Unobstructed	☐ Check Satellite and Compass Status
☐ Antennas Properly Positioned	☐ Check RC Battery Level	☐ Set RTH Location And Height
☐ Turn on Aircraft	☐ Check Aircraft Battery Level	☐ Check Camera Settings

Takeoff Checklist

☐ Check Launch site is Clear for Takeoff	☐ Takeoff and Hover	☐ Check Flight Controls, Make Sure They Respond As Expected
☐ Start the motors	☐ Make Sure The Aircraft Is Stable While Hovering	☐ Start Recording Video

Post Flight Checklist

☐ Remove Battery From Aircraft	☐ Repack All Equipment
☐ Install Gimbal Guard	☐ **Complete The Flight Log**

FLIGHT | **73**

FLIGHT PLAN

PILOT NAME: ....   FAA ID: ....

ADDRESS: ....   PHONE: ....

VISUAL OBSERVER(S): ....

LOCATION: ....

DATE: ....   AIRCRAFT TYPE/NAME: ....

PLANNED TIME: ....   AIRCRAFT CERTIFICATE N°: ....

ESTIMATED FLIGHT DURATION: ....   FLIGHT TYPE: ....

AIRPORTS WITHIN 5 MILES: ....

WAIVERS APPLIED FOR: ....

FLIGHT DESCRIPTION/ROUTE: ....

....

....

FLIGHT RECORD

FLIGHT 1

TAKEOFF LOC.: ....   LAUNCH TIME: ....   FLIGHT NOTES: ....

LANDING LOC.: ....   LANDING TIME: ....

BATTERY VOLTAGE: ....   ELAPSED TIME: ....

FLIGHT 2

TAKEOFF LOC.: ....   LAUNCH TIME: ....   FLIGHT NOTES: ....

LANDING LOC.: ....   LANDING TIME: ....

BATTERY VOLTAGE: ....   ELAPSED TIME: ....

FLIGHT 3

TAKEOFF LOC.: ....   LAUNCH TIME: ....   FLIGHT NOTES: ....

LANDING LOC.: ....   LANDING TIME: ....

BATTERY VOLTAGE: ....   ELAPSED TIME: ....

FLIGHT 4

TAKEOFF LOC.: ....   LAUNCH TIME: ....   FLIGHT NOTES: ....

LANDING LOC.: ....   LANDING TIME: ....

BATTERY VOLTAGE: ....   ELAPSED TIME: ....

GENERAL NOTES: ....

....

....

Flight Checklist

☐ Airport(s) Notified	☐ UAV Batteries Charged	☐ Gimbal Protector Installed
☐ Location is OK To Fly	Battery 1 volts:	☐ Propellers Packed
☐ Weather Forecast OK	Battery 2 volts:	☐ Cables Packed
Temperature:	Battery 3 volts:	☐ Camera Filters Packed
Wind:	Battery 4 volts:	☐ Sun Shade Packed
Precipitation:	☐ Controller Charged	☐ Tools Packed
☐ Firmware up-to-date	☐ Tablet Charged	☐ Flight Plan designed/entered in Software
☐ Memory Card Formatted	☐ Mobile Phone Charged	☐ Logbook Packed

Launch Site Checklist

☐ Verify Weather is OK To Fly	☐ Check For Obstacles, Interferences
Temperature:	☐ Check For Nearby Human Activity/ Dangerous
Wind:	☐ Verify Launch Pad is Down-wind From Observers
Precipitation:	☐ Launch Pad/Barriers Placed
☐ **Safety Briefing**	

Equipment Checklist

☐ Airframe/Landing Gear Inspected	☐ Battery Installed
☐ Propellers Inspected/ Attached	☐ Gimbal/Lens Protector Removed
☐ Controller/Tablet Assembled	
☐ Memory Card Installed	☐ Camera Filters Installed

Pre-Flight Checklist

☐ Aircraft Placed on Lauch Pad	☐ Check The Aircraft Status LEDs	☐ Check Flight Mode Switch (P-Mode)
☐ Turn On Remote Controller/ Tablet/DJI Pilot App	☐ Verify the Gimbal is Level, Can Move Unobstructed	☐ Check Satellite and Compass Status
☐ Antennas Properly Positioned	☐ Check RC Battery Level	☐ Set RTH Location And Height
☐ Turn on Aircraft	☐ Check Aircraft Battery Level	☐ Check Camera Settings

Takeoff Checklist

☐ Check Launch site is Clear for Takeoff	☐ Takeoff and Hover	☐ Check Flight Controls, Make Sure They Respond As Expected
☐ Start the motors	☐ Make Sure The Aircraft Is Stable While Hovering	☐ Start Recording Video

Post Flight Checklist

☐ Remove Battery From Aircraft	☐ Repack All Equipment
☐ Install Gimbal Guard	☐ **Complete The Flight Log**

FLIGHT | 74

FLIGHT PLAN

PILOT NAME: .... FAA ID: ....

ADDRESS: .... PHONE: ....

VISUAL OBSERVER(S): ....

LOCATION: ....

DATE: .... AIRCRAFT TYPE/NAME: ....

PLANNED TIME: .... AIRCRAFT CERTIFICATE N°: ....

ESTIMATED FLIGHT DURATION: .... FLIGHT TYPE: ....

AIRPORTS WITHIN 5 MILES: ....

WAIVERS APPLIED FOR: ....

FLIGHT DESCRIPTION/ROUTE: ....

....

....

FLIGHT RECORD

FLIGHT 1
TAKEOFF LOC.: .... LAUNCH TIME: .... FLIGHT NOTES: ....

LANDING LOC.: .... LANDING TIME: ....

BATTERY VOLTAGE: .... ELAPSED TIME: ....

FLIGHT 2
TAKEOFF LOC.: .... LAUNCH TIME: .... FLIGHT NOTES: ....

LANDING LOC.: .... LANDING TIME: ....

BATTERY VOLTAGE: .... ELAPSED TIME: ....

FLIGHT 3
TAKEOFF LOC.: .... LAUNCH TIME: .... FLIGHT NOTES: ....

LANDING LOC.: .... LANDING TIME: ....

BATTERY VOLTAGE: .... ELAPSED TIME: ....

FLIGHT 4
TAKEOFF LOC.: .... LAUNCH TIME: .... FLIGHT NOTES: ....

LANDING LOC.: .... LANDING TIME: ....

BATTERY VOLTAGE: .... ELAPSED TIME: ....

GENERAL NOTES: ....

....

....

Flight Checklist

☐ Airport(s) Notified	☐ UAV Batteries Charged	☐ Gimbal Protector Installed
☐ Location is OK To Fly	Battery 1 volts:	☐ Propellers Packed
☐ Weather Forecast OK	Battery 2 volts:	☐ Cables Packed
Temperature:	Battery 3 volts:	☐ Camera Filters Packed
Wind:	Battery 4 volts:	☐ Sun Shade Packed
Precipitation:	☐ Controller Charged	☐ Tools Packed
☐ Firmware up-to-date	☐ Tablet Charged	☐ Flight Plan designed/entered in Software
☐ Memory Card Formatted	☐ Mobile Phone Charged	☐ Logbook Packed

Launch Site Checklist

☐ Verify Weather is OK To Fly	☐ Check For Obstacles, Interferences
Temperature:	☐ Check For Nearby Human Activity/ Dangerous
Wind:	☐ Verify Launch Pad Is Down-wind From Observers
Precipitation:	☐ Launch Pad/Barriers Placed
☐ **Safety Briefing**	

Equipment Checklist

☐ Airframe/Landing Gear Inspected	☐ Battery Installed
☐ Propellers Inspected/ Attached	☐ Gimbal/Lens Protector Removed
☐ Controller/Tablet Assembled	
☐ Memory Card Installed	☐ Camera Filters Installed

Pre-Flight Checklist

☐ Aircraft Placed on Lauch Pad	☐ Check The Aircraft Status LEDs	☐ Check Flight Mode Switch (P-Mode)
☐ Turn On Remote Controller/ Tablet/DJI Pilot App	☐ Verify the Gimbal is Level, Can Move Unobstructed	☐ Check Satellite and Compass Status
☐ Antennas Properly Positioned	☐ Check RC Battery Level	☐ Set RTH Location And Height
☐ Turn on Aircraft	☐ Check Aircraft Battery Level	☐ Check Camera Settings

Takeoff Checklist

☐ Check Launch site is Clear for Takeoff	☐ Takeoff and Hover	☐ Check Flight Controls, Make Sure They Respond As Expected
☐ Start the motors	☐ Make Sure The Aircraft Is Stable While Hovering	☐ Start Recording Video

Post Flight Checklist

☐ Remove Battery From Aircraft	☐ Repack All Equipment
☐ Install Gimbal Guard	☐ **Complete The Flight Log**

Flight Plan

Pilot Name: .... FAA ID: ....

Address: .... Phone: ....

Visual Observer(s): ....

Location: ....

Date: .... Aircraft Type/Name: ....

Planned Time: .... Aircraft Certificate n°: ....

Estimated Flight Duration: .... Flight Type: ....

Airports Within 5 Miles: ....

Waivers Applied For: ....

Flight Description/Route: ....

....

....

Flight Record

Flight 1
Takeoff Loc.: .... Launch Time: .... Flight Notes: ....
Landing Loc.: .... Landing Time: ....
Battery Voltage: .... Elapsed Time: ....

Flight 2
Takeoff Loc.: .... Launch Time: .... Flight Notes: ....
Landing Loc.: .... Landing Time: ....
Battery Voltage: .... Elapsed Time: ....

Flight 3
Takeoff Loc.: .... Launch Time: .... Flight Notes: ....
Landing Loc.: .... Landing Time: ....
Battery Voltage: .... Elapsed Time: ....

Flight 4
Takeoff Loc.: .... Launch Time: .... Flight Notes: ....
Landing Loc.: .... Landing Time: ....
Battery Voltage: .... Elapsed Time: ....

General Notes: ....

....

....

FLIGHT CHECKLIST

☐ Airport(s) Notified	☐ UAV Batteries Charged	☐ Gimbal Protector Installed
☐ Location is OK To Fly	Battery 1 volts:	☐ Propellers Packed
☐ Weather Forecast OK	Battery 2 volts:	☐ Cables Packed
Temperature:	Battery 3 volts:	☐ Camera Filters Packed
Wind:	Battery 4 volts:	☐ Sun Shade Packed
Precipitation:	☐ Controller Charged	☐ Tools Packed
☐ Firmware up-to-date	☐ Tablet Charged	☐ Flight Plan designed/entered in Software
☐ Memory Card Formatted	☐ Mobile Phone Charged	☐ Logbook Packed

LAUNCH SITE CHECKLIST

☐ Verify Weather is OK To Fly	☐ Check For Obstacles, Interferences
Temperature:	☐ Check For Nearby Human Activity/ Dangerous
Wind:	☐ Verify Launch Pad Is Down-wind From Observers
Precipitation:	☐ Launch Pad/Barriers Placed
☐ **Safety Briefing**	

EQUIPMENT CHECKLIST

☐ Airframe/Landing Gear Inspected	☐ Battery Installed
☐ Propellers Inspected/ Attached	☐ Gimbal/Lens Protector Removed
☐ Controller/Tablet Assembled	
☐ Memory Card Installed	☐ Camera Filters Installed

PRE-FLIGHT CHECKLIST

☐ Aircraft Placed on Lauch Pad	☐ Check The Aircraft Status LEDs	☐ Check Flight Mode Switch (P-Mode)
☐ Turn On Remote Controller/ Tablet/DJI Pilot App	☐ Verify the Gimbal is Level, Can Move Unobstructed	☐ Check Satellite and Compass Status
☐ Antennas Properly Positioned	☐ Check RC Battery Level	☐ Set RTH Location And Height
☐ Turn on Aircraft	☐ Check Aircraft Battery Level	☐ Check Camera Settings

TAKEOFF CHECKLIST

☐ Check Launch site is Clear for Takeoff	☐ Takeoff and Hover	☐ Check Flight Controls, Make Sure They Respond As Expected
☐ Start the motors	☐ Make Sure The Aircraft Is Stable While Hovering	☐ Start Recording Video

POST FLIGHT CHECKLIST

☐ Remove Battery From Aircraft	☐ Repack All Equipment
☐ Install Gimbal Guard	☐ **Complete The Flight Log**

FLIGHT | 76

FLIGHT PLAN

PILOT NAME: ....   FAA ID: ....

ADDRESS: ....   PHONE: ....

VISUAL OBSERVER(S): ....

LOCATION: ....

DATE: ....   AIRCRAFT TYPE/NAME: ....

PLANNED TIME: ....   AIRCRAFT CERTIFICATE N°: ....

ESTIMATED FLIGHT DURATION: ....   FLIGHT TYPE: ....

AIRPORTS WITHIN 5 MILES: ....

WAIVERS APPLIED FOR: ....

FLIGHT DESCRIPTION/ROUTE: ....

....

....

FLIGHT RECORD

FLIGHT 1

TAKEOFF LOC.:	LAUNCH TIME:	FLIGHT NOTES: ....
LANDING LOC.:	LANDING TIME:	....
BATTERY VOLTAGE:	ELAPSED TIME:	....

FLIGHT 2

TAKEOFF LOC.:	LAUNCH TIME:	FLIGHT NOTES: ....
LANDING LOC.:	LANDING TIME:	....
BATTERY VOLTAGE:	ELAPSED TIME:	....

FLIGHT 3

TAKEOFF LOC.:	LAUNCH TIME:	FLIGHT NOTES: ....
LANDING LOC.:	LANDING TIME:	....
BATTERY VOLTAGE:	ELAPSED TIME:	....

FLIGHT 4

TAKEOFF LOC.:	LAUNCH TIME:	FLIGHT NOTES: ....
LANDING LOC.:	LANDING TIME:	....
BATTERY VOLTAGE:	ELAPSED TIME:	....

GENERAL NOTES: ....

....

....

Flight Checklist

☐ Airport(s) Notified	☐ UAV Batteries Charged	☐ Gimbal Protector Installed
☐ Location is OK To Fly	Battery 1 volts:	☐ Propellers Packed
☐ Weather Forecast OK	Battery 2 volts:	☐ Cables Packed
Temperature:	Battery 3 volts:	☐ Camera Filters Packed
Wind:	Battery 4 volts:	☐ Sun Shade Packed
Precipitation:	☐ Controller Charged	☐ Tools Packed
☐ Firmware up-to-date	☐ Tablet Charged	☐ Flight Plan designed/entered in Software
☐ Memory Card Formatted	☐ Mobile Phone Charged	☐ Logbook Packed

Launch Site Checklist

☐ Verify Weather is OK To Fly	☐ Check For Obstacles, Interferences
Temperature:	☐ Check For Nearby Human Activity/ Dangerous
Wind:	☐ Verify Launch Pad Is Down-wind From Observers
Precipitation:	☐ Launch Pad/Barriers Placed
☐ **Safety Briefing**	

Equipment Checklist

☐ Airframe/Landing Gear Inspected	☐ Battery Installed
☐ Propellers Inspected/ Attached	☐ Gimbal/Lens Protector Removed
☐ Controller/Tablet Assembled	
☐ Memory Card Installed	☐ Camera Filters Installed

Pre-Flight Checklist

☐ Aircraft Placed on Lauch Pad	☐ Check The Aircraft Status LEDs	☐ Check Flight Mode Switch (P-Mode)
☐ Turn On Remote Controller/ Tablet/DJI Pilot App	☐ Verify the Gimbal is Level, Can Move Unobstructed	☐ Check Satellite and Compass Status
☐ Antennas Properly Positioned	☐ Check RC Battery Level	☐ Set RTH Location And Height
☐ Turn on Aircraft	☐ Check Aircraft Battery Level	☐ Check Camera Settings

Takeoff Checklist

☐ Check Launch site is Clear for Takeoff	☐ Takeoff and Hover	☐ Check Flight Controls, Make Sure They Respond As Expected
☐ Start the motors	☐ Make Sure The Aircraft Is Stable While Hovering	☐ Start Recording Video

Post Flight Checklist

☐ Remove Battery From Aircraft	☐ Repack All Equipment
☐ Install Gimbal Guard	☐ **Complete The Flight Log**

FLIGHT 77

FLIGHT PLAN

PILOT NAME: .... FAA ID: ....

ADDRESS: .... PHONE: ....

VISUAL OBSERVER(S): ....

LOCATION: ....

DATE: .... AIRCRAFT TYPE/NAME: ....

PLANNED TIME: .... AIRCRAFT CERTIFICATE N°: ....

ESTIMATED FLIGHT DURATION: .... FLIGHT TYPE: ....

AIRPORTS WITHIN 5 MILES: ....

WAIVERS APPLIED FOR: ....

FLIGHT DESCRIPTION/ROUTE: ....

....

....

FLIGHT RECORD

FLIGHT 1

TAKEOFF LOC.: .... LAUNCH TIME: .... FLIGHT NOTES: ....

LANDING LOC.: .... LANDING TIME: ....

BATTERY VOLTAGE: .... ELAPSED TIME: ....

FLIGHT 2

TAKEOFF LOC.: .... LAUNCH TIME: .... FLIGHT NOTES: ....

LANDING LOC.: .... LANDING TIME: ....

BATTERY VOLTAGE: .... ELAPSED TIME: ....

FLIGHT 3

TAKEOFF LOC.: .... LAUNCH TIME: .... FLIGHT NOTES: ....

LANDING LOC.: .... LANDING TIME: ....

BATTERY VOLTAGE: .... ELAPSED TIME: ....

FLIGHT 4

TAKEOFF LOC.: .... LAUNCH TIME: .... FLIGHT NOTES: ....

LANDING LOC.: .... LANDING TIME: ....

BATTERY VOLTAGE: .... ELAPSED TIME: ....

GENERAL NOTES: ....

....

....

Flight Checklist

☐ Airport(s) Notified	☐ UAV Batteries Charged	☐ Gimbal Protector Installed
☐ Location is OK To Fly	Battery 1 volts:	☐ Propellers Packed
☐ Weather Forecast OK	Battery 2 volts:	☐ Cables Packed
Temperature:	Battery 3 volts:	☐ Camera Filters Packed
Wind:	Battery 4 volts:	☐ Sun Shade Packed
Precipitation:	☐ Controller Charged	☐ Tools Packed
☐ Firmware up-to-date	☐ Tablet Charged	☐ Flight Plan designed/entered in Software
☐ Memory Card Formatted	☐ Mobile Phone Charged	☐ Logbook Packed

Launch Site Checklist

☐ Verify Weather is OK To Fly	☐ Check For Obstacles, Interferences
Temperature:	☐ Check For Nearby Human Activity/ Dangerous
Wind:	☐ Verify Launch Pad Is Down-wind From Observers
Precipitation:	
☐ **Safety Briefing**	☐ Launch Pad/Barriers Placed

Equipment Checklist

☐ Airframe/Landing Gear Inspected	☐ Battery Installed
☐ Propellers Inspected/ Attached	☐ Gimbal/Lens Protector Removed
☐ Controller/Tablet Assembled	
☐ Memory Card Installed	☐ Camera Filters Installed

Pre-Flight Checklist

☐ Aircraft Placed on Lauch Pad	☐ Check The Aircraft Status LEDs	☐ Check Flight Mode Switch (P-Mode)
☐ Turn On Remote Controller/ Tablet/DJI Pilot App	☐ Verify the Gimbal is Level, Can Move Unobstructed	☐ Check Satellite and Compass Status
☐ Antennas Properly Positioned	☐ Check RC Battery Level	☐ Set RTH Location And Height
☐ Turn on Aircraft	☐ Check Aircraft Battery Level	☐ Check Camera Settings

Takeoff Checklist

☐ Check Launch site is Clear for Takeoff	☐ Takeoff and Hover	☐ Check Flight Controls, Make Sure They Respond As Expected
☐ Start the motors	☐ Make Sure The Aircraft Is Stable While Hovering	☐ Start Recording Video

Post Flight Checklist

☐ Remove Battery From Aircraft	☐ Repack All Equipment
☐ Install Gimbal Guard	☐ **Complete The Flight Log**

FLIGHT PLAN

PILOT NAME: .... FAA ID: ....

ADDRESS: .... PHONE: ....

VISUAL OBSERVER(S): ....

LOCATION: ....

DATE: .... AIRCRAFT TYPE/NAME: ....

PLANNED TIME: .... AIRCRAFT CERTIFICATE N°: ....

ESTIMATED FLIGHT DURATION: .... FLIGHT TYPE: ....

AIRPORTS WITHIN 5 MILES: ....

WAIVERS APPLIED FOR: ....

FLIGHT DESCRIPTION/ROUTE: ....

....

....

FLIGHT RECORD

FLIGHT 1
TAKEOFF LOC.: .... LAUNCH TIME: .... FLIGHT NOTES: ....
LANDING LOC.: .... LANDING TIME: ....
BATTERY VOLTAGE: .... ELAPSED TIME: ....

FLIGHT 2
TAKEOFF LOC.: .... LAUNCH TIME: .... FLIGHT NOTES: ....
LANDING LOC.: .... LANDING TIME: ....
BATTERY VOLTAGE: .... ELAPSED TIME: ....

FLIGHT 3
TAKEOFF LOC.: .... LAUNCH TIME: .... FLIGHT NOTES: ....
LANDING LOC.: .... LANDING TIME: ....
BATTERY VOLTAGE: .... ELAPSED TIME: ....

FLIGHT 4
TAKEOFF LOC.: .... LAUNCH TIME: .... FLIGHT NOTES: ....
LANDING LOC.: .... LANDING TIME: ....
BATTERY VOLTAGE: .... ELAPSED TIME: ....

GENERAL NOTES: ....

....

....

FLIGHT CHECKLIST

☐ Airport(s) Notified	☐ UAV Batteries Charged	☐ Gimbal Protector Installed
☐ Location is OK To Fly	Battery 1 volts:	☐ Propellers Packed
☐ Weather Forecast OK	Battery 2 volts:	☐ Cables Packed
Temperature:	Battery 3 volts:	☐ Camera Filters Packed
Wind:	Battery 4 volts:	☐ Sun Shade Packed
Precipitation:	☐ Controller Charged	☐ Tools Packed
☐ Firmware up-to-date	☐ Tablet Charged	☐ Flight Plan designed/entered in Software
☐ Memory Card Formatted	☐ Mobile Phone Charged	☐ Logbook Packed

LAUNCH SITE CHECKLIST

☐ Verify Weather is OK To Fly	☐ Check For Obstacles, Interferences
Temperature:	☐ Check For Nearby Human Activity/ Dangerous
Wind:	☐ Verify Launch Pad is Down-wind From Observers
Precipitation:	☐ Launch Pad/Barriers Placed
☐ **Safety Briefing**	

EQUIPMENT CHECKLIST

☐ Airframe/Landing Gear Inspected	☐ Battery Installed
☐ Propellers Inspected/ Attached	☐ Gimbal/Lens Protector Removed
☐ Controller/Tablet Assembled	
☐ Memory Card Installed	☐ Camera Filters Installed

PRE-FLIGHT CHECKLIST

☐ Aircraft Placed on Lauch Pad	☐ Check The Aircraft Status LEDs	☐ Check Flight Mode Switch (P-Mode)
☐ Turn On Remote Controller/ Tablet/DJI Pilot App	☐ Verify the Gimbal is Level, Can Move Unobstructed	☐ Check Satellite and Compass Status
☐ Antennas Properly Positioned	☐ Check RC Battery Level	☐ Set RTH Location And Height
☐ Turn on Aircraft	☐ Check Aircraft Battery Level	☐ Check Camera Settings

TAKEOFF CHECKLIST

☐ Check Launch site is Clear for Takeoff	☐ Takeoff and Hover	☐ Check Flight Controls, Make Sure They Respond As Expected
☐ Start the motors	☐ Make Sure The Aircraft Is Stable While Hovering	☐ Start Recording Video

POST FLIGHT CHECKLIST

☐ Remove Battery From Aircraft	☐ Repack All Equipment
☐ Install Gimbal Guard	☐ **Complete The Flight Log**

FLIGHT | 79

FLIGHT PLAN

PILOT NAME: ....   FAA ID: ....

ADDRESS: ....   PHONE: ....

VISUAL OBSERVER(S): ....

LOCATION: ....

DATE: ....   AIRCRAFT TYPE/NAME: ....

PLANNED TIME: ....   AIRCRAFT CERTIFICATE N°: ....

ESTIMATED FLIGHT DURATION: ....   FLIGHT TYPE: ....

AIRPORTS WITHIN 5 MILES: ....

WAIVERS APPLIED FOR: ....

FLIGHT DESCRIPTION/ROUTE: ....

....

....

FLIGHT RECORD

FLIGHT 1

TAKEOFF LOC.: ....   LAUNCH TIME: ....   FLIGHT NOTES: ....

LANDING LOC.: ....   LANDING TIME: ....

BATTERY VOLTAGE: ....   ELAPSED TIME: ....

FLIGHT 2

TAKEOFF LOC.: ....   LAUNCH TIME: ....   FLIGHT NOTES: ....

LANDING LOC.: ....   LANDING TIME: ....

BATTERY VOLTAGE: ....   ELAPSED TIME: ....

FLIGHT 3

TAKEOFF LOC.: ....   LAUNCH TIME: ....   FLIGHT NOTES: ....

LANDING LOC.: ....   LANDING TIME: ....

BATTERY VOLTAGE: ....   ELAPSED TIME: ....

FLIGHT 4

TAKEOFF LOC.: ....   LAUNCH TIME: ....   FLIGHT NOTES: ....

LANDING LOC.: ....   LANDING TIME: ....

BATTERY VOLTAGE: ....   ELAPSED TIME: ....

GENERAL NOTES: ....

....

....

Flight Checklist

☐ Airport(s) Notified	☐ UAV Batteries Charged	☐ Gimbal Protector Installed
☐ Location is OK To Fly	Battery 1 volts:	☐ Propellers Packed
☐ Weather Forecast OK	Battery 2 volts:	☐ Cables Packed
Temperature:	Battery 3 volts:	☐ Camera Filters Packed
Wind:	Battery 4 volts:	☐ Sun Shade Packed
Precipitation:	☐ Controller Charged	☐ Tools Packed
☐ Firmware up-to-date	☐ Tablet Charged	☐ Flight Plan designed/entered in Software
☐ Memory Card Formatted	☐ Mobile Phone Charged	☐ Logbook Packed

Launch Site Checklist

☐ Verify Weather is OK To Fly	☐ Check For Obstacles, Interferences
Temperature:	☐ Check For Nearby Human Activity/ Dangerous
Wind:	☐ Verify Launch Pad Is Down-wind From Observers
Precipitation:	
☐ **Safety Briefing**	☐ Launch Pad/Barriers Placed

Equipment Checklist

☐ Airframe/Landing Gear Inspected	☐ Battery Installed
☐ Propellers Inspected/ Attached	☐ Gimbal/Lens Protector Removed
☐ Controller/Tablet Assembled	
☐ Memory Card Installed	☐ Camera Filters Installed

Pre-Flight Checklist

☐ Aircraft Placed on Lauch Pad	☐ Check The Aircraft Status LEDs	☐ Check Flight Mode Switch (P-Mode)
☐ Turn On Remote Controller/ Tablet/DJI Pilot App	☐ Verify the Gimbal is Level, Can Move Unobstructed	☐ Check Satellite and Compass Status
☐ Antennas Properly Positioned	☐ Check RC Battery Level	☐ Set RTH Location And Height
☐ Turn on Aircraft	☐ Check Aircraft Battery Level	☐ Check Camera Settings

Takeoff Checklist

☐ Check Launch site is Clear for Takeoff	☐ Takeoff and Hover	☐ Check Flight Controls, Make Sure They Respond As Expected
☐ Start the motors	☐ Make Sure The Aircraft Is Stable While Hovering	☐ Start Recording Video

Post Flight Checklist

☐ Remove Battery From Aircraft	☐ Repack All Equipment
☐ Install Gimbal Guard	☐ **Complete The Flight Log**

FLIGHT PLAN

PILOT NAME: .... FAA ID: ....

ADDRESS: .... PHONE: ....

VISUAL OBSERVER(S): ....

LOCATION: ....

DATE: .... AIRCRAFT TYPE/NAME: ....

PLANNED TIME: .... AIRCRAFT CERTIFICATE N°: ....

ESTIMATED FLIGHT DURATION: .... FLIGHT TYPE: ....

AIRPORTS WITHIN 5 MILES: ....

WAIVERS APPLIED FOR: ....

FLIGHT DESCRIPTION/ROUTE: ....

....

....

FLIGHT RECORD

FLIGHT 1

TAKEOFF LOC.: .... LAUNCH TIME: .... FLIGHT NOTES: ....

LANDING LOC.: .... LANDING TIME: ....

BATTERY VOLTAGE: .... ELAPSED TIME: ....

FLIGHT 2

TAKEOFF LOC.: .... LAUNCH TIME: .... FLIGHT NOTES: ....

LANDING LOC.: .... LANDING TIME: ....

BATTERY VOLTAGE: .... ELAPSED TIME: ....

FLIGHT 3

TAKEOFF LOC.: .... LAUNCH TIME: .... FLIGHT NOTES: ....

LANDING LOC.: .... LANDING TIME: ....

BATTERY VOLTAGE: .... ELAPSED TIME: ....

FLIGHT 4

TAKEOFF LOC.: .... LAUNCH TIME: .... FLIGHT NOTES: ....

LANDING LOC.: .... LANDING TIME: ....

BATTERY VOLTAGE: .... ELAPSED TIME: ....

GENERAL NOTES: ....

....

....

FLIGHT CHECKLIST

☐ Airport(s) Notified	☐ UAV Batteries Charged	☐ Gimbal Protector Installed
☐ Location is OK To Fly	Battery 1 volts:	☐ Propellers Packed
☐ Weather Forecast OK	Battery 2 volts:	☐ Cables Packed
Temperature:	Battery 3 volts:	☐ Camera Filters Packed
Wind:	Battery 4 volts:	☐ Sun Shade Packed
Precipitation:	☐ Controller Charged	☐ Tools Packed
☐ Firmware up-to-date	☐ Tablet Charged	☐ Flight Plan designed/entered in Software
☐ Memory Card Formatted	☐ Mobile Phone Charged	☐ Logbook Packed

LAUNCH SITE CHECKLIST

☐ Verify Weather is OK To Fly	☐ Check For Obstacles, Interferences
Temperature:	☐ Check For Nearby Human Activity/ Dangerous
Wind:	☐ Verify Launch Pad Is Down-wind From Observers
Precipitation:	
☐ **Safety Briefing**	☐ Launch Pad/Barriers Placed

EQUIPMENT CHECKLIST

☐ Airframe/Landing Gear Inspected	☐ Battery Installed
☐ Propellers Inspected/ Attached	☐ Gimbal/Lens Protector Removed
☐ Controller/Tablet Assembled	
☐ Memory Card Installed	☐ Camera Filters Installed

PRE-FLIGHT CHECKLIST

☐ Aircraft Placed on Lauch Pad	☐ Check The Aircraft Status LEDs	☐ Check Flight Mode Switch (P-Mode)
☐ Turn On Remote Controller/ Tablet/DJI Pilot App	☐ Verify the Gimbal is Level, Can Move Unobstructed	☐ Check Satellite and Compass Status
☐ Antennas Properly Positioned	☐ Check RC Battery Level	☐ Set RTH Location And Height
☐ Turn on Aircraft	☐ Check Aircraft Battery Level	☐ Check Camera Settings

TAKEOFF CHECKLIST

☐ Check Launch site is Clear for Takeoff	☐ Takeoff and Hover	☐ Check Flight Controls, Make Sure They Respond As Expected
☐ Start the motors	☐ Make Sure The Aircraft Is Stable While Hovering	☐ Start Recording Video

POST FLIGHT CHECKLIST

☐ Remove Battery From Aircraft	☐ Repack All Equipment
☐ Install Gimbal Guard	☐ **Complete The Flight Log**

FLIGHT PLAN

PILOT NAME: .... FAA ID: ....

ADDRESS: .... PHONE: ....

VISUAL OBSERVER(S): ....

LOCATION: ....

DATE: .... AIRCRAFT TYPE/NAME: ....

PLANNED TIME: .... AIRCRAFT CERTIFICATE N°: ....

ESTIMATED FLIGHT DURATION: .... FLIGHT TYPE: ....

AIRPORTS WITHIN 5 MILES: ....

WAIVERS APPLIED FOR: ....

FLIGHT DESCRIPTION/ROUTE: ....

....

....

FLIGHT RECORD

FLIGHT 1

TAKEOFF LOC.: .... LAUNCH TIME: .... FLIGHT NOTES: ....

LANDING LOC.: .... LANDING TIME: ....

BATTERY VOLTAGE: .... ELAPSED TIME: ....

FLIGHT 2

TAKEOFF LOC.: .... LAUNCH TIME: .... FLIGHT NOTES: ....

LANDING LOC.: .... LANDING TIME: ....

BATTERY VOLTAGE: .... ELAPSED TIME: ....

FLIGHT 3

TAKEOFF LOC.: .... LAUNCH TIME: .... FLIGHT NOTES: ....

LANDING LOC.: .... LANDING TIME: ....

BATTERY VOLTAGE: .... ELAPSED TIME: ....

FLIGHT 4

TAKEOFF LOC.: .... LAUNCH TIME: .... FLIGHT NOTES: ....

LANDING LOC.: .... LANDING TIME: ....

BATTERY VOLTAGE: .... ELAPSED TIME: ....

GENERAL NOTES: ....

....

....

Flight Checklist

☐ Airport(s) Notified	☐ UAV Batteries Charged	☐ Gimbal Protector Installed
☐ Location is OK To Fly	Battery 1 volts:	☐ Propellers Packed
☐ Weather Forecast OK	Battery 2 volts:	☐ Cables Packed
Temperature:	Battery 3 volts:	☐ Camera Filters Packed
Wind:	Battery 4 volts:	☐ Sun Shade Packed
Precipitation:	☐ Controller Charged	☐ Tools Packed
☐ Firmware up-to-date	☐ Tablet Charged	☐ Flight Plan designed/entered in Software
☐ Memory Card Formatted	☐ Mobile Phone Charged	☐ Logbook Packed

Launch Site Checklist

☐ Verify Weather is OK To Fly	☐ Check For Obstacles, Interferences
Temperature:	☐ Check For Nearby Human Activity/ Dangerous
Wind:	☐ Verify Launch Pad is Down-wind From Observers
Precipitation:	☐ Launch Pad/Barriers Placed
☐ **Safety Briefing**	

Equipment Checklist

☐ Airframe/Landing Gear Inspected	☐ Battery Installed
☐ Propellers Inspected/ Attached	☐ Gimbal/Lens Protector Removed
☐ Controller/Tablet Assembled	
☐ Memory Card Installed	☐ Camera Filters Installed

Pre-Flight Checklist

☐ Aircraft Placed on Lauch Pad	☐ Check The Aircraft Status LEDs	☐ Check Flight Mode Switch (P-Mode)
☐ Turn On Remote Controller/ Tablet/DJI Pilot App	☐ Verify the Gimbal is Level, Can Move Unobstructed	☐ Check Satellite and Compass Status
☐ Antennas Properly Positioned	☐ Check RC Battery Level	☐ Set RTH Location And Height
☐ Turn on Aircraft	☐ Check Aircraft Battery Level	☐ Check Camera Settings

Takeoff Checklist

☐ Check Launch site is Clear for Takeoff	☐ Takeoff and Hover	☐ Check Flight Controls, Make Sure They Respond As Expected
☐ Start the motors	☐ Make Sure The Aircraft Is Stable While Hovering	☐ Start Recording Video

Post Flight Checklist

☐ Remove Battery From Aircraft	☐ Repack All Equipment
☐ Install Gimbal Guard	☐ **Complete The Flight Log**

FLIGHT 82

FLIGHT PLAN

PILOT NAME: .... FAA ID: ....

ADDRESS: .... PHONE: ....

VISUAL OBSERVER(S): ....

LOCATION: ....

DATE: .... AIRCRAFT TYPE/NAME: ....

PLANNED TIME: .... AIRCRAFT CERTIFICATE N°: ....

ESTIMATED FLIGHT DURATION: .... FLIGHT TYPE: ....

AIRPORTS WITHIN 5 MILES: ....

WAIVERS APPLIED FOR: ....

FLIGHT DESCRIPTION/ROUTE: ....

....

....

FLIGHT RECORD

FLIGHT 1
TAKEOFF LOC.: .... LAUNCH TIME: .... FLIGHT NOTES: ....

LANDING LOC.: .... LANDING TIME: ....

BATTERY VOLTAGE: .... ELAPSED TIME: ....

FLIGHT 2
TAKEOFF LOC.: .... LAUNCH TIME: .... FLIGHT NOTES: ....

LANDING LOC.: .... LANDING TIME: ....

BATTERY VOLTAGE: .... ELAPSED TIME: ....

FLIGHT 3
TAKEOFF LOC.: .... LAUNCH TIME: .... FLIGHT NOTES: ....

LANDING LOC.: .... LANDING TIME: ....

BATTERY VOLTAGE: .... ELAPSED TIME: ....

FLIGHT 4
TAKEOFF LOC.: .... LAUNCH TIME: .... FLIGHT NOTES: ....

LANDING LOC.: .... LANDING TIME: ....

BATTERY VOLTAGE: .... ELAPSED TIME: ....

GENERAL NOTES: ....

....

....

Flight Checklist

☐ Airport(s) Notified	☐ UAV Batteries Charged	☐ Gimbal Protector Installed
☐ Location is OK To Fly	Battery 1 volts:	☐ Propellers Packed
☐ Weather Forecast OK	Battery 2 volts:	☐ Cables Packed
Temperature:	Battery 3 volts:	☐ Camera Filters Packed
Wind:	Battery 4 volts:	☐ Sun Shade Packed
Precipitation:	☐ Controller Charged	☐ Tools Packed
☐ Firmware up-to-date	☐ Tablet Charged	☐ Flight Plan designed/entered in Software
☐ Memory Card Formatted	☐ Mobile Phone Charged	☐ Logbook Packed

Launch Site Checklist

☐ Verify Weather is OK To Fly	☐ Check For Obstacles, Interferences
Temperature:	☐ Check For Nearby Human Activity/ Dangerous
Wind:	☐ Verify Launch Pad Is Down-wind From Observers
Precipitation:	☐ Launch Pad/Barriers Placed
☐ **Safety Briefing**	

Equipment Checklist

☐ Airframe/Landing Gear Inspected	☐ Battery Installed
☐ Propellers Inspected/ Attached	☐ Gimbal/Lens Protector Removed
☐ Controller/Tablet Assembled	
☐ Memory Card Installed	☐ Camera Filters Installed

Pre-Flight Checklist

☐ Aircraft Placed on Lauch Pad	☐ Check The Aircraft Status LEDs	☐ Check Flight Mode Switch (P-Mode)
☐ Turn On Remote Controller/ Tablet/DJI Pilot App	☐ Verify the Gimbal is Level, Can Move Unobstructed	☐ Check Satellite and Compass Status
☐ Antennas Properly Positioned	☐ Check RC Battery Level	☐ Set RTH Location And Height
☐ Turn on Aircraft	☐ Check Aircraft Battery Level	☐ Check Camera Settings

Takeoff Checklist

☐ Check Launch site is Clear for Takeoff	☐ Takeoff and Hover	☐ Check Flight Controls, Make Sure They Respond As Expected
☐ Start the Motors	☐ Make Sure The Aircraft Is Stable While Hovering	☐ Start Recording Video

Post Flight Checklist

☐ Remove Battery From Aircraft	☐ Repack All Equipment
☐ Install Gimbal Guard	☐ **Complete The Flight Log**

Flight Plan

PILOT NAME: .... FAA ID: ....

ADDRESS: .... PHONE: ....

VISUAL OBSERVER(S): ....

LOCATION: ....

DATE: .... AIRCRAFT TYPE/NAME: ....

PLANNED TIME: .... AIRCRAFT CERTIFICATE N°: ....

ESTIMATED FLIGHT DURATION: .... FLIGHT TYPE: ....

AIRPORTS WITHIN 5 MILES: ....

WAIVERS APPLIED FOR: ....

FLIGHT DESCRIPTION/ROUTE: ....

....

....

Flight Record

FLIGHT 1

TAKEOFF LOC.: .... LAUNCH TIME: .... FLIGHT NOTES: ....

LANDING LOC.: .... LANDING TIME: ....

BATTERY VOLTAGE: .... ELAPSED TIME: ....

FLIGHT 2

TAKEOFF LOC.: .... LAUNCH TIME: .... FLIGHT NOTES: ....

LANDING LOC.: .... LANDING TIME: ....

BATTERY VOLTAGE: .... ELAPSED TIME: ....

FLIGHT 3

TAKEOFF LOC.: .... LAUNCH TIME: .... FLIGHT NOTES: ....

LANDING LOC.: .... LANDING TIME: ....

BATTERY VOLTAGE: .... ELAPSED TIME: ....

FLIGHT 4

TAKEOFF LOC.: .... LAUNCH TIME: .... FLIGHT NOTES: ....

LANDING LOC.: .... LANDING TIME: ....

BATTERY VOLTAGE: .... ELAPSED TIME: ....

GENERAL NOTES: ....

....

....

Flight Checklist

☐ Airport(s) Notified	☐ UAV Batteries Charged	☐ Gimbal Protector Installed
☐ Location is OK To Fly	Battery 1 volts:	☐ Propellers Packed
☐ Weather Forecast OK	Battery 2 volts:	☐ Cables Packed
Temperature:	Battery 3 volts:	☐ Camera Filters Packed
Wind:	Battery 4 volts:	☐ Sun Shade Packed
Precipitation:	☐ Controller Charged	☐ Tools Packed
☐ Firmware up-to-date	☐ Tablet Charged	☐ Flight Plan designed/entered in Software
☐ Memory Card Formatted	☐ Mobile Phone Charged	☐ Logbook Packed

Launch Site Checklist

☐ Verify Weather is OK To Fly	☐ Check For Obstacles, Interferences
Temperature:	☐ Check For Nearby Human Activity/ Dangerous
Wind:	☐ Verify Launch Pad Is Down-wind From Observers
Precipitation:	☐ Launch Pad/Barriers Placed
☐ **Safety Briefing**	

Equipment Checklist

☐ Airframe/Landing Gear Inspected	☐ Battery Installed
☐ Propellers Inspected/ Attached	☐ Gimbal/Lens Protector Removed
☐ Controller/Tablet Assembled	
☐ Memory Card Installed	☐ Camera Filters Installed

Pre-Flight Checklist

☐ Aircraft Placed on Lauch Pad	☐ Check The Aircraft Status LEDs	☐ Check Flight Mode Switch (P-Mode)
☐ Turn On Remote Controller/ Tablet/DJI Pilot App	☐ Verify the Gimbal is Level, Can Move Unobstructed	☐ Check Satellite and Compass Status
☐ Antennas Properly Positioned	☐ Check RC Battery Level	☐ Set RTH Location And Height
☐ Turn on Aircraft	☐ Check Aircraft Battery Level	☐ Check Camera Settings

Takeoff Checklist

☐ Check Launch site is Clear for Takeoff	☐ Takeoff and Hover	☐ Check Flight Controls, Make Sure They Respond As Expected
☐ Start the motors	☐ Make Sure The Aircraft Is Stable While Hovering	☐ Start Recording Video

Post Flight Checklist

☐ Remove Battery From Aircraft	☐ Repack All Equipment
☐ Install Gimbal Guard	☐ **Complete The Flight Log**

FLIGHT 84

FLIGHT PLAN

PILOT NAME: .... FAA ID: ....

ADDRESS: .... PHONE: ....

VISUAL OBSERVER(S): ....

LOCATION: ....

DATE: .... AIRCRAFT TYPE/NAME: ....

PLANNED TIME: .... AIRCRAFT CERTIFICATE N°: ....

ESTIMATED FLIGHT DURATION: .... FLIGHT TYPE: ....

AIRPORTS WITHIN 5 MILES: ....

WAIVERS APPLIED FOR: ....

FLIGHT DESCRIPTION/ROUTE: ....

....

....

FLIGHT RECORD

FLIGHT 1
TAKEOFF LOC.: .... LAUNCH TIME: .... FLIGHT NOTES: ....

LANDING LOC.: .... LANDING TIME: ....

BATTERY VOLTAGE: .... ELAPSED TIME: ....

FLIGHT 2
TAKEOFF LOC.: .... LAUNCH TIME: .... FLIGHT NOTES: ....

LANDING LOC.: .... LANDING TIME: ....

BATTERY VOLTAGE: .... ELAPSED TIME: ....

FLIGHT 3
TAKEOFF LOC.: .... LAUNCH TIME: .... FLIGHT NOTES: ....

LANDING LOC.: .... LANDING TIME: ....

BATTERY VOLTAGE: .... ELAPSED TIME: ....

FLIGHT 4
TAKEOFF LOC.: .... LAUNCH TIME: .... FLIGHT NOTES: ....

LANDING LOC.: .... LANDING TIME: ....

BATTERY VOLTAGE: .... ELAPSED TIME: ....

GENERAL NOTES: ....

....

....

Flight Checklist

☐ Airport(s) Notified	☐ UAV Batteries Charged	☐ Gimbal Protector Installed
☐ Location is OK To Fly	Battery 1 volts:	☐ Propellers Packed
☐ Weather Forecast OK	Battery 2 volts:	☐ Cables Packed
Temperature:	Battery 3 volts:	☐ Camera Filters Packed
Wind:	Battery 4 volts:	☐ Sun Shade Packed
Precipitation:	☐ Controller Charged	☐ Tools Packed
☐ Firmware up-to-date	☐ Tablet Charged	☐ Flight Plan designed/entered in Software
☐ Memory Card Formatted	☐ Mobile Phone Charged	☐ Logbook Packed

Launch Site Checklist

☐ Verify Weather is OK To Fly	☐ Check For Obstacles, Interferences
Temperature:	☐ Check For Nearby Human Activity/ Dangerous
Wind:	☐ Verify Launch Pad Is Down-wind From Observers
Precipitation:	☐ Launch Pad/Barriers Placed
☐ **Safety Briefing**	

Equipment Checklist

☐ Airframe/Landing Gear Inspected	☐ Battery Installed
☐ Propellers Inspected/ Attached	☐ Gimbal/Lens Protector Removed
☐ Controller/Tablet Assembled	
☐ Memory Card Installed	☐ Camera Filters Installed

Pre-Flight Checklist

☐ Aircraft Placed on Lauch Pad	☐ Check The Aircraft Status LEDs	☐ Check Flight Mode Switch (P-Mode)
☐ Turn On Remote Controller/ Tablet/DJI Pilot App	☐ Verify the Gimbal is Level, Can Move Unobstructed	☐ Check Satellite and Compass Status
☐ Antennas Properly Positioned	☐ Check RC Battery Level	☐ Set RTH Location And Height
☐ Turn on Aircraft	☐ Check Aircraft Battery Level	☐ Check Camera Settings

Takeoff Checklist

☐ Check Launch site is Clear for Takeoff	☐ Takeoff and Hover	☐ Check Flight Controls, Make Sure They Respond As Expected
☐ Start the motors	☐ Make Sure The Aircraft Is Stable While Hovering	☐ Start Recording Video

Post Flight Checklist

☐ Remove Battery From Aircraft	☐ Repack All Equipment
☐ Install Gimbal Guard	☐ **Complete The Flight Log**

FLIGHT PLAN

PILOT NAME: .... FAA ID: ....

ADDRESS: .... PHONE: ....

VISUAL OBSERVER(S): ....

LOCATION: ....

DATE: .... AIRCRAFT TYPE/NAME: ....

PLANNED TIME: .... AIRCRAFT CERTIFICATE N°: ....

ESTIMATED FLIGHT DURATION: .... FLIGHT TYPE: ....

AIRPORTS WITHIN 5 MILES: ....

WAIVERS APPLIED FOR: ....

FLIGHT DESCRIPTION/ROUTE: ....

....

....

FLIGHT RECORD

FLIGHT 1

TAKEOFF LOC.: .... LAUNCH TIME: .... FLIGHT NOTES: ....

LANDING LOC.: .... LANDING TIME: ....

BATTERY VOLTAGE: .... ELAPSED TIME: ....

FLIGHT 2

TAKEOFF LOC.: .... LAUNCH TIME: .... FLIGHT NOTES: ....

LANDING LOC.: .... LANDING TIME: ....

BATTERY VOLTAGE: .... ELAPSED TIME: ....

FLIGHT 3

TAKEOFF LOC.: .... LAUNCH TIME: .... FLIGHT NOTES: ....

LANDING LOC.: .... LANDING TIME: ....

BATTERY VOLTAGE: .... ELAPSED TIME: ....

FLIGHT 4

TAKEOFF LOC.: .... LAUNCH TIME: .... FLIGHT NOTES: ....

LANDING LOC.: .... LANDING TIME: ....

BATTERY VOLTAGE: .... ELAPSED TIME: ....

GENERAL NOTES: ....

....

....

Flight Checklist

☐ Airport(s) Notified	☐ UAV Batteries Charged	☐ Gimbal Protector Installed
☐ Location is OK To Fly	Battery 1 volts:	☐ Propellers Packed
☐ Weather Forecast OK	Battery 2 volts:	☐ Cables Packed
Temperature:	Battery 3 volts:	☐ Camera Filters Packed
Wind:	Battery 4 volts:	☐ Sun Shade Packed
Precipitation:	☐ Controller Charged	☐ Tools Packed
☐ Firmware up-to-date	☐ Tablet Charged	☐ Flight Plan designed/entered in Software
☐ Memory Card Formatted	☐ Mobile Phone Charged	☐ Logbook Packed

Launch Site Checklist

☐ Verify Weather is OK To Fly	☐ Check For Obstacles, Interferences
Temperature:	☐ Check For Nearby Human Activity/ Dangerous
Wind:	☐ Verify Launch Pad Is Down-wind From Observers
Precipitation:	☐ Launch Pad/Barriers Placed
☐ **Safety Briefing**	

Equipment Checklist

☐ Airframe/Landing Gear Inspected	☐ Battery Installed
☐ Propellers Inspected/ Attached	☐ Gimbal/Lens Protector Removed
☐ Controller/Tablet Assembled	
☐ Memory Card Installed	☐ Camera Filters Installed

Pre-Flight Checklist

☐ Aircraft Placed on Lauch Pad	☐ Check The Aircraft Status LEDs	☐ Check Flight Mode Switch (P-Mode)
☐ Turn On Remote Controller/ Tablet/DJI Pilot App	☐ Verify the Gimbal is Level, Can Move Unobstructed	☐ Check Satellite and Compass Status
☐ Antennas Properly Positioned	☐ Check RC Battery Level	☐ Set RTH Location And Height
☐ Turn on Aircraft	☐ Check Aircraft Battery Level	☐ Check Camera Settings

Takeoff Checklist

☐ Check Launch site is Clear for Takeoff	☐ Takeoff and Hover	☐ Check Flight Controls, Make Sure They Respond As Expected
☐ Start the motors	☐ Make Sure The Aircraft Is Stable While Hovering	☐ Start Recording Video

Post Flight Checklist

☐ Remove Battery From Aircraft	☐ Repack All Equipment
☐ Install Gimbal Guard	☐ **Complete The Flight Log**

FLIGHT PLAN

PILOT NAME: .... FAA ID: ....

ADDRESS: .... PHONE: ....

VISUAL OBSERVER(S): ....

LOCATION: ....

DATE: .... AIRCRAFT TYPE/NAME: ....

PLANNED TIME: .... AIRCRAFT CERTIFICATE N°: ....

ESTIMATED FLIGHT DURATION: .... FLIGHT TYPE: ....

AIRPORTS WITHIN 5 MILES: ....

WAIVERS APPLIED FOR: ....

FLIGHT DESCRIPTION/ROUTE: ....

....

....

FLIGHT RECORD

FLIGHT 1

TAKEOFF LOC.: .... LAUNCH TIME: .... FLIGHT NOTES: ....

LANDING LOC.: .... LANDING TIME: ....

BATTERY VOLTAGE: .... ELAPSED TIME: ....

FLIGHT 2

TAKEOFF LOC.: .... LAUNCH TIME: .... FLIGHT NOTES: ....

LANDING LOC.: .... LANDING TIME: ....

BATTERY VOLTAGE: .... ELAPSED TIME: ....

FLIGHT 3

TAKEOFF LOC.: .... LAUNCH TIME: .... FLIGHT NOTES: ....

LANDING LOC.: .... LANDING TIME: ....

BATTERY VOLTAGE: .... ELAPSED TIME: ....

FLIGHT 4

TAKEOFF LOC.: .... LAUNCH TIME: .... FLIGHT NOTES: ....

LANDING LOC.: .... LANDING TIME: ....

BATTERY VOLTAGE: .... ELAPSED TIME: ....

GENERAL NOTES: ....

....

....

FLIGHT CHECKLIST

☐ Airport(s) Notified	☐ UAV Batteries Charged	☐ Gimbal Protector Installed
☐ Location is OK To Fly	Battery 1 volts:	☐ Propellers Packed
☐ Weather Forecast OK	Battery 2 volts:	☐ Cables Packed
Temperature:	Battery 3 volts:	☐ Camera Filters Packed
Wind:	Battery 4 volts:	☐ Sun Shade Packed
Precipitation:	☐ Controller Charged	☐ Tools Packed
☐ Firmware up-to-date	☐ Tablet Charged	☐ Flight Plan designed/entered in Software
☐ Memory Card Formatted	☐ Mobile Phone Charged	☐ Logbook Packed

LAUNCH SITE CHECKLIST

☐ Verify Weather is OK To Fly	☐ Check For Obstacles, Interferences
Temperature:	☐ Check For Nearby Human Activity/ Dangerous
Wind:	☐ Verify Launch Pad Is Down-wind From Observers
Precipitation:	☐ Launch Pad/Barriers Placed
☐ **Safety Briefing**	

EQUIPMENT CHECKLIST

☐ Airframe/Landing Gear Inspected	☐ Battery Installed
☐ Propellers Inspected/ Attached	☐ Gimbal/Lens Protector Removed
☐ Controller/Tablet Assembled	
☐ Memory Card Installed	☐ Camera Filters Installed

PRE-FLIGHT CHECKLIST

☐ Aircraft Placed on Lauch Pad	☐ Check The Aircraft Status LEDs	☐ Check Flight Mode Switch (P-Mode)
☐ Turn On Remote Controller/ Tablet/DJI Pilot App	☐ Verify the Gimbal is Level, Can Move Unobstructed	☐ Check Satellite and Compass Status
☐ Antennas Properly Positioned	☐ Check RC Battery Level	☐ Set RTH Location And Height
☐ Turn on Aircraft	☐ Check Aircraft Battery Level	☐ Check Camera Settings

TAKEOFF CHECKLIST

☐ Check Launch site is Clear for Takeoff	☐ Takeoff and Hover	☐ Check Flight Controls, Make Sure They Respond As Expected
☐ Start the motors	☐ Make Sure The Aircraft Is Stable While Hovering	☐ Start Recording Video

POST FLIGHT CHECKLIST

☐ Remove Battery From Aircraft	☐ Repack All Equipment
☐ Install Gimbal Guard	☐ **Complete The Flight Log**

FLIGHT PLAN

PILOT NAME: .... FAA ID: ....

ADDRESS: .... PHONE: ....

VISUAL OBSERVER(S): ....

LOCATION: ....

DATE: .... AIRCRAFT TYPE/NAME: ....

PLANNED TIME: .... AIRCRAFT CERTIFICATE N°: ....

ESTIMATED FLIGHT DURATION: .... FLIGHT TYPE: ....

AIRPORTS WITHIN 5 MILES: ....

WAIVERS APPLIED FOR: ....

FLIGHT DESCRIPTION/ROUTE: ....

....

....

FLIGHT RECORD

FLIGHT 1

TAKEOFF LOC.: .... LAUNCH TIME: .... FLIGHT NOTES: ....

LANDING LOC.: .... LANDING TIME: ....

BATTERY VOLTAGE: .... ELAPSED TIME: ....

FLIGHT 2

TAKEOFF LOC.: .... LAUNCH TIME: .... FLIGHT NOTES: ....

LANDING LOC.: .... LANDING TIME: ....

BATTERY VOLTAGE: .... ELAPSED TIME: ....

FLIGHT 3

TAKEOFF LOC.: .... LAUNCH TIME: .... FLIGHT NOTES: ....

LANDING LOC.: .... LANDING TIME: ....

BATTERY VOLTAGE: .... ELAPSED TIME: ....

FLIGHT 4

TAKEOFF LOC.: .... LAUNCH TIME: .... FLIGHT NOTES: ....

LANDING LOC.: .... LANDING TIME: ....

BATTERY VOLTAGE: .... ELAPSED TIME: ....

GENERAL NOTES: ....

....

....

Flight Checklist

☐ Airport(s) Notified	☐ UAV Batteries Charged	☐ Gimbal Protector Installed
☐ Location is OK To Fly	Battery 1 volts:	☐ Propellers Packed
☐ Weather Forecast OK	Battery 2 volts:	☐ Cables Packed
Temperature:	Battery 3 volts:	☐ Camera Filters Packed
Wind:	Battery 4 volts:	☐ Sun Shade Packed
Precipitation:	☐ Controller Charged	☐ Tools Packed
☐ Firmware up-to-date	☐ Tablet Charged	☐ Flight Plan designed/entered in Software
☐ Memory Card Formatted	☐ Mobile Phone Charged	☐ Logbook Packed

Launch Site Checklist

☐ Verify Weather is OK To Fly	☐ Check For Obstacles, Interferences
Temperature:	☐ Check For Nearby Human Activity/ Dangerous
Wind:	☐ Verify Launch Pad Is Down-wind From Observers
Precipitation:	☐ Launch Pad/Barriers Placed
☐ **Safety Briefing**	

Equipment Checklist

☐ Airframe/Landing Gear Inspected	☐ Battery Installed
☐ Propellers Inspected/ Attached	☐ Gimbal/Lens Protector Removed
☐ Controller/Tablet Assembled	
☐ Memory Card Installed	☐ Camera Filters Installed

Pre-Flight Checklist

☐ Aircraft Placed on Lauch Pad	☐ Check The Aircraft Status LEDs	☐ Check Flight Mode Switch (P-Mode)
☐ Turn On Remote Controller/ Tablet/DJI Pilot App	☐ Verify the Gimbal is Level, Can Move Unobstructed	☐ Check Satellite and Compass Status
☐ Antennas Properly Positioned	☐ Check RC Battery Level	☐ Set RTH Location And Height
☐ Turn on Aircraft	☐ Check Aircraft Battery Level	☐ Check Camera Settings

Takeoff Checklist

☐ Check Launch site is Clear for Takeoff	☐ Takeoff and Hover	☐ Check Flight Controls, Make Sure They Respond As Expected
☐ Start the motors	☐ Make Sure The Aircraft Is Stable While Hovering	☐ Start Recording Video

Post Flight Checklist

☐ Remove Battery From Aircraft	☐ Repack All Equipment
☐ Install Gimbal Guard	☐ **Complete The Flight Log**

FLIGHT PLAN

PILOT NAME: ....   FAA ID: ....

ADDRESS: ....   PHONE: ....

VISUAL OBSERVER(S): ....

LOCATION: ....

DATE: ....   AIRCRAFT TYPE/NAME: ....

PLANNED TIME: ....   AIRCRAFT CERTIFICATE N°: ....

ESTIMATED FLIGHT DURATION: ....   FLIGHT TYPE: ....

AIRPORTS WITHIN 5 MILES: ....

WAIVERS APPLIED FOR: ....

FLIGHT DESCRIPTION/ROUTE: ....

....

....

FLIGHT RECORD

FLIGHT 1

TAKEOFF LOC.: ....   LAUNCH TIME: ....   FLIGHT NOTES: ....

LANDING LOC.: ....   LANDING TIME: ....

BATTERY VOLTAGE: ....   ELAPSED TIME: ....

FLIGHT 2

TAKEOFF LOC.: ....   LAUNCH TIME: ....   FLIGHT NOTES: ....

LANDING LOC.: ....   LANDING TIME: ....

BATTERY VOLTAGE: ....   ELAPSED TIME: ....

FLIGHT 3

TAKEOFF LOC.: ....   LAUNCH TIME: ....   FLIGHT NOTES: ....

LANDING LOC.: ....   LANDING TIME: ....

BATTERY VOLTAGE: ....   ELAPSED TIME: ....

FLIGHT 4

TAKEOFF LOC.: ....   LAUNCH TIME: ....   FLIGHT NOTES: ....

LANDING LOC.: ....   LANDING TIME: ....

BATTERY VOLTAGE: ....   ELAPSED TIME: ....

GENERAL NOTES: ....

....

....

Flight Checklist

☐ Airport(s) Notified	☐ UAV Batteries Charged	☐ Gimbal Protector Installed
☐ Location is OK To Fly	Battery 1 volts:	☐ Propellers Packed
☐ Weather Forecast OK	Battery 2 volts:	☐ Cables Packed
Temperature:	Battery 3 volts:	☐ Camera Filters Packed
Wind:	Battery 4 volts:	☐ Sun Shade Packed
Precipitation:	☐ Controller Charged	☐ Tools Packed
☐ Firmware up-to-date	☐ Tablet Charged	☐ Flight Plan designed/entered in Software
☐ Memory Card Formatted	☐ Mobile Phone Charged	☐ Logbook Packed

Launch Site Checklist

☐ Verify Weather is OK To Fly	☐ Check For Obstacles, Interferences
Temperature:	☐ Check For Nearby Human Activity/ Dangerous
Wind:	☐ Verify Launch Pad Is Down-wind From Observers
Precipitation:	☐ Launch Pad/Barriers Placed
☐ **Safety Briefing**	

Equipment Checklist

☐ Airframe/Landing Gear Inspected	☐ Battery Installed
☐ Propellers Inspected/ Attached	☐ Gimbal/Lens Protector Removed
☐ Controller/Tablet Assembled	
☐ Memory Card Installed	☐ Camera Filters Installed

Pre-Flight Checklist

☐ Aircraft Placed on Lauch Pad	☐ Check The Aircraft Status LEDs	☐ Check Flight Mode Switch (P-Mode)
☐ Turn On Remote Controller/ Tablet/DJI Pilot App	☐ Verify the Gimbal is Level, Can Move Unobstructed	☐ Check Satellite and Compass Status
☐ Antennas Properly Positioned	☐ Check RC Battery Level	☐ Set RTH Location And Height
☐ Turn on Aircraft	☐ Check Aircraft Battery Level	☐ Check Camera Settings

Takeoff Checklist

☐ Check Launch site is Clear for Takeoff	☐ Takeoff and Hover	☐ Check Flight Controls, Make Sure They Respond As Expected
☐ Start the motors	☐ Make Sure The Aircraft Is Stable While Hovering	☐ Start Recording Video

Post Flight Checklist

☐ Remove Battery From Aircraft	☐ Repack All Equipment
☐ Install Gimbal Guard	☐ **Complete The Flight Log**

FLIGHT 89

FLIGHT PLAN

PILOT NAME: .... FAA ID: ....

ADDRESS: .... PHONE: ....

VISUAL OBSERVER(S): ....

LOCATION: ....

DATE: .... AIRCRAFT TYPE/NAME: ....

PLANNED TIME: .... AIRCRAFT CERTIFICATE N°: ....

ESTIMATED FLIGHT DURATION: .... FLIGHT TYPE: ....

AIRPORTS WITHIN 5 MILES: ....

WAIVERS APPLIED FOR: ....

FLIGHT DESCRIPTION/ROUTE: ....

....

....

FLIGHT RECORD

FLIGHT 1

TAKEOFF LOC.: .... LAUNCH TIME: .... FLIGHT NOTES: ....

LANDING LOC.: .... LANDING TIME: ....

BATTERY VOLTAGE: .... ELAPSED TIME: ....

FLIGHT 2

TAKEOFF LOC.: .... LAUNCH TIME: .... FLIGHT NOTES: ....

LANDING LOC.: .... LANDING TIME: ....

BATTERY VOLTAGE: .... ELAPSED TIME: ....

FLIGHT 3

TAKEOFF LOC.: .... LAUNCH TIME: .... FLIGHT NOTES: ....

LANDING LOC.: .... LANDING TIME: ....

BATTERY VOLTAGE: .... ELAPSED TIME: ....

FLIGHT 4

TAKEOFF LOC.: .... LAUNCH TIME: .... FLIGHT NOTES: ....

LANDING LOC.: .... LANDING TIME: ....

BATTERY VOLTAGE: .... ELAPSED TIME: ....

GENERAL NOTES: ....

....

....

Flight Checklist

☐ Airport(s) Notified	☐ UAV Batteries Charged	☐ Gimbal Protector Installed
☐ Location is OK To Fly	Battery 1 volts:	☐ Propellers Packed
☐ Weather Forecast OK	Battery 2 volts:	☐ Cables Packed
Temperature:	Battery 3 volts:	☐ Camera Filters Packed
Wind:	Battery 4 volts:	☐ Sun Shade Packed
Precipitation:	☐ Controller Charged	☐ Tools Packed
☐ Firmware up-to-date	☐ Tablet Charged	☐ Flight Plan designed/entered in Software
☐ Memory Card Formatted	☐ Mobile Phone Charged	☐ Logbook Packed

Launch Site Checklist

☐ Verify Weather is OK To Fly	☐ Check For Obstacles, Interferences
Temperature:	☐ Check For Nearby Human Activity/ Dangerous
Wind:	☐ Verify Launch Pad Is Down-wind From Observers
Precipitation:	☐ Launch Pad/Barriers Placed
☐ **Safety Briefing**	

Equipment Checklist

☐ Airframe/Landing Gear Inspected	☐ Battery Installed
☐ Propellers Inspected/ Attached	☐ Gimbal/Lens Protector Removed
☐ Controller/Tablet Assembled	
☐ Memory Card Installed	☐ Camera Filters Installed

Pre-Flight Checklist

☐ Aircraft Placed on Lauch Pad	☐ Check The Aircraft Status LEDs	☐ Check Flight Mode Switch (P-Mode)
☐ Turn On Remote Controller/ Tablet/DJI Pilot App	☐ Verify the Gimbal is Level, Can Move Unobstructed	☐ Check Satellite and Compass Status
☐ Antennas Properly Positioned	☐ Check RC Battery Level	☐ Set RTH Location And Height
☐ Turn on Aircraft	☐ Check Aircraft Battery Level	☐ Check Camera Settings

Takeoff Checklist

☐ Check Launch site is Clear for Takeoff	☐ Takeoff and Hover	☐ Check Flight Controls, Make Sure They Respond As Expected
☐ Start the motors	☐ Make Sure The Aircraft Is Stable While Hovering	☐ Start Recording Video

Post Flight Checklist

☐ Remove Battery From Aircraft	☐ Repack All Equipment
☐ Install Gimbal Guard	☐ **Complete The Flight Log**

FLIGHT PLAN

PILOT NAME: ....   FAA ID: ....

ADDRESS: ....   PHONE: ....

VISUAL OBSERVER(S): ....

LOCATION: ....

DATE: ....   AIRCRAFT TYPE/NAME: ....

PLANNED TIME: ....   AIRCRAFT CERTIFICATE n°: ....

ESTIMATED FLIGHT DURATION: ....   FLIGHT TYPE: ....

AIRPORTS WITHIN 5 MILES: ....

WAIVERS APPLIED FOR: ....

FLIGHT DESCRIPTION/ROUTE: ....
....
....

FLIGHT RECORD

FLIGHT 1

TAKEOFF LOC.: ....   LAUNCH TIME: ....   FLIGHT NOTES: ....

LANDING LOC.: ....   LANDING TIME: ....

BATTERY VOLTAGE: ....   ELAPSED TIME: ....

FLIGHT 2

TAKEOFF LOC.: ....   LAUNCH TIME: ....   FLIGHT NOTES: ....

LANDING LOC.: ....   LANDING TIME: ....

BATTERY VOLTAGE: ....   ELAPSED TIME: ....

FLIGHT 3

TAKEOFF LOC.: ....   LAUNCH TIME: ....   FLIGHT NOTES: ....

LANDING LOC.: ....   LANDING TIME: ....

BATTERY VOLTAGE: ....   ELAPSED TIME: ....

FLIGHT 4

TAKEOFF LOC.: ....   LAUNCH TIME: ....   FLIGHT NOTES: ....

LANDING LOC.: ....   LANDING TIME: ....

BATTERY VOLTAGE: ....   ELAPSED TIME: ....

GENERAL NOTES: ....
....
....

Flight Checklist

☐ Airport(s) Notified	☐ UAV Batteries Charged	☐ Gimbal Protector Installed
☐ Location is OK To Fly	Battery 1 volts:	☐ Propellers Packed
☐ Weather Forecast OK	Battery 2 volts:	☐ Cables Packed
Temperature:	Battery 3 volts:	☐ Camera Filters Packed
Wind:	Battery 4 volts:	☐ Sun Shade Packed
Precipitation:	☐ Controller Charged	☐ Tools Packed
☐ Firmware up-to-date	☐ Tablet Charged	☐ Flight Plan designed/entered in Software
☐ Memory Card Formatted	☐ Mobile Phone Charged	☐ Logbook Packed

Launch Site Checklist

☐ Verify Weather is OK To Fly	☐ Check For Obstacles, Interferences
Temperature:	☐ Check For Nearby Human Activity/ Dangerous
Wind:	☐ Verify Launch Pad Is Down-wind From Observers
Precipitation:	☐ Launch Pad/Barriers Placed
☐ **Safety Briefing**	

Equipment Checklist

☐ Airframe/Landing Gear Inspected	☐ Battery Installed
☐ Propellers Inspected/ Attached	☐ Gimbal/Lens Protector Removed
☐ Controller/Tablet Assembled	
☐ Memory Card Installed	☐ Camera Filters Installed

Pre-Flight Checklist

☐ Aircraft Placed on Lauch Pad	☐ Check The Aircraft Status LEDs	☐ Check Flight Mode Switch (P-Mode)
☐ Turn On Remote Controller/ Tablet/DJI Pilot App	☐ Verify the Gimbal is Level, Can Move Unobstructed	☐ Check Satellite and Compass Status
☐ Antennas Properly Positioned	☐ Check RC Battery Level	☐ Set RTH Location And Height
☐ Turn on Aircraft	☐ Check Aircraft Battery Level	☐ Check Camera Settings

Takeoff Checklist

☐ Check Launch site is Clear for Takeoff	☐ Takeoff and Hover	☐ Check Flight Controls, Make Sure They Respond As Expected
☐ Start the motors	☐ Make Sure The Aircraft Is Stable While Hovering	☐ Start Recording Video

Post Flight Checklist

☐ Remove Battery From Aircraft	☐ Repack All Equipment
☐ Install Gimbal Guard	☐ **Complete The Flight Log**

FLIGHT 91

FLIGHT PLAN

PILOT NAME: .... FAA ID: ....

ADDRESS: .... PHONE: ....

VISUAL OBSERVER(S): ....

LOCATION: ....

DATE: .... AIRCRAFT TYPE/NAME: ....

PLANNED TIME: .... AIRCRAFT CERTIFICATE N°: ....

ESTIMATED FLIGHT DURATION: .... FLIGHT TYPE: ....

AIRPORTS WITHIN 5 MILES: ....

WAIVERS APPLIED FOR: ....

FLIGHT DESCRIPTION/ROUTE: ....

....

....

FLIGHT RECORD

	FLIGHT 1		
TAKEOFF LOC.:	LAUNCH TIME:	FLIGHT NOTES: ....
LANDING LOC.:	LANDING TIME:	....
BATTERY VOLTAGE:	ELAPSED TIME:	....

	FLIGHT 2		
TAKEOFF LOC.:	LAUNCH TIME:	FLIGHT NOTES: ....
LANDING LOC.:	LANDING TIME:	....
BATTERY VOLTAGE:	ELAPSED TIME:	....

	FLIGHT 3		
TAKEOFF LOC.:	LAUNCH TIME:	FLIGHT NOTES: ....
LANDING LOC.:	LANDING TIME:	....
BATTERY VOLTAGE:	ELAPSED TIME:	....

	FLIGHT 4		
TAKEOFF LOC.:	LAUNCH TIME:	FLIGHT NOTES: ....
LANDING LOC.:	LANDING TIME:	....
BATTERY VOLTAGE:	ELAPSED TIME:	....

GENERAL NOTES: ....

....

....

Flight Checklist

☐ Airport(s) Notified	☐ UAV Batteries Charged	☐ Gimbal Protector Installed
☐ Location is OK To Fly	Battery 1 volts:	☐ Propellers Packed
☐ Weather Forecast OK	Battery 2 volts:	☐ Cables Packed
Temperature:	Battery 3 volts:	☐ Camera Filters Packed
Wind:	Battery 4 volts:	☐ Sun Shade Packed
Precipitation:	☐ Controller Charged	☐ Tools Packed
☐ Firmware up-to-date	☐ Tablet Charged	☐ Flight Plan designed/entered in Software
☐ Memory Card Formatted	☐ Mobile Phone Charged	☐ Logbook Packed

Launch Site Checklist

☐ Verify Weather is OK To Fly	☐ Check For Obstacles, Interferences
Temperature:	☐ Check For Nearby Human Activity/ Dangerous
Wind:	☐ Verify Launch Pad Is Down-wind From Observers
Precipitation:	☐ Launch Pad/Barriers Placed
☐ **Safety Briefing**	

Equipment Checklist

☐ Airframe/Landing Gear Inspected	☐ Battery Installed
☐ Propellers Inspected/ Attached	☐ Gimbal/Lens Protector Removed
☐ Controller/Tablet Assembled	
☐ Memory Card Installed	☐ Camera Filters Installed

Pre-Flight Checklist

☐ Aircraft Placed on Lauch Pad	☐ Check The Aircraft Status LEDs	☐ Check Flight Mode Switch (P-Mode)
☐ Turn On Remote Controller/ Tablet/DJI Pilot App	☐ Verify the Gimbal is Level, Can Move Unobstructed	☐ Check Satellite and Compass Status
☐ Antennas Properly Positioned	☐ Check RC Battery Level	☐ Set RTH Location And Height
☐ Turn on Aircraft	☐ Check Aircraft Battery Level	☐ Check Camera Settings

Takeoff Checklist

☐ Check Launch site is Clear for Takeoff	☐ Takeoff and Hover	☐ Check Flight Controls, Make Sure They Respond As Expected
☐ Start the motors	☐ Make Sure The Aircraft Is Stable While Hovering	☐ Start Recording Video

Post Flight Checklist

☐ Remove Battery From Aircraft	☐ Repack All Equipment
☐ Install Gimbal Guard	☐ **Complete The Flight Log**

FLIGHT PLAN

PILOT NAME: .... FAA ID: ....

ADDRESS: .... PHONE: ....

VISUAL OBSERVER(S): ....

LOCATION: ....

DATE: .... AIRCRAFT TYPE/NAME: ....

PLANNED TIME: .... AIRCRAFT CERTIFICATE n°: ....

ESTIMATED FLIGHT DURATION: .... FLIGHT TYPE: ....

AIRPORTS WITHIN 5 MILES: ....

WAIVERS APPLIED FOR: ....

FLIGHT DESCRIPTION/ROUTE: ....

....

....

FLIGHT RECORD

FLIGHT 1

TAKEOFF LOC.: .... LAUNCH TIME: .... FLIGHT NOTES: ....

LANDING LOC.: .... LANDING TIME: ....

BATTERY VOLTAGE: .... ELAPSED TIME: ....

FLIGHT 2

TAKEOFF LOC.: .... LAUNCH TIME: .... FLIGHT NOTES: ....

LANDING LOC.: .... LANDING TIME: ....

BATTERY VOLTAGE: .... ELAPSED TIME: ....

FLIGHT 3

TAKEOFF LOC.: .... LAUNCH TIME: .... FLIGHT NOTES: ....

LANDING LOC.: .... LANDING TIME: ....

BATTERY VOLTAGE: .... ELAPSED TIME: ....

FLIGHT 4

TAKEOFF LOC.: .... LAUNCH TIME: .... FLIGHT NOTES: ....

LANDING LOC.: .... LANDING TIME: ....

BATTERY VOLTAGE: .... ELAPSED TIME: ....

GENERAL NOTES: ....

....

....

Flight Checklist

☐ Airport(s) Notified	☐ UAV Batteries Charged	☐ Gimbal Protector Installed
☐ Location is OK To Fly	Battery 1 volts:	☐ Propellers Packed
☐ Weather Forecast OK	Battery 2 volts:	☐ Cables Packed
Temperature:	Battery 3 volts:	☐ Camera Filters Packed
Wind:	Battery 4 volts:	☐ Sun Shade Packed
Precipitation:	☐ Controller Charged	☐ Tools Packed
☐ Firmware up-to-date	☐ Tablet Charged	☐ Flight Plan designed/entered in Software
☐ Memory Card Formatted	☐ Mobile Phone Charged	☐ Logbook Packed

Launch Site Checklist

☐ Verify Weather is OK To Fly	☐ Check For Obstacles, Interferences
Temperature:	☐ Check For Nearby Human Activity/ Dangerous
Wind:	☐ Verify Launch Pad Is Down-wind From Observers
Precipitation:	☐ Launch Pad/Barriers Placed
☐ **Safety Briefing**	

Equipment Checklist

☐ Airframe/Landing Gear Inspected	☐ Battery Installed
☐ Propellers Inspected/ Attached	☐ Gimbal/Lens Protector Removed
☐ Controller/Tablet Assembled	
☐ Memory Card Installed	☐ Camera Filters Installed

Pre-Flight Checklist

☐ Aircraft Placed on Lauch Pad	☐ Check The Aircraft Status LEDs	☐ Check Flight Mode Switch (P-Mode)
☐ Turn On Remote Controller/ Tablet/DJI Pilot App	☐ Verify the Gimbal is Level, Can Move Unobstructed	☐ Check Satellite and Compass Status
☐ Antennas Properly Positioned	☐ Check RC Battery Level	☐ Set RTH Location And Height
☐ Turn on Aircraft	☐ Check Aircraft Battery Level	☐ Check Camera Settings

Takeoff Checklist

☐ Check Launch site is Clear for Takeoff	☐ Takeoff and Hover	☐ Check Flight Controls, Make Sure They Respond As Expected
☐ Start the motors	☐ Make Sure The Aircraft Is Stable While Hovering	☐ Start Recording Video

Post Flight Checklist

☐ Remove Battery From Aircraft	☐ Repack All Equipment
☐ Install Gimbal Guard	☐ **Complete The Flight Log**

FLIGHT PLAN

PILOT NAME: .... FAA ID: ....

ADDRESS: .... PHONE: ....

VISUAL OBSERVER(S): ....

LOCATION: ....

DATE: .... AIRCRAFT TYPE/NAME: ....

PLANNED TIME: .... AIRCRAFT CERTIFICATE N°: ....

ESTIMATED FLIGHT DURATION: .... FLIGHT TYPE: ....

AIRPORTS WITHIN 5 MILES: ....

WAIVERS APPLIED FOR: ....

FLIGHT DESCRIPTION/ROUTE: ....

....

....

FLIGHT RECORD

FLIGHT 1

TAKEOFF LOC.: .... LAUNCH TIME: .... FLIGHT NOTES: ....

LANDING LOC.: .... LANDING TIME: ....

BATTERY VOLTAGE: .... ELAPSED TIME: ....

FLIGHT 2

TAKEOFF LOC.: .... LAUNCH TIME: .... FLIGHT NOTES: ....

LANDING LOC.: .... LANDING TIME: ....

BATTERY VOLTAGE: .... ELAPSED TIME: ....

FLIGHT 3

TAKEOFF LOC.: .... LAUNCH TIME: .... FLIGHT NOTES: ....

LANDING LOC.: .... LANDING TIME: ....

BATTERY VOLTAGE: .... ELAPSED TIME: ....

FLIGHT 4

TAKEOFF LOC.: .... LAUNCH TIME: .... FLIGHT NOTES: ....

LANDING LOC.: .... LANDING TIME: ....

BATTERY VOLTAGE: .... ELAPSED TIME: ....

GENERAL NOTES: ....

....

....

Flight Checklist

☐ Airport(s) Notified	☐ UAV Batteries Charged	☐ Gimbal Protector Installed
☐ Location is OK To Fly	Battery 1 volts:	☐ Propellers Packed
☐ Weather Forecast OK	Battery 2 volts:	☐ Cables Packed
Temperature:	Battery 3 volts:	☐ Camera Filters Packed
Wind:	Battery 4 volts:	☐ Sun Shade Packed
Precipitation:	☐ Controller Charged	☐ Tools Packed
☐ Firmware up-to-date	☐ Tablet Charged	☐ Flight Plan designed/entered in Software
☐ Memory Card Formatted	☐ Mobile Phone Charged	☐ Logbook Packed

Launch Site Checklist

☐ Verify Weather is OK To Fly	☐ Check For Obstacles, Interferences
Temperature:	☐ Check For Nearby Human Activity/ Dangerous
Wind:	☐ Verify Launch Pad Is Down-wind From Observers
Precipitation:	☐ Launch Pad/Barriers Placed
☐ **Safety Briefing**	

Equipment Checklist

☐ Airframe/Landing Gear Inspected	☐ Battery Installed
☐ Propellers Inspected/ Attached	☐ Gimbal/Lens Protector Removed
☐ Controller/Tablet Assembled	
☐ Memory Card Installed	☐ Camera Filters Installed

Pre-Flight Checklist

☐ Aircraft Placed on Lauch Pad	☐ Check The Aircraft Status LEDs	☐ Check Flight Mode Switch (P-Mode)
☐ Turn On Remote Controller/ Tablet/DJI Pilot App	☐ Verify the Gimbal is Level, Can Move Unobstructed	☐ Check Satellite and Compass Status
☐ Antennas Properly Positioned	☐ Check RC Battery Level	☐ Set RTH Location And Height
☐ Turn on Aircraft	☐ Check Aircraft Battery Level	☐ Check Camera Settings

Takeoff Checklist

☐ Check Launch site is Clear for Takeoff	☐ Takeoff and Hover	☐ Check Flight Controls, Make Sure They Respond As Expected
☐ Start the motors	☐ Make Sure The Aircraft Is Stable While Hovering	☐ Start Recording Video

Post Flight Checklist

☐ Remove Battery From Aircraft	☐ Repack All Equipment
☐ Install Gimbal Guard	☐ **Complete The Flight Log**

FLIGHT PLAN

PILOT NAME: .... FAA ID: ....

ADDRESS: .... PHONE: ....

VISUAL OBSERVER(S): ....

LOCATION: ....

DATE: .... AIRCRAFT TYPE/NAME: ....

PLANNED TIME: .... AIRCRAFT CERTIFICATE N°: ....

ESTIMATED FLIGHT DURATION: .... FLIGHT TYPE: ....

AIRPORTS WITHIN 5 MILES: ....

WAIVERS APPLIED FOR: ....

FLIGHT DESCRIPTION/ROUTE: ....

....

....

FLIGHT RECORD

FLIGHT 1

TAKEOFF LOC.: .... LAUNCH TIME: .... FLIGHT NOTES: ....

LANDING LOC.: .... LANDING TIME: ....

BATTERY VOLTAGE: .... ELAPSED TIME: ....

FLIGHT 2

TAKEOFF LOC.: .... LAUNCH TIME: .... FLIGHT NOTES: ....

LANDING LOC.: .... LANDING TIME: ....

BATTERY VOLTAGE: .... ELAPSED TIME: ....

FLIGHT 3

TAKEOFF LOC.: .... LAUNCH TIME: .... FLIGHT NOTES: ....

LANDING LOC.: .... LANDING TIME: ....

BATTERY VOLTAGE: .... ELAPSED TIME: ....

FLIGHT 4

TAKEOFF LOC.: .... LAUNCH TIME: .... FLIGHT NOTES: ....

LANDING LOC.: .... LANDING TIME: ....

BATTERY VOLTAGE: .... ELAPSED TIME: ....

GENERAL NOTES: ....

....

....

Flight Checklist

☐ Airport(s) Notified	☐ UAV Batteries Charged	☐ Gimbal Protector Installed
☐ Location is OK To Fly	Battery 1 volts:	☐ Propellers Packed
☐ Weather Forecast OK	Battery 2 volts:	☐ Cables Packed
Temperature:	Battery 3 volts:	☐ Camera Filters Packed
Wind:	Battery 4 volts:	☐ Sun Shade Packed
Precipitation:	☐ Controller Charged	☐ Tools Packed
☐ Firmware up-to-date	☐ Tablet Charged	☐ Flight Plan designed/entered in Software
☐ Memory Card Formatted	☐ Mobile Phone Charged	☐ Logbook Packed

Launch Site Checklist

☐ Verify Weather is OK To Fly	☐ Check For Obstacles, Interferences
Temperature:	☐ Check For Nearby Human Activity/ Dangerous
Wind:	☐ Verify Launch Pad Is Down-wind From Observers
Precipitation:	☐ Launch Pad/Barriers Placed
☐ **Safety Briefing**	

Equipment Checklist

☐ Airframe/Landing Gear Inspected	☐ Battery Installed
☐ Propellers Inspected/ Attached	☐ Gimbal/Lens Protector Removed
☐ Controller/Tablet Assembled	
☐ Memory Card Installed	☐ Camera Filters Installed

Pre-Flight Checklist

☐ Aircraft Placed on Lauch Pad	☐ Check The Aircraft Status LEDs	☐ Check Flight Mode Switch (P-Mode)
☐ Turn On Remote Controller/ Tablet/DJI Pilot App	☐ Verify the Gimbal is Level, Can Move Unobstructed	☐ Check Satellite and Compass Status
☐ Antennas Properly Positioned	☐ Check RC Battery Level	☐ Set RTH Location And Height
☐ Turn on Aircraft	☐ Check Aircraft Battery Level	☐ Check Camera Settings

Takeoff Checklist

☐ Check Launch site is Clear for Takeoff	☐ Takeoff and Hover	☐ Check Flight Controls, Make Sure They Respond As Expected
☐ Start the motors	☐ Make Sure The Aircraft Is Stable While Hovering	☐ Start Recording Video

Post Flight Checklist

☐ Remove Battery From Aircraft	☐ Repack All Equipment
☐ Install Gimbal Guard	☐ **Complete The Flight Log**

FLIGHT PLAN

PILOT NAME: .... FAA ID: ....

ADDRESS: .... PHONE: ....

VISUAL OBSERVER(S): ....

LOCATION: ....

DATE: .... AIRCRAFT TYPE/NAME: ....

PLANNED TIME: .... AIRCRAFT CERTIFICATE N°: ....

ESTIMATED FLIGHT DURATION: .... FLIGHT TYPE: ....

AIRPORTS WITHIN 5 MILES: ....

WAIVERS APPLIED FOR: ....

FLIGHT DESCRIPTION/ROUTE: ....

....

....

FLIGHT RECORD

FLIGHT 1
TAKEOFF LOC.: .... LAUNCH TIME: .... FLIGHT NOTES: ....
LANDING LOC.: .... LANDING TIME: ....
BATTERY VOLTAGE: .... ELAPSED TIME: ....

FLIGHT 2
TAKEOFF LOC.: .... LAUNCH TIME: .... FLIGHT NOTES: ....
LANDING LOC.: .... LANDING TIME: ....
BATTERY VOLTAGE: .... ELAPSED TIME: ....

FLIGHT 3
TAKEOFF LOC.: .... LAUNCH TIME: .... FLIGHT NOTES: ....
LANDING LOC.: .... LANDING TIME: ....
BATTERY VOLTAGE: .... ELAPSED TIME: ....

FLIGHT 4
TAKEOFF LOC.: .... LAUNCH TIME: .... FLIGHT NOTES: ....
LANDING LOC.: .... LANDING TIME: ....
BATTERY VOLTAGE: .... ELAPSED TIME: ....

GENERAL NOTES: ....

....

....

Flight Checklist

☐ Airport(s) Notified	☐ UAV Batteries Charged	☐ Gimbal Protector Installed
☐ Location is OK To Fly	Battery 1 volts:	☐ Propellers Packed
☐ Weather Forecast OK	Battery 2 volts:	☐ Cables Packed
Temperature:	Battery 3 volts:	☐ Camera Filters Packed
Wind:	Battery 4 volts:	☐ Sun Shade Packed
Precipitation:	☐ Controller Charged	☐ Tools Packed
☐ Firmware up-to-date	☐ Tablet Charged	☐ Flight Plan designed/entered in Software
☐ Memory Card Formatted	☐ Mobile Phone Charged	☐ Logbook Packed

Launch Site Checklist

☐ Verify Weather is OK To Fly	☐ Check For Obstacles, Interferences
Temperature:	☐ Check For Nearby Human Activity/ Dangerous
Wind:	☐ Verify Launch Pad Is Down-wind From Observers
Precipitation:	
☐ **Safety Briefing**	☐ Launch Pad/Barriers Placed

Equipment Checklist

☐ Airframe/Landing Gear Inspected	☐ Battery Installed
☐ Propellers Inspected/ Attached	☐ Gimbal/Lens Protector Removed
☐ Controller/Tablet Assembled	
☐ Memory Card Installed	☐ Camera Filters Installed

Pre-Flight Checklist

☐ Aircraft Placed on Lauch Pad	☐ Check The Aircraft Status LEDs	☐ Check Flight Mode Switch (P-Mode)
☐ Turn On Remote Controller/ Tablet/DJI Pilot App	☐ Verify the Gimbal is Level, Can Move Unobstructed	☐ Check Satellite and Compass Status
☐ Antennas Properly Positioned	☐ Check RC Battery Level	☐ Set RTH Location And Height
☐ Turn on Aircraft	☐ Check Aircraft Battery Level	☐ Check Camera Settings

Takeoff Checklist

☐ Check Launch site is Clear for Takeoff	☐ Takeoff and Hover	☐ Check Flight Controls, Make Sure They Respond As Expected
☐ Start the motors	☐ Make Sure The Aircraft Is Stable While Hovering	☐ Start Recording Video

Post Flight Checklist

☐ Remove Battery From Aircraft	☐ Repack All Equipment
☐ Install Gimbal Guard	☐ **Complete The Flight Log**

FLIGHT PLAN

PILOT NAME: .... FAA ID: ....

ADDRESS: .... PHONE: ....

VISUAL OBSERVER(S): ....

LOCATION: ....

DATE: .... AIRCRAFT TYPE/NAME: ....

PLANNED TIME: .... AIRCRAFT CERTIFICATE N°: ....

ESTIMATED FLIGHT DURATION: .... FLIGHT TYPE: ....

AIRPORTS WITHIN 5 MILES: ....

WAIVERS APPLIED FOR: ....

FLIGHT DESCRIPTION/ROUTE: ....

....

....

FLIGHT RECORD

FLIGHT 1

TAKEOFF LOC.: .... LAUNCH TIME: .... FLIGHT NOTES: ....

LANDING LOC.: .... LANDING TIME: ....

BATTERY VOLTAGE: .... ELAPSED TIME: ....

FLIGHT 2

TAKEOFF LOC.: .... LAUNCH TIME: .... FLIGHT NOTES: ....

LANDING LOC.: .... LANDING TIME: ....

BATTERY VOLTAGE: .... ELAPSED TIME: ....

FLIGHT 3

TAKEOFF LOC.: .... LAUNCH TIME: .... FLIGHT NOTES: ....

LANDING LOC.: .... LANDING TIME: ....

BATTERY VOLTAGE: .... ELAPSED TIME: ....

FLIGHT 4

TAKEOFF LOC.: .... LAUNCH TIME: .... FLIGHT NOTES: ....

LANDING LOC.: .... LANDING TIME: ....

BATTERY VOLTAGE: .... ELAPSED TIME: ....

GENERAL NOTES: ....

....

....

Flight Checklist

☐ Airport(s) Notified	☐ UAV Batteries Charged	☐ Gimbal Protector Installed
☐ Location is OK To Fly	Battery 1 volts:	☐ Propellers Packed
☐ Weather Forecast OK	Battery 2 volts:	☐ Cables Packed
Temperature:	Battery 3 volts:	☐ Camera Filters Packed
Wind:	Battery 4 volts:	☐ Sun Shade Packed
Precipitation:	☐ Controller Charged	☐ Tools Packed
☐ Firmware up-to-date	☐ Tablet Charged	☐ Flight Plan designed/entered in Software
☐ Memory Card Formatted	☐ Mobile Phone Charged	☐ Logbook Packed

Launch Site Checklist

☐ Verify Weather is OK To Fly	☐ Check For Obstacles, Interferences
Temperature:	☐ Check For Nearby Human Activity/ Dangerous
Wind:	☐ Verify Launch Pad Is Down-wind From Observers
Precipitation:	☐ Launch Pad/Barriers Placed
☐ **Safety Briefing**	

Equipment Checklist

☐ Airframe/Landing Gear Inspected	☐ Battery Installed
☐ Propellers Inspected/ Attached	☐ Gimbal/Lens Protector Removed
☐ Controller/Tablet Assembled	
☐ Memory Card Installed	☐ Camera Filters Installed

Pre-Flight Checklist

☐ Aircraft Placed on Lauch Pad	☐ Check The Aircraft Status LEDs	☐ Check Flight Mode Switch (P-Mode)
☐ Turn On Remote Controller/ Tablet/DJI Pilot App	☐ Verify the Gimbal is Level, Can Move Unobstructed	☐ Check Satellite and Compass Status
☐ Antennas Properly Positioned	☐ Check RC Battery Level	☐ Set RTH Location And Height
☐ Turn on Aircraft	☐ Check Aircraft Battery Level	☐ Check Camera Settings

Takeoff Checklist

☐ Check Launch site is Clear for Takeoff	☐ Takeoff and Hover	☐ Check Flight Controls, Make Sure They Respond As Expected
☐ Start the motors	☐ Make Sure The Aircraft Is Stable While Hovering	☐ Start Recording Video

Post Flight Checklist

☐ Remove Battery From Aircraft	☐ Repack All Equipment
☐ Install Gimbal Guard	☐ **Complete The Flight Log**

Flight Plan

Pilot Name: .... FAA ID: ....

Address: .... Phone: ....

Visual Observer(s): ....

Location: ....

Date: .... Aircraft Type/Name: ....

Planned Time: .... Aircraft Certificate n°: ....

Estimated Flight Duration: .... Flight Type: ....

Airports Within 5 Miles: ....

Waivers Applied For: ....

Flight Description/Route: ....

....

....

Flight Record

Flight 1

Takeoff Loc.: .... Launch Time: .... Flight Notes: ....

Landing Loc.: .... Landing Time: ....

Battery Voltage: .... Elapsed Time: ....

Flight 2

Takeoff Loc.: .... Launch Time: .... Flight Notes: ....

Landing Loc.: .... Landing Time: ....

Battery Voltage: .... Elapsed Time: ....

Flight 3

Takeoff Loc.: .... Launch Time: .... Flight Notes: ....

Landing Loc.: .... Landing Time: ....

Battery Voltage: .... Elapsed Time: ....

Flight 4

Takeoff Loc.: .... Launch Time: .... Flight Notes: ....

Landing Loc.: .... Landing Time: ....

Battery Voltage: .... Elapsed Time: ....

General Notes: ....

....

....

Flight Checklist

☐ Airport(s) Notified	☐ UAV Batteries Charged	☐ Gimbal Protector Installed
☐ Location is OK To Fly	Battery 1 volts:	☐ Propellers Packed
☐ Weather Forecast OK	Battery 2 volts:	☐ Cables Packed
Temperature:	Battery 3 volts:	☐ Camera Filters Packed
Wind:	Battery 4 volts:	☐ Sun Shade Packed
Precipitation:	☐ Controller Charged	☐ Tools Packed
☐ Firmware up-to-date	☐ Tablet Charged	☐ Flight Plan designed/entered in Software
☐ Memory Card Formatted	☐ Mobile Phone Charged	☐ Logbook Packed

Launch Site Checklist

☐ Verify Weather is OK To Fly	☐ Check For Obstacles, Interferences
Temperature:	☐ Check For Nearby Human Activity/ Dangerous
Wind:	☐ Verify Launch Pad Is Down-wind From Observers
Precipitation:	☐ Launch Pad/Barriers Placed
☐ **Safety Briefing**	

Equipment Checklist

☐ Airframe/Landing Gear Inspected	☐ Battery Installed
☐ Propellers Inspected/ Attached	☐ Gimbal/Lens Protector Removed
☐ Controller/Tablet Assembled	
☐ Memory Card Installed	☐ Camera Filters Installed

Pre-Flight Checklist

☐ Aircraft Placed on Lauch Pad	☐ Check The Aircraft Status LEDs	☐ Check Flight Mode Switch (P-Mode)
☐ Turn On Remote Controller/ Tablet/DJI Pilot App	☐ Verify the Gimbal is Level, Can Move Unobstructed	☐ Check Satellite and Compass Status
☐ Antennas Properly Positioned	☐ Check RC Battery Level	☐ Set RTH Location And Height
☐ Turn on Aircraft	☐ Check Aircraft Battery Level	☐ Check Camera Settings

Takeoff Checklist

☐ Check Launch site is Clear for Takeoff	☐ Takeoff and Hover	☐ Check Flight Controls, Make Sure They Respond As Expected
☐ Start the motors	☐ Make Sure The Aircraft Is Stable While Hovering	☐ Start Recording Video

Post Flight Checklist

☐ Remove Battery From Aircraft	☐ Repack All Equipment
☐ Install Gimbal Guard	☐ **Complete The Flight Log**

FLIGHT PLAN

PILOT NAME: .... FAA ID: ....

ADDRESS: .... PHONE: ....

VISUAL OBSERVER(S): ....

LOCATION: ....

DATE: .... AIRCRAFT TYPE/NAME: ....

PLANNED TIME: .... AIRCRAFT CERTIFICATE N°: ....

ESTIMATED FLIGHT DURATION: .... FLIGHT TYPE: ....

AIRPORTS WITHIN 5 MILES: ....

WAIVERS APPLIED FOR: ....

FLIGHT DESCRIPTION/ROUTE: ....

....

....

FLIGHT RECORD

FLIGHT 1

TAKEOFF LOC.: .... LAUNCH TIME: .... FLIGHT NOTES: ....

LANDING LOC.: .... LANDING TIME: ....

BATTERY VOLTAGE: .... ELAPSED TIME: ....

FLIGHT 2

TAKEOFF LOC.: .... LAUNCH TIME: .... FLIGHT NOTES: ....

LANDING LOC.: .... LANDING TIME: ....

BATTERY VOLTAGE: .... ELAPSED TIME: ....

FLIGHT 3

TAKEOFF LOC.: .... LAUNCH TIME: .... FLIGHT NOTES: ....

LANDING LOC.: .... LANDING TIME: ....

BATTERY VOLTAGE: .... ELAPSED TIME: ....

FLIGHT 4

TAKEOFF LOC.: .... LAUNCH TIME: .... FLIGHT NOTES: ....

LANDING LOC.: .... LANDING TIME: ....

BATTERY VOLTAGE: .... ELAPSED TIME: ....

GENERAL NOTES: ....

....

....

Flight Checklist

☐ Airport(s) Notified	☐ UAV Batteries Charged	☐ Gimbal Protector Installed
☐ Location is OK To Fly	Battery 1 volts:	☐ Propellers Packed
☐ Weather Forecast OK	Battery 2 volts:	☐ Cables Packed
Temperature:	Battery 3 volts:	☐ Camera Filters Packed
Wind:	Battery 4 volts:	☐ Sun Shade Packed
Precipitation:	☐ Controller Charged	☐ Tools Packed
☐ Firmware up-to-date	☐ Tablet Charged	☐ Flight Plan designed/entered in Software
☐ Memory Card Formatted	☐ Mobile Phone Charged	☐ Logbook Packed

Launch Site Checklist

☐ Verify Weather is OK To Fly	☐ Check For Obstacles, Interferences
Temperature:	☐ Check For Nearby Human Activity/ Dangerous
Wind:	☐ Verify Launch Pad Is Down-wind From Observers
Precipitation:	☐ Launch Pad/Barriers Placed
☐ **Safety Briefing**	

Equipment Checklist

☐ Airframe/Landing Gear Inspected	☐ Battery Installed
☐ Propellers Inspected/ Attached	☐ Gimbal/Lens Protector Removed
☐ Controller/Tablet Assembled	
☐ Memory Card Installed	☐ Camera Filters Installed

Pre-Flight Checklist

☐ Aircraft Placed on Lauch Pad	☐ Check The Aircraft Status LEDs	☐ Check Flight Mode Switch (P-Mode)
☐ Turn On Remote Controller/ Tablet/DJI Pilot App	☐ Verify the Gimbal is Level, Can Move Unobstructed	☐ Check Satellite and Compass Status
☐ Antennas Properly Positioned	☐ Check RC Battery Level	☐ Set RTH Location And Height
☐ Turn on Aircraft	☐ Check Aircraft Battery Level	☐ Check Camera Settings

Takeoff Checklist

☐ Check Launch site is Clear for Takeoff	☐ Takeoff and Hover	☐ Check Flight Controls, Make Sure They Respond As Expected
☐ Start the motors	☐ Make Sure The Aircraft Is Stable While Hovering	☐ Start Recording Video

Post Flight Checklist

☐ Remove Battery From Aircraft	☐ Repack All Equipment
☐ Install Gimbal Guard	☐ **Complete The Flight Log**

FLIGHT **99**

Flight Plan

Pilot Name: .... FAA ID: ....

Address: .... Phone: ....

Visual Observer(s): ....

Location: ....

Date: .... Aircraft Type/Name: ....

Planned Time: .... Aircraft Certificate n°: ....

Estimated Flight Duration: .... Flight Type: ....

Airports Within 5 Miles: ....

Waivers Applied For: ....

Flight Description/Route: ....

....

....

Flight Record

FLIGHT 1

Takeoff Loc.: .... Launch Time: .... Flight Notes: ....

Landing Loc.: .... Landing Time: ....

Battery Voltage: .... Elapsed Time: ....

FLIGHT 2

Takeoff Loc.: .... Launch Time: .... Flight Notes: ....

Landing Loc.: .... Landing Time: ....

Battery Voltage: .... Elapsed Time: ....

FLIGHT 3

Takeoff Loc.: .... Launch Time: .... Flight Notes: ....

Landing Loc.: .... Landing Time: ....

Battery Voltage: .... Elapsed Time: ....

FLIGHT 4

Takeoff Loc.: .... Launch Time: .... Flight Notes: ....

Landing Loc.: .... Landing Time: ....

Battery Voltage: .... Elapsed Time: ....

General Notes: ....

....

....

Flight Checklist

☐ Airport(s) Notified	☐ UAV Batteries Charged	☐ Gimbal Protector Installed
☐ Location is OK To Fly	Battery 1 volts:	☐ Propellers Packed
☐ Weather Forecast OK	Battery 2 volts:	☐ Cables Packed
Temperature:	Battery 3 volts:	☐ Camera Filters Packed
Wind:	Battery 4 volts:	☐ Sun Shade Packed
Precipitation:	☐ Controller Charged	☐ Tools Packed
☐ Firmware up-to-date	☐ Tablet Charged	☐ Flight Plan designed/entered in Software
☐ Memory Card Formatted	☐ Mobile Phone Charged	☐ Logbook Packed

Launch Site Checklist

☐ Verify Weather is OK To Fly	☐ Check For Obstacles, Interferences
Temperature:	☐ Check For Nearby Human Activity/ Dangerous
Wind:	☐ Verify Launch Pad Is Down-wind From Observers
Precipitation:	
☐ **Safety Briefing**	☐ Launch Pad/Barriers Placed

Equipment Checklist

☐ Airframe/Landing Gear Inspected	☐ Battery Installed
☐ Propellers Inspected/ Attached	☐ Gimbal/Lens Protector Removed
☐ Controller/Tablet Assembled	
☐ Memory Card Installed	☐ Camera Filters Installed

Pre-Flight Checklist

☐ Aircraft Placed on Lauch Pad	☐ Check The Aircraft Status LEDs	☐ Check Flight Mode Switch (P-Mode)
☐ Turn On Remote Controller/ Tablet/DJI Pilot App	☐ Verify the Gimbal is Level, Can Move Unobstructed	☐ Check Satellite and Compass Status
☐ Antennas Properly Positioned	☐ Check RC Battery Level	☐ Set RTH Location And Height
☐ Turn on Aircraft	☐ Check Aircraft Battery Level	☐ Check Camera Settings

Takeoff Checklist

☐ Check Launch site is Clear for Takeoff	☐ Takeoff and Hover	☐ Check Flight Controls, Make Sure They Respond As Expected
☐ Start the motors	☐ Make Sure The Aircraft Is Stable While Hovering	☐ Start Recording Video

Post Flight Checklist

☐ Remove Battery From Aircraft	☐ Repack All Equipment
☐ Install Gimbal Guard	☐ **Complete The Flight Log**

FLIGHT 100

FLIGHT PLAN

PILOT NAME: .... FAA ID: ....

ADDRESS: .... PHONE: ....

VISUAL OBSERVER(S): ....

LOCATION: ....

DATE: .... AIRCRAFT TYPE/NAME: ....

PLANNED TIME: .... AIRCRAFT CERTIFICATE N°: ....

ESTIMATED FLIGHT DURATION: .... FLIGHT TYPE: ....

AIRPORTS WITHIN 5 MILES: ....

WAIVERS APPLIED FOR: ....

FLIGHT DESCRIPTION/ROUTE: ....

....

....

FLIGHT RECORD

FLIGHT 1

TAKEOFF LOC.: .... LAUNCH TIME: .... FLIGHT NOTES: ....

LANDING LOC.: .... LANDING TIME: ....

BATTERY VOLTAGE: .... ELAPSED TIME: ....

FLIGHT 2

TAKEOFF LOC.: .... LAUNCH TIME: .... FLIGHT NOTES: ....

LANDING LOC.: .... LANDING TIME: ....

BATTERY VOLTAGE: .... ELAPSED TIME: ....

FLIGHT 3

TAKEOFF LOC.: .... LAUNCH TIME: .... FLIGHT NOTES: ....

LANDING LOC.: .... LANDING TIME: ....

BATTERY VOLTAGE: .... ELAPSED TIME: ....

FLIGHT 4

TAKEOFF LOC.: .... LAUNCH TIME: .... FLIGHT NOTES: ....

LANDING LOC.: .... LANDING TIME: ....

BATTERY VOLTAGE: .... ELAPSED TIME: ....

GENERAL NOTES: ....

....

....

Flight Checklist

☐ Airport(s) Notified	☐ UAV Batteries Charged	☐ Gimbal Protector Installed
☐ Location is OK To Fly	Battery 1 volts:	☐ Propellers Packed
☐ Weather Forecast OK	Battery 2 volts:	☐ Cables Packed
Temperature:	Battery 3 volts:	☐ Camera Filters Packed
Wind:	Battery 4 volts:	☐ Sun Shade Packed
Precipitation:	☐ Controller Charged	☐ Tools Packed
☐ Firmware up-to-date	☐ Tablet Charged	☐ Flight Plan designed/entered in Software
☐ Memory Card Formatted	☐ Mobile Phone Charged	☐ Logbook Packed

Launch Site Checklist

☐ Verify Weather is OK To Fly	☐ Check For Obstacles, Interferences
Temperature:	☐ Check For Nearby Human Activity/ Dangerous
Wind:	☐ Verify Launch Pad Is Down-wind From Observers
Precipitation:	☐ Launch Pad/Barriers Placed
☐ **Safety Briefing**	

Equipment Checklist

☐ Airframe/Landing Gear Inspected	☐ Battery Installed
☐ Propellers Inspected/ Attached	☐ Gimbal/Lens Protector Removed
☐ Controller/Tablet Assembled	
☐ Memory Card Installed	☐ Camera Filters Installed

Pre-Flight Checklist

☐ Aircraft Placed on Lauch Pad	☐ Check The Aircraft Status LEDs	☐ Check Flight Mode Switch (P-Mode)
☐ Turn On Remote Controller/ Tablet/DJI Pilot App	☐ Verify the Gimbal is Level, Can Move Unobstructed	☐ Check Satellite and Compass Status
☐ Antennas Properly Positioned	☐ Check RC Battery Level	☐ Set RTH Location And Height
☐ Turn on Aircraft	☐ Check Aircraft Battery Level	☐ Check Camera Settings

Takeoff Checklist

☐ Check Launch site is Clear for Takeoff	☐ Takeoff and Hover	☐ Check Flight Controls, Make Sure They Respond As Expected
☐ Start the motors	☐ Make Sure The Aircraft Is Stable While Hovering	☐ Start Recording Video

Post Flight Checklist

☐ Remove Battery From Aircraft	☐ Repack All Equipment
☐ Install Gimbal Guard	☐ **Complete The Flight Log**

Notes

NOTES

NOTES

Made in the USA
Las Vegas, NV
05 February 2024

85333175R00120